NEWCASTLE/BLOODAXE POETRY SERIES: 11

OUT OF BOUNDS

NEWCASTLE/BLOODAXE POETRY SERIES

NEWCASTLE / BLOODAXE POETRY SERIES: 11

OUT OF BOUNDS

BRITISH BLACK & ASIAN POETS

EDITED BY
JACKIE KAY
JAMES PROCTER
& GEMMA ROBINSON

BLOODAXE BOOKS

Introduction & selection © copyright
Jackie Kay, James Procter, Gemma Robinson.

ISBN: 978 1 85224 929 8

First published 2012 by
Department of English Literary & Linguistic Studies,
Newcastle University,
Newcastle upon Tyne NE1 7RU,
in association with
Bloodaxe Books Ltd,
Highgreen,
Tarset,
Northumberland NE48 1RP.

www.bloodaxebooks.com

For further information about Bloodaxe titles
please visit our website or write to
the above address for a catalogue.

Cover design: Neil Astley & Pamela Robertson-Pearce.

Printed in Great Britain by Bell & Bain Limited, Glasgow, Scotland.

CONTENTS

NORTH

OUT OF BOUNDS

Let us make our own map of the sprawl, / its life and ours
JOHN SIDDIQUE

If you like, consider this anthology as an invitation to travel from north to south, bookended by the Shetland Isles and the Isle of Wight. Or if you prefer, read it as a transnational trek between the three nations of Scotland, Wales and England and the global communities caught in Britain's imperial past and present. Or take a stroll through the distinct localities, zig-zagging the regions of the three countries that make up this island.

The poems here present a map of Britain. Written by the many black and Asian poets who have lived and lingered in, who have passed through or been born into, its landscapes, these poems offer a fresh look at the country – a chorography in voice and print. If all anthologies offer readers ways to make a journey, they also limit the roads that we can take. *Out of Bounds* offers these same promises and restrictions. But by explicitly plotting its various routes and cul-de-sacs, this collection also strives to open up the very boundaries which have historically disconnected poets from place. If alienation, unbelonging and dislocation remain key aspects of black and Asian experiences in Britain, what such terms simultaneously conceal are the rich and manifold attachments to place, region, city and landscape offered here.

The itineraries that we provide are mappable in an empirical sense, but the various twists and turns they evoke signpost what is essentially an imagined, imaginative journey, a sequence curious to our sense of how we might move in, and move through, poetry from north to south, country to country, region to region and locale to locale.

Compass Points

North, south, east and west. These absolute cardinal directions suggest the possibility of something precise, and the precision crafted in these poems is the lyric, dramatic and narrative voices that speak of place. For some, place is circumscribed by generalised national spaces of Scotland, Wales, England and Britain. For others, place is geological structure, physical contour, political border, a building, an art work, personal history or a site of memory binding the poet to Britain. In wanting to understand the natural, built and imagined environments of this contradictory territory through poetry, we recognise that we have imposed a collective identity of 'British black and Asian poets' upon all the writers here. The extent to which each might accept this imposition is varied: from Derek Walcott's critical examination in *Midsummer* of the traveller's transience alongside familial connections with Warwick and Warwickshire, to Daljit Nagra's self-identification in Kwame Dawes's and Peepal Tree Press's innovative *Red* anthology – a recent and revitalising return to anthologising black British poetry. What kept us, as editors, motivated despite our discontents about the imposition of identity was the belief that the poems question the idea of an easy or singular identity, nimbly dealing with the triple bind of ethnic, geographical and poetic belonging. This collective body of work should not be read as an attempt to create a canon or construct an identity, but rather as a means by which we – as readers, as poets – can contemplate, trouble, embrace and reject the categories of our living and being.

A time line seems to emerge, particularly in the London poems. These poems form the largest non-national or non–regional area and we have ordered them by journeys north and south of the Thames, from west to east. In the earliest poems we find the metropolis as metonym for the rest of the country, as the 'arrivants' (to use Kamau Brathwaite's term) confront the capital of empire.[1] Claude McKay (who lived in London between 1919 and 1921) reveals in his autobiography, 'I felt entirely out of sympathy with the English environment. [...] the feeling of London was so harshly unfriendly to me that sometimes I was happy in the embrace of the enfolding fog'.[2] In contrast, for Una Marson (who first lived in London in 1932), returning in 1964 allowed her to 'let the solid peace and security of this lovely old city sink again into my heart'.[3] Between these two extremes London and England come into focus. Wole Soyinka's famous 'Telephone Conversation' dramatises the racism of arrival and dwelling in London. For George Lamming

1. See Edward [Kamau] Brathwaite: *The Arrivants, A New World Trilogy: Rights of Passage, Islands, Masks* (Oxford: Oxford University Press, 1973).
2. Claude McKay: *A Long Way from Home* (1937), ed. Gene Andrew Jarrett (Rutgers: Rutgers University Press, 2007), p. 56.
3. Una Marson: 'London Revisited', *Jamaica Gleaner*, 28 February 1965.

in 'Swans' there is the drama of being a spectator and a visitor, seeing and being seen by the 'imperturbable birds' in the 'howling city'. John Lyons voices the bathos of emigration, of what Louise Bennett comically terms 'colonisation in reverse': 'Well, ah lan up in Englan, / Victoria Station, London. / D I S M A L !'.[4]

For Kamau Brathwaite, London is not the centre, but just one stop in a list of international departures and arrivals – New York, Florida, Panama, Canada, Mississippi, Glasgow – that make up a global network of the African and Caribbean diaspora. Alongside its position in this list, London is found in poems that grapple with it as a generalised site and a fragmented city. *Out of Bounds* moves through the landmarks of the capital to hear the lives of Notting Hill and the dub voices of Brixton. By the time we reach the youngest poets collected here, London is still polymorphous in its ability to stage the public and private dramas of belonging, but its particularities have been reworked by a new generation. The brutal end of a romance plays out on Hampstead Heath (Ashna Sarkar) where once it was the locus of 'Apartheid Britain' (Zhana), the transposed and overlaid photographs of a lover are haunted by the Circle Line and St Paul's (Jay Bernard); the pull of music comes not from McKay's sounds of 'La Paloma' in Soho, but from Peckham Rye's now demolished Lazerdrome nightclub (Jacob Sam-La Rose) or Berwick Street and the travelling 'world of bass' (Kayo Chingonyi).

However, it is by moving beyond the bounds of London that this collection stakes its claim to occupy new ground. An earlier generation of settlers and visitors (from McKay to Bennett) strayed only rarely from the English metropolis in their poetry, but recent decades have seen a proliferation of poetry presented from the point of view of the national, regional and local realms beyond London. This does not amount to a narrowing of vision, the regional as parochial; on the contrary it opens up the counties and countries of Britain to their post-colonial heritage. London no longer lords over the national landscape, but becomes one site among many. *Out of Bounds* registers a broader set of poetic attachments to landscape, attachments that today are nationwide, but emphatically not nation-bound.

4. See Louise Bennett: 'Colonisation in Reverse', *Jamaica Labrish* (Kingston: Sangsters, 1990).

Scotland

We start in the Scottish Islands and Highlands, move from Aberdeen south to Fife and Edinburgh before going off to Glasgow, via the Campsie Fells, the west of Scotland and then heading south. Our search for the most northerly reaches comes with provisos. If we enter the wild in 'Scotland', we find it is (in the words of Kathleen Jamie) 'not a place to stride over but a force requiring constant negotiation'. Certainly we can find 'the theatrically empty places' but as Jamie, and the other poets here remind us, 'wild and not-wild is a false distinction, in this ancient, contested country'.[5] In 'Campsie Fells' Imtiaz Dharker describes an extended family 'set free out of solid homes / for one Sunday morning, / catapulted into the countryside'. Her question – 'What were we like, on that / Scottish field, up in the hills, / navigating the cow pats' – is multiply answered as the locations called up in the poem move between field, house, stream, and long-departed village. The wild can be found everywhere: in the 'yob' confrontations of Kukomo Rocks's 'Shopping Trip in Fife', in the Kala Pani-Skye-inspired curry-making unorthodoxy of Maya Chowdhry's 'Hurry Curry', in Tariq Latif's seawall-leaping 'lads', in 'After Lights over Girvan', in the mirage-like M8 of Gary Singh's 'India Gate', in Raman Mundair's ghostly 'Shetland Muse', in Suhayl Saadi's 'wild peacock reeds of the cold green river' in his paradisial, saturated Glasgow, in Sudesh Mishra's lone swan in 'Suva; Skye' and Vahni Capildeo's 'Shell', where (a note to the editors tells us) we view the Isle of Arran from Barassie and Troon, but are reminded by the poet that 'no names for you pass muster'.

The conceptually blurred edges between the urban, rural, sub-urban and wild undermine what might be categorised as cultivated, wilderness or wasteland. And these peculiar histories of human encounter contain within them contentious designations of other-ness that inspire many poets. But more than this, combinations of past and present, here and there, familiar and strange, home and exile surface as persistent themes in these poems, alongside the varied terrain of wilderness and cultivation. Leila Aboulela's 'When I first came to Scotland' registers hurt with the land itself; Maud Sulter's poems distil the desire for romantic and political flight.

5. Kathleen Jamie: 'A Lone Enraptured Male', *London Review of Books*, 6 March 2008, pp. 25-27, http://www.lrb.co.uk/v30/n05/kathleen-jamie/a-lone-enraptured-male.

Sometimes, the poems act as channels that mark new-found and surprising alliances (such as Grace Nichols's inter-textual request to Kathleen Jamie for 'Sheba-Scottish relations' and Roger Robinson's quieter reckoning of his father's life and work).

Personal and national histories breathe the life of then into the now of poetry, and we find identity forged in family tricks for cutting pomegranates, the new seafaring lives of a generation of 'Lascar Johnnies' (Imtiaz Dharker), the intricacies of sporting allegiances (Bashabi Fraser, Sudeep Sen), and in the 'footnotes' of Edinburgh's taxidermy, where John Edmonstone, and his student, Charles Darwin, join as 'each other's missing link' (John Agard). Maya Chowdhry, in 'Four Corners', asks 'How can I have grown up in the Second City of Empire / amidst its decaying shell?', and tries to imagine an identity beyond 'East and West' / 'North and South'. For Roger Robinson identities are literally translated across location: ' "Lukeit theis evrybuddy" / and then the conversion: "All of allyuh, check dis out nuh".' Written between Trinidad Creole and Scottish accents, Punjabi in Glasgow ports, the language of medicine in Edinburgh, the goodbyes of Bollywood (*Alvida, Alvida*), these poems of particular, shifting connection might, following Raman Mundair, be called poems of the 'shoormal' – Shetland dialect for 'where the shore meets the sea'.

North

As we enter the North of England we descend the east coast from Northumberland to Hull. It is a winding journey that takes us from Whitley Bay via Newcastle and Durham, to Bridlington and beyond. A sharp right turn then takes the reader out of the north east and on a scenic route inland, via the Lake District (from Keswick to Kendal), to Yorkshire's rural and (post-) industrial heartlands: Leeds, Bradford, Haworth, Huddersfield, Hebden Bridge, and finally south to Sheffield. From here, we head westwards and northwards, over the rising backbone of the Pennines (see Lyons' 'Drinking up the Drizzle') and into Lancashire. From the county town of Lancaster we roughly follow the M6 southbound, taking in Blackpool, Preston, Wigan, Bolton and Rochdale, before a lingering stop off in Manchester. Heading out of the self-proclaimed capital of the north takes us through Salford and Altrincham and to our final northern destination of Liverpool and the River Mersey. Along the way we visit Durham Cathedral, the Baltic, Angel of the North,

17

Bamburgh Castle; museums and galleries in Keswick and Manchester, the West Yorkshire Playhouse, and Harewood House.

The regional landscape is forced to open up in these poems and accommodate new and unexpected settings. John Lyons twins Yorkshire's blackbird with Trinidad's humming bird, immortelles with silver birch, the Pennines point to the Himalayas. Lumb Bank evokes India's cotton fields and Caribbean cane fields (Merle Collins). In and around Manchester, the Tower Blocks of Hulme recall a Delhi skyline (Maya Chowdhry). For Lemn Sissay Mill Towns stretch to Africa, and the New World seeps into Manchester through the gaps between its paving stones (see also Kei Miller's poetic counterpointing of Manchester and Jamaica). In Romesh Gunesekera's 'Turning Point', migrant memories circle out of regional and national bounds, before converging on a Manchester flat. Poets like Grace Nichols, Dorothea Smartt and Jack Mapanje remind us that the ghosts of slavery haunt the local landscapes of the north, Hull, Lancaster and Bridlington. Such historical journeys are retraced through the itineraries of these poems, which often compose place and landscape not from the perspective of the native or settled speaker, but *en route*, on the move, between places. There's the fleeting glimpse of the Angel of the North, or Hull from an InterCity train in the work of Nichols.

Other poems also signal a sense of dwelling, of being a lingering, internal presence. Memory is not simply migratory in the poems gathered here, but is evoked in ways that signal new kinds of accommodation within the north. In Ibrahiim's snapshot of Leeds or in the childhood memories of Sheree Mack, Nabila Jameel and Michelle Scalley-Clarke's poems, the past is not elsewhere, but *here*, in the north. We have D.S. Marriott's poetic dedication to the memory of Ena Sharples, an early star of Britain's most famous northern soap opera, *Coronation Street*. 'Forty years he's been walking these streets. Maybe more', states the speaker in Tajinder Singh Hayer's 'Holy Man'. In R. Parthasarathy's 'Northern City' the once alienating northern drizzle is mellowed by memory and what the speaker, now five years on, reveals is a growing 'affection' for a Leeds that was once merely 'ugly and wet' with its dirty 'puddles' of children in lanes. The 'again' of Merle Collins's visit to Yorkshire suggests a repeat journey that might be both routine and estranging. Although within the national imagination the north has (too) often been allowed to appear remote from the multicultural cosmopolis of London, landscape emerges across the poems of this section no longer necessarily foreign but familiar. 'Toxteth my dwelling place,' states Levi Tafari. 'I love Moss Side' is the refrain that runs through Pete Kalu's 'The Poet's Song'. Or as John Siddique puts it in 'Map of Rochdale': 'Let us make our own map of the sprawl, / its life and ours.'

As well as places, the poems of this section are packed with references to weather. Recurring images of rain, sleet, snow and ice, of brisk sea winds and slumbering mists greet the reader. These abundant meteorological metaphors operate on one level as shortcuts to a national repertoire of established images about regional English landscape, and the wuthering north. Understood as pathetic fallacy, the often bleak and tumultuous settings of these poems suggest the newcomer's vulnerability within inhospitable or isolating environs. However, such expressions of unbelonging rarely go unqualified in the poems gathered here, and are often undercut by associations the poems establish between romance and weather. Potentially lonely climatic conditions are repeatedly countered by the presence of lovers, friends, and chance encounters (Kayo Chingonyi, Fred D'Aguiar), human bonds that are in turn echoed in attachments to place. As Merle Collins has it in one of her Lumb Bank poems: 'Warmth might just / sometimes / be found in misty cold.'

Other poets seem to thaw the frigid north through tropical images of sunshine, spice and sand. Bridlington suggests the Sahara in Jack Mapanje's coastal poem; there's a sense of irony about the prawn korma and boiled rice at Bamburgh ('Denouement'), that bursts into overt comedy in SuAndi's 'Bolton Safari'. Elsewhere, Yorkshire's village mill stones and moss flecked dry stone walls 'course' into 'long stretches of sandy beach, rows of cane rustling with crows and cranes, long runways of singing surf'.

Wales

After the Isle of Man and the north-west we arrive in Wales, where we move north to south, criss-crossing the mountains, valleys and coast from Colwyn Bay to Cardiff. If Scotland is dreich and frozen, Wales is rain-soaked and mountain-misted: both places have inspired their own elegies and paeans to the elements. In 'Welsh Postcard' Raman Mundair turns traveller to send messages of 'soft / focus humpback isles' of 'disappearing /

seas in salty blurs'. Tinashe Mushakavanhu's wet-weather trip to the Green Man Festival leaves 'spirits scalded', and Moniza Alvi recalls the harshness and delicacy of 'the hills of Llandogo / where the sleet falls like blossom'. From Rhyl, Colwyn Bay, Llandudno, Trefor, Snowdon, the Brecon Beacons, Llandogo, Cardiff, Tiger Bay to Barry, the horizon in these poems is measured by the affiliations and forces (elemental, human, technological, linguistic) that bring into focus home ground, foreign territory and the spaces in-between. While the local is pronounced within many of the poems in this collection, there is nothing entirely discrete about our geographical divisions, and many of the poems that we have situated in Scotland, Northern England, Wales, the Midlands or Southern England speak across to other places, regions and cities. In 'Montbretia, Wales' Maggie Harris makes a writer's pilgrimage to Ireland, finding not only a Celtic fringe of poets but ocean-leaping flowers that 'house-hunted *me*' in Wales, 'head aflame / with madness, wild, frantic, blazing poetry'.

The first poem in the Wales section is oriented looking out from the 'North Wales coast', and Patience Agbabi's parenthetical insertion in 'North(West)ern' reveals those compass points that lead to affiliations across borders. Here it is the 'Northern Soul Mecca' of the Wigan Casino that pulls in people to dance to the music of Detroit and Chicago 'where transatlantic bass / beat blacker than blue in glittering mono'. Agbabi side-steps the supremacist views of the white skinheads who became linked to the scene of 'regular all-night Soul extravaganza for up to 1500 fans' and instead remembers on Colwyn Bay pier a new and incongruous site of Soul – a place of imaginative connections, from where 'my heart was break / dancing on the road to Wigan Casino'.[6] In 'Postmod' Agbabi comically transposes 'Rhyl / '82' for '*Brighton Beach 1963*' and this lightness of poetic touch continues in Maggie Harris where the sight of llamas in Cwmpengraig links with Peru and Guyana to create 'an echo between us, of continents'.

The scale and idiom of family and home shapes the poems about Wales just as it does elsewhere. 'Dis gurl gon walk my grandmother say / And walk I walk from Guyana to West Wales', writes Maggie Harris, juxtaposing Guyanese 'oceans and slave bones' with 'bruk

6. See Les Back & Vron Ware: *Out of Whiteness: Colour, Politics and Culture* (Chicago: University of Chicago Press, 2001), p. 102.

down cottages and hills'. Water is swapped for land, but these are intimate Atlantic histories – 20th-century immigrant imagining emigrating mill worker – and are crafted in the contrasting realisms of sat-nav, quadrant and footfall. Elsewhere, Marsden Falcon and Sadi Husain articulate the bravado of youth as it clashes with cultural expectations. Labi Siffre looks to a future beyond interloping and autochthony for definitions of Welshness and Tishani Doshi's contemplative sestina conjures the inherited memories of a Welsh childhood. For Eric Ngalle Charles the Welsh landscape reminds him of the giant legends of Cameroon, and so mountain and sea become characters in his story of exile and 'home-coming'. The journeying Derek Walcott conjures other fictional powers: Arthurian Avalon and the borderland poetry of William Langland's Plowman surface on 'the skittering ridges of Wales', as the warring past blurs into the rainy present. Literary geographies and intimate relationships continue, as Grace Nichols weeps for R.S. Thomas, Leon Charles celebrates the shape-shifting Taliesin for forging 'rainbow Wales' in Tiger Bay, and Moniza Alvi's Aunt Lukbir speaks of Jane Austen, 'remembered from an overseas degree' against the Cardiff backdrop of 'garden fence and roses'. Tariq Latif and John Siddique, meanwhile, encourage us to pull back from human culture, and re-imagine ourselves, small, and romantically inclined in the face of a more powerful nature.

Midlands

From Wales we travel to England's Midlands and a sequence of poems that moves across Stoke, Leicester and Birmingham, the Malvern Hills and the snaking Severn. Once again, we find ourselves confronted by a series of poems that are themselves *en route*, whether by bus (Kimberly Trusty), or boat (David Dabydeen). However, there is more to these 'Middle Lands' (Carol Leeming) poems than a set of journeys between places and what we also encounter in this section is a shift in register, as accents subtly but surely shift.

'It all happens here duck' says Jean, directing the theatre restaurant in Trusty's 'New Vic Theatre Poem'. This local term of affection is one that Jean 'Binta' Breeze, otherwise famous for her sorties into creole dialect, riffs on in 'Mi Duck'. The use of regional register is not unique to the Midlands, of course. You only need to look at the Yorkshire soundings of Daljit Nagra's 'Raju t'Wonder Dog', or 'Frame Yourself' by Seni Seneviratne (a

Yorkshire expression meaning sort yourself out), or the casual manner in which the proper noun 'Manchester' becomes 'Manny' (Jeff Caffrey); or Mundair's 'My mouth toiled to accommodate the rough musicality of Mancunian vowels'. We are reminded through such examples of the extent to which the poems of this collection aren't simply about place, they are about the *language* of place, language which does not just note the foreign, but which comes to accommodate difference and acts as marker of regional belonging. Within such poems a new twist is given to Dabydeen's broader observation in 'Coolie Odyssey': 'Now that peasantry is in vogue, / Poetry bubbles from peat bogs, / People strain for the old folk's fatal gobs / Coughed up in grates North or North East / 'Tween bouts o' living dialect'. Through dialect, the poets of this collection do not so much evoke a modish authenticity as suggest how language becomes fresh and new on different tongues, in different places. It is in the Midlands, perhaps more than anywhere else in *Out of Bounds*, that the range between regional English dialect, Indian expressions and African Caribbean creole is most pronounced and varied. Beyond the silences and 'bitten tongue' of Gunesekera's 'Frontliners' we have Hindi along the River Severn in Solanki's 'The Jar' ('*Shri Ram jaya Ram jaya jaya*'), and 'achar' in Smethwick, thanks to Roshan Doug. Then there's a modified African Caribbean in the 'Natty Dread' of Selassie's poem set in the 'concrete jungle' of Birmingham: Evvryweh Iman guh / All Isee is concrete / Cum mek wi step it / Uppah freeman street'.

Other kinds of cartographic connection can be traced through these poems: there's the tactile terms of Doug's 'Slow Motion' with its emphasis on intimacy in the Malvern Hills, there's Benjamin Zephaniah's image of a 'Jamaican hand' on an 'Ethiopian heart' in a 'Brummie chest', there's Gunesekra's tropicalised Sherwood, and the juxtaposition of territories in Carol Leeming's image of muezzin calls rising over the terraced houses of Highfields in Leicester. There is 'race' to be found too in the 'ale-coloured' skies that hang over Warwickshire in Walcott's Midlands series, a sequence of poems that repeatedly ties the local rural landscape (inns, chapels and hedges) to other national sites of urban conflict (Brixton) and beyond that, to the West Indies. In addition to these hyphenated worlds and identities, we find more emphatic and apparently (although appearances can be deceptive) unambiguous connections to place: in the unexpected hint at what it might mean to 'proudly be Birmingham' at the end of Roi Kwabena's 'Location: Re', or in the humour in the poetic literalism of Hubbard's 'Take the girl out of Notts, but you can't take Notts out of the girl!'

South

In *South* we regroup a final time, heading east to start southern England in Norfolk and sweep west through Oxford to Bristol, before cutting back east to travel through Berkshire to London's sprawl, and finally along the south coast. Here the poems strike at, resist, accommodate and work out (sometimes uneasy) attachments to the language and iconography of southern Englishness. London of the British Empire and its immigrants loom large, and the historical domination of England and its south is streaked through these poems. 'That side is Wales and all the world / beyond, this side is England' declares Rajat Kumar Biswas's friend, Cambridge. Standing firmly in Clapham Common, John Agard's now famous 'simple immigrant' assaults 'de Queen's English', and importantly offers a located 'self-defence' against an equally locatable place of linguistic power: the Oxford that is synonymous with dons and dictionaries. Twenty-five years on and Oxford remains a site of contradictions (as in Christian Campbell's 'Oxfraud') or, as Vahni Capildeo captures in 'La Poetessa', a repository for particular kinds of exaggerated, whimsical Englishness: 'English her name, English her language, English her absobloomburylutely witty garments'. For Stuart Hall, reminiscing on Radio 4's *Desert Island Discs* in 2000, it was notions of Britain and black British, not isolating England and Englishness, that offered a first generation Jamaican migrant and sociologist of multicultures a way to make a place in this new world. The gaps between experiences of first, second and third generations are marked in all the sections here, but in poems about the south of England the challenge of entrenched Englishness, the myth of the purity of English culture, is a creative grist that links poets across a period of ninety years.

A poetry of place for England, Scotland and Wales reveals poetic forms that are myriad. We have Fred D'Aguiar's sonnets, Maya Chowdhry's and Tishani Doshi's sestinas, Derek Walcott's elastic pentameters and hexameters, Jean 'Binta' Breeze's dramatic mono-logue, the rhyming of rap and performance poetry, the shape poems of Vahni Capildeo and Tawona Sithole, Bernardine Evaristo's and Sudeep Sen's couplets, and Linton Kwesi Johnson's dub beats, but for the most part this is an anthology of free verse, where poems assert the freedom to create internal rhythms and rhymes that cross the line and the layout of the page. There is no easy relationship between place, form and metre here. Kamau Brathwaite may have famously declared that 'the hurricane does not roar in pentameters', and that the rhythms of English poetry cannot account for the rhythms of Caribbean poetry. But Brathwaite's further question – 'how do you get a rhythm which approximates the natural experience, the environmental experience?' – is complicated by a poetry which finds no fixed British 'environmental experience'.[7] Grace Nichols writes a loose iambic pentameter in the opening line of 'Hurricane Hits England': 'It took a hurricane, to bring her closer'. Remembering the hurricane-force winds that battered the south coast of England in 1987, Nichols reframes her own subjectivity 'to the landscape', and in doing so reframes Brathwaite's comments: this hurricane might roar in pentameter, but it roars otherwise too. 'I'm riding the mystery of your storm', she writes, working between the pentameter and the 4-stress line; this environment offers no stable poetic metre, as Brathwaite suggests, and Nichols shows that the rhythms and locales of her environmental poetry are open to variation.

The wild returns in the south through weather, but also in the landscapes that are home to the East Anglian waters and fenland birds in Judith Lal's work and Sudeep Sen's writerly, rural Devonshire moors. But as elsewhere, the wild and the non-wild merge to have their urban and political forms here too, their pejorative and liberating resonances, their timescales and contexts. Explosive and apparently polite racisms are narrated and fought against: in the Brixton riots, during a National Front invasion of Acklam Hall, in the aftermath of the New Cross fire and at Kenwood Ladies Pond. The unruliness of the 'sus laws' and community policing in inner city London and the 'Insohrekshan' they provoke (Desmond Johnson, Marsha Prescod, Linton Kwesi Johnson), are joined by a different kind of policing at the National Portrait Gallery (Kwame Dawes) and by the post-9/11 fears and injustices found in Shamshad Khan's 'Isosceles'. Within this poetry of resistance, traditions of

---

7. Edward Kamau Brathwaite: *History of the Voice: The Development of Nation Language in Anglophone Caribbean Poetry* (London and Port of Spain: New Beacon, 1984), p. 10.

individualism and community activism emerge out of the crowd, but this individuality and collectivity is rewardingly hard to define. If London becomes for Moniza Alvi 'the double city', a sense of hybridity and in-betweenness is not restricted to this capital. In Welwyn Garden City, Bristol, Westbirton Arboretum, along the Dorset and Devon coast uneasy accommodations take place. And as if to mark the contradiction, Louisa Adjoa Parker writes of those 'with *not from here* etched / like tribal markings into their skin' but she and Karen McCarthy Woolf still remain in Dorset and Devon to write a poetry of belonging in the landscapes of coastal holiday-making. Throughout the collection pleasure abounds at the island's peripheries from Whitley Bay and Blackpool Pleasure Beach to Paignton, jostling for recognition alongside the more overtly political poetry of protest above.

A world of proper nouns bursts into the poetic language that helps focus the landscapes of the south: Moongazer, Huracan, Oya, Hattie, Shango, Bedford van, Whitstabubble, Heathrow, H.M. Customs, Earl Grey, Acklam Hall, National Front, Tendulkar, Black Uhuru, the Go-Go's, McDonalds, Common/wealth, Demerara, Muslim, Samaritan, Woolworth, V&A, Portrait Gallery, Insohrekshan, Leroy Harris, Swamp Eighty-Wan, Sofrano B, New Cross, SOAS, Mandeville, Coromantyn, Ballygunge, Kali, Big Ben, Tom Waits, Hungerford Bridge, Kiranjit, Lord Taylor, Gucci, Toussaint L'Ouverture, Sunrise Radio, Bollywood, Rama, Divali, Sita, Pizza Hut, Eidh, Vasaikhi, Odysseus, Saxon, White Ladies Road, Black Boy's Hill, Mohammed, Homer, Hannibal, Jesus, Junkanoo, Tingumology, Abaco, Merton College, MOMA, M&S, Forster, Marabar, Dolcis, Pied Piper. If some of these names are more familiar than others (and we could draw up separate and overlapping lists for each of our geographical sections), it should provoke us to read and to wonder about the neologisms and nouns that speak of people, place and culture. Like Vanley Burke's iconic 1970s photograph, 'Boy with Flag', taken in Handsworth Park, Birmingham, these words (and the Union Flag that flies on his bike) all speak of identity, but it is in their permutations and patterning that we search for poetic meaning.

Beyond the bounds
Of course, there are locations that this anthology obscures. By gathering a poetry of place we have necessarily ignored where

poets were born, live and work, and the kinds of connections that these bring to our reckoning of place. More than this, anthologies also flatten those sources in which poems are first materially located through publication. In that respect this anthology is only the visible tip of the manifold and impressive work of poets, publishers, arts councils, local councils, museums, galleries, community groups, writing retreats, festivals, writing collectives, blogospheres, magazines and journals. We encourage you to take another journey, to search the acknowledgements and biographies to find the original contours of this poetry as they first came into focus for us.

Above all, though, this anthology is an invitation to make a map – an alternative A-Z of poetic Britain. It should be one that makes sense for our 21st-century sensibilities, but in the light of the multiple pasts and cultures of this small island (in Andrea Levy's phrase). If place has become virtual, digital, reproduced, simulated, generic in our age of supermodernity (the world of the web, of internauts, of film and photograph, of repeating high streets, 'non-places' of airport, supermarket, motorway) it also remains elemental and imaginative as well as material.[8] Here are poems of air, water, fire and earth. From the extremes of hot and cold, wet and dry, we find a world by turns blazing and blustering, dusty and mud-splattered, salty and stony. When the 'human-centred cosmos' (to use the words of the Guyanese visionary Wilson Harris) fails us – as it can in times of crisis, riot or persecution as much as in the everyday – these poets do not reject humanity, but look instead for a world that connects more than just people.[9] It is then that these collected poets make the world anew for us, reassert its familiarity, invoke its strangeness, create a vocabulary, rhythm and chorus of voices which remind us that this place, these places, this contested territory, will be shared in more ways than we can ever know.

JACKIE KAY
JAMES PROCTER
GEMMA ROBINSON

8. See Marc Augé: *Non-Lieux, Introduction à une anthropologie de la surmodernité* (1992); *Non-Places: Introduction to an Anthropology of Supermodernity*, tr. John Howe (London: Verso, 1995).
9. See Wilson Harris: *Jonestown* (London: Faber, 1996), p. 97.

SCOTLAND

RAMAN MUNDAIR

Shetland Muse
(My Craft or Sullen Art)

Outside dark molasses
absorbs the last juice
from a misshapen tangerine
and pours thick across the vale.
The wind furious at being
ignored whips the ocean to a roar.

Soon, the gloaming begins
and something in my lower back
stirs and, later, something
lying beneath my skin moves
and my hand casts spells
that appear garbled on the page.

Throughout the night, the moon,
just out of reach, plays with the sheep –
hide and seek – their bustle torsos
a strange comfort in a landscape
void of trees. While most sleep,
my ink luminous marks magic true.

RAMAN MUNDAIR

from Stories fae da Shoormal

1

Here. Hear da ice craack.
Be still. Wir forever
on da move. Dis rodd
gengs naewye, dis rodd
gengs aawye. Da onnly
thing daat truly flaows is da sea.

Da sea lonnlie, da sea,
da sea seduces, da sea,
da sea screms, da sea,
da sea senses, da sea,
da sea, da sea. In me drems

der a rodd; it gengs on
laang, laang – forever. Unlichted,
unshadowed, I canna see
mysel, bit I kyen, Ah'm dere. Un-alon,
awaash o me, awaash o midnicht
blue. Da skies waash ower me.

Da ice craacks, da Arctic tundra
shivers, readjusts hits spines,
sends secret messages idda dialect
tae hits nerve-endins in Shetlan.
Dir ley lines here
vibratin, crackin – electric.

2

Strange hoo far awa
memories come tae be – laek waves
laevin da shore.
      Wha wis da wumman?
      Wha wis da man?
We met idda shoormal.
Dee. Dee. Dee.
Du wis my fire
wance – my man
o' da waves. Du cam,
rested upo my shore.
I wis dy first
I wis dy harbour.
Bit my love, my selkie
man, du wis
      run agrund. Aach,
         siccan a sad thing for a sailor.
An noo my love, da sea
is my rodd, da rodd my sea.

I traivel on, traivel on, traivel
on, for my love
wisna meant tae be.
Da ocean,
da waves,
da shoormal –
dis is noo my place,
my warmin space, my
restin, my faimily.

3

unidentified-unknown-unseen-unheard-unvoiced
unopened-unrecognisable-disappeared-silent
suppressed-lost-forgotten-stolen-unmemoried
stilled-haunted-unspoken-memory-still-past-mystery

Du doesna mind
Ah'm forgotten
I donnt exist
Du's med me inveesible

Dis is my mindin
Dis camera, my umbilical ee
Dis is my memory
Reliable, dis doesna lee

unidentified-unknown-unseen-unheard-unvoiced
unopened-unrecognisable-disappeared-silent
suppressed-lost-forgotten-stolen-unmemoried
stilled-haunted-unspoken-memory-still-past-mystery

4

Here, you hae ta be waatchful.
Norden lichts happen
when you're sleepin.
Whaals sail by,
oot a sicht ahint ferries, tankers.
Be ever alert,
meteor shooers cascade
ahint your back, whispers

echo alang Da Esplanade,
transparent lives – while da days
pass, markit be *Da Shetland Times*.

RAMAN MUNDAIR

Sheep Hill, Fair Isle

I begin sheepishly.
      Feel with fingers,
attempt to *roo*

your softness taut
in struggle. I soothe
      with lullaby;

you settle. In no time
at all the shear's song
reveals your baby skin.

      You free yourself
of me. Hoof away. My fingers
lanolin soft with your memory.

MAYA CHOWDHRY

Hurry Curry

rain heralds her arrival
she pours herself into the land
in the post office she discovers *Pataks Original Mild Curry
Paste* and begins blending
the ready-made with the soon to be made
her grandmother's words sizzling you can't make a curry in a hurry

she lowers the heat and adds the paste in a hurry
imperialism gives rise to the recipe's arrival
resisting the way curry had to be made
dissension – the right to her roots on the mother-land
the Kala Pani and Sound of Skye blending
could she put haggis in a curry

could she resist her birthright of curry
would her grandmother's ghost know it was with haste and a hurry
of blending
that this soil felt her arrival
in the mountains and vales of this land
until in the earth's womb a pact was made

and on her table acceptable ready-made?
lowering the tone with her curry
giving her tolerability in this land
if *Tescos* could do it in a hurry
globalised food had its arrival
aisles of ready-meals blending

chicken and tikka masala blending
allegiances made
departure and arrival
of the colonial curry
judgments made in a hurry
about who can migrate to the land

harvest the land
through blending
and mixing in a hurry
until the recipe is made
a bastardised curry
makes its arrival

blending promises made
we land a new kind of curry
hurry to await its arrival

SUDESH MISHRA

Suva; Skye

A half-spent
mosquito coil
mounted on an upended fork
buoyed
inside a squat jar
brimming with smoky water
is nothing
like the swan he saw
that neutral day
arching
its ancient ashen neck
upon the flood
of a loch
crammed with brilliant sky.
Nothing like.

RIZWAN AKHTAR

Aberdonian winter

I

Beneath a dark sky there are no shades
only a white web of black barks
the snowy morning is touch illuminated
by the surreal peripheries on the horizon
the city holds to its frozen centre
the old structures settle in the stoned silence,
wind-shattered a crow perches on the antennae.

II

The crusted pavement is a forensic sheet
the town is a map of footprints, a prowler
from the beyond only adds to its obscurity,
the snow freezes his directions but melts
in the prolonged pauses, the wind leaves him
scattered on a road going everywhere.

III

A slow spooky rain determines the status
of the wanderer; the accent gurgles with
distant streams, tongues rinse in the alien tides
the teeth sparkle in the Northern mirrors
the buds are brown, the enamel is white.

IV

The church is cobbled into nuptial solemnity
kilt-wearing men play pipes, the groom whips
the last flakes (he cruises past) from the bride's lips
the guests disperse mutely.

JACKIE KAY

Granite

I found the quine and I found the loon
in the sparkling granite toon,
jist as the haar wis comin doon,
jist as the cloud had slaired the moon.

The faither's face is set in stane,
the mither cries and's all alane.
I've wandered richt up Gaelic Lane
doon Union Street and back agane.

Jist as granite comes fray *grain*,
gin they'll be grown folk search in vain,
tracking doon the past in the rain,
as lang as you'd ca' a stane a stane.

KOKUMO ROCKS

Shopping Trip Tesco in Fife

A woman woke up
Washed dressed
Fed the kids
The husband
The rabbit
Just like every morning
She went shopping
For bread milk
Cat food
Just like every morning

Passers by got in her way

Buses swept right past her

Yobs shouted

Hey black bitch
Just like every morning

Next day she watched television

It spoke of riots in Britain

Black fighting white

She listened well
That morning
She went shopping yet again
For bread milk
Cat food
She got jostled pushed
From the corner of her eye
She saw the familiar pack

Hey die black black bitch they screamed
But things seemed different that morning

She turned she started

Started forward
Rage rising
She shook

She choked
She stuttered
She spoke

She raised her arm
Hand made into a fist
Hand met jaw
Thud crack
One yob landed on deck

Blood spilled
The woman walked on
Smiled
Collected the milk
The bread
The cat food
Just like every morning

ROGER ROBINSON

Sleep

It becomes clear to you
the night your father asks you
to wake him up to see
his favourite film on TV,
and despite cups of coffee
bright lights and company
he is asleep
with his dark rimmed glasses
tilted on his face before
the opening credits.

And there
hearing the drag of his snore
and watching the uncomfortably
crooked angle of his neck,
you see him at nineteen,
taking care of his four brothers
and one sister and studying
for a scholarship while working
nights pushing dead bodies
at the local morgue, and he's tired
but he can't stop because he'll
be the first in their family
to go to university and he can't
let them down.

At twenty-one
he's in class at Stirling University
wondering if he can afford the batteries
for his warehouseman's torch
so he can study on the job tonight.
Nobody told him Scotland
would be this cold, and it's
so lonely sometimes but he
has to pass these exams
or he'll be out.

At twenty-two you're born.
Your mother works the night shift
at the hospital, and he tries to read
between your two a.m. squeals
and he picks you up
in the hand not holding the book
and smiles and rocks you to sleep.

Twenty-five now,
and working late five nights a week
trying to snatch a few promotions,
and somehow he thought
it might be a bit easier with his degree,
and he really needs
to move his wife and kids
into a place of their own.

And for the next twenty years
he battles on his job every day
just so you could be comfortable
and have the space to be what you want.

And then you know
that he's never had much time for this
for rest, for sleep.
You prop his head with a pillow,
gingerly pull off his glasses
and stare at him
snoring, loudly,
beautifully.

ROGER ROBINSON

Conversion

Over dinner mum remembers
that I was six when we moved
back to Trinidad.

She said people would ask
my name and I would say
'Hhrroaja Hrrroabinsin'

and people would chuckle
at the black boy
with the Scottish accent.

One day she woke
to see me in the bedroom
mirror in blue y-fronts,

practising the accent
with full hand and facial
gestures. First in Scottish:

'Lukeit theis evrybuddy'
and then the conversion:
'All of allyuh, check dis out nuh.'

MAUD SULTER

Scots Triptych

Passion Plays

Passion plays on the lips
like guilt preys on the mind.

Having left you
not five minutes ago
I try to remember

Your eyes – piercing
your broad smile and your
built for speed hips

Fearful that not having you near me
my memory will deceive me.

That the opportunity was there
to touch you
caress you
to kiss those bold black lips

Yet denied myself the pleasure
Erzulie hear me sister

The train bullets through
a dark dank tunnel
close my eyes   purse my lips
heart pumping fast   in anticipation

Of your mouth moist touching mine
the charge between us
makes me start back
in to my corner seat.

Tomorrow my candy   my caramel sweet
we two in Edinburgh shall meet
dressed in black flowing low
to throw myself wildly in to the abyss

You take me and make me whatever you wish
forty-eight hours   as one   in beauty
and grace
Remembering more than your Damballah like
face   a serpent shall keep vigil until
you return to claim me   my sweetest
Aida Ouedo snakes to Papa.

Drich Day

Ice cold steel gray sky ahead
entering the Kingdom of Fife

Walk through ruins
of castles ancient, a priory
tombstones cold as death itself
of people past, children lost
to disease poverty the harsh
reality of life

Sea a blanket of September sorrows
unremitting drich and drizzle
permeates our light outerwear

Walking the links at St Andrews
we kissed holding each to the other
treasuring the moment
for the sake of itself
nothing between us and Denmark
except that tomorrow you leave me.

If Leaving You

If leaving you
was as easy
as the falling
in love
with
a
total
stranger

– not total

our blackness
a bond
before speech
or encounter

I could walk
from you now
into the hustle
and bustle

of Waverley
station
and checking
my ticket
– depart.

JOHN AGARD

The Ascent of John Edmonstone
(The freed black slave who taught Darwin taxidermy at Edinburgh – 1826.)

My name rings no bell
in the ears of science
but footnotes know me well –

footnotes where history
shows its true colours
and passing reference is flesh

for I am John Edmonstone,
whose name is little known
to evolution's white ladder.

But Darwin will remember me,
just say the black man who taught him
Egypt's ancient art of taxidermy.

To think that we should meet
in Edinburgh of all places
few doors apart on Lothian Street.

No mention then of savage races.
In those days we were two bird-stuffers
mounting mortality in feathers.

We were each other's missing link
colleagues upright on the chain of being
a pair of wingless apes condemned to think.

SUDEEP SEN

Over May Day

(for Angus Calder)

The drunkenness of things being various
LOUIS MacNEICE

At Edinburgh's Carlton Cricket Pavilion, we sat
brooding over Scotland's heavy air on May Day, over
    how the sixth seam swung unpredictably and
the ball kept low, as were the runs, over after over.

At a corner pub last year on a November night
when the air outside was frozen
    still, thick froth overflowed the endless pints'
brim, as we carefully constructed the World XI.

At Leven Terrace's kitchen with port and coffee,
and later in the study, we debated about CD-ROMS, faxes,
    over the legitimacy of performance poetry,
about history, datelines, deadlines and continents.

At Netherbow Theatre on a Thursday night
when I read poems from my new book under arc-lights
    half-blinded, I composed this one in my mind
as I watched you scanning the lines with your wife;

I thought to myself, if the world were a game
of limited-over cricket, there would almost always
    be a result at the end, except of course in the case
of a tie. No hesitancy, no areas of monotonous greys

    where most people spend their lives. Nothing
is sealed until the last over is carved
    deceptively with the racing cork, on the outfield
undulations of a gently stretched corrugated turf.

IRFAN MERCHANT

The World Is More Real Than It Is

I was sat alone in the café along the street
from Edinburgh Central Mosque
reading *The Satanic Verses* discreetly
when I came to that bit about
How does newness come into the world?
I paused, glanced up and out
the window, and as I stared
the street stared back, absurdly bright,
the crossroad's grid and arrows
too perfect, as if in Toytown
or freshly painted yellow and white
though I had not seen
man, nor beast, nor machine.
My eyes were as wide as salmon.
I reeled them in
and it was then the babble began.

The chairs, all higgledy-piggledy
took up the great question
as the ghosts of former occupants –
students with theory and Penguin Classics,
young mothers shushing kids,
lovers leaning closer together
and a cluster of men dressed as Freud
contested this and that;
when a man at the edge in a yellow hat
and an anorak folded like wings
unfolded his lips from a cigarette
and like an angel began to sing:

The man at the edge in a yellow hat
and an anorak folded like wings
will unfold his lips from his cigarette
and this is what he will sing

44

IMTIAZ DHARKER

Campsie Fells

What did we look like?
A band of gypsies
set free out of solid homes
for one Sunday morning,
catapulted into the countryside,
a caravan.
All the families, Auntie Ameena,
Uncle Ramzan, a variety of children
in flowered frocks and wide shalwars,
clothes that responded to the wind.

What were we like, on that
Scottish field, up in the hills,
navigating the cow-pats,
paddling in sweet streams?

The children made daisy chains.
Azaan
shone a buttercup beneath our chins
to check if we loved butter.

And when the picnic was opened out,
the competition began, between
the families.
Who brought boiled eggs and sandwiches,
who made kebabs and tikkas with chutney.
The thermos flasks of tea,
all made up with sugar and with milk.

My mother settled like a queen,
a sculpture, took possession of that field,
spread all her goods around her.

The green sharpened.
The sun always blazed,
The long evenings never grew cold.

The Aunties began to speak
about old films, *Alvida, Alvida*
sang bits of songs
that always sounded sad,
Tum bhi kho gaye, hum bhi kho gaye.
Lines of remembered poems
made Uncle Asif cry.
Azaan asked, 'If you mind so much,
why don't you go back?'

Uncle Asif, wiping his eyes, replied,
'Our families are scattered. My brothers
and their wives are here. The village has changed.
My uncles have moved to town.
I'm not sure if anyone knows us any more.
And would you go get Zenab
out of the cow-shit and wash your hands
before you touch those chips?'

Afterwards we washed the cups.
Our names splashed in the stream,
no questions asked.

TARIQ LATIF

Western Ferry

These elemental men crossing the Clyde
labour seven days a week, all year round,
go back and forth in all weather and tides

collect tickets from passengers who drive
on the ferry and yearn for solid ground.
These elemental men crossing the Clyde

have a firm footing whatever the ride.
They smile, chat and joke and turning around
go back and forth in all weather and tides.

The men park the cars right up to the sides.
Mocking the notion of being lost or found
these elemental men crossing the Clyde

read the light like braille, sense the gentle glide
of isotherms in the bones which like sound
go back and forth in all weather and tides.

On some days, parties of the groom and bride
make the journey, a dead soul pays one pound.
These elemental men crossing the Clyde
go back and forth in all weather and tides.

LEILA ABOULELA

When I First Came to Scotland...

I pushed open the door that said 'Black Bastards' in pen, and
stepped into the mosque. A woman was taking off her shoes,
untying laces, left shoe then right. I greeted her and after she
replied, I said, 'Where can I get soap and water to clean the
words off the door?'

She said, 'Leave it now, we must be quick.'

I took off my shoes and hurried after her down corridors thick
with toddlers, little girls in long braids, fights over bubble-gum.

When I reached the hall, I heard a loud voice, 'Straighten the
lines! Straighten the lines and pray as if this is the last prayer.'

MAYA CHOWDHRY

Four Corners

'Empire of the East' in bold letters on the torn rusty hold
of a once grand ship   now despatched
to a steel graveyard   its ruling days over

How can I have grown in the Second City of the Empire
amidst its decaying shell? Why does my heart split
with every panel that's torn from its structure?

Outside the Trades House on Glassford Street
I fancy mysel'a weaver o'the Weaver's Guild
I wind down the plaid streets connecting
Campbells to McDonalds   Stuarts to McLarens
a woman in a head scarf on Bothwell Street stares
at me   do I look lost?
do I look like I've na hame?

On Saracen Street I gaze up at the tenements
dripping with stories of Merchant Traders
an'immigrants wondering whether
I'm the product of a marriage of East and West
North and South   or something in between

An equinox
where day and night are equal
where the sun rises in Mumbai
and sets over Glasgow

IMTIAZ DHARKER

Being good in Glasgow

FARIDA:

I did it all: read the Koran
five times at the seamen's club
that masqueraded as a mosque on Sundays,
kept the rosas,
fasted from dawn right through
the endless Scottish dusk,
definitely never drank. Ate
fish and chips when all my
friends had hamburgers. If
I even thought of a pig I'd
spit.

I was really full of shit.

I got fed up with being good.
It must have been a put-on anyway,
because I was hungry to be bad,
like craving food.

What I wanted, really, deep down, was sin.
To open the front door
in the middle of the morning
and let the devil in.

IMTIAZ DHARKER

from Lascar Johnnie 1930

In the 1930s, twenty percent of Britain's maritime labour force was made up of Indian seamen, called Lascars. Many stayed on at ports like Glasgow, some as itinerant salesmen, peddling their wares in remote parts of Scotland.

Lascar

I am invisible, in a ship manned
by invisible men, hands without names.
The captain does not see us,
but there are times when the ship does,
when it forgets its cargo of cotton,
loses its grip on sugar and tobacco,
and reshapes itself around its living load.

This is when it lifts a little
and the water slips
into the road I travel every night,
cradled by sugarcane, overhung
with tamarind. The air
has the sting of the songs we sing,
sharp with the taste of Jhelum.

Water cannot satisfy my tongue.
My thirst needs broad Punjabi,
my feet scrabble for flat earth, the plains.
Sometimes leaving America,
sometimes coming in to Glasgow,
I see another shoreline, sprung
with palms.

The captain chooses not to hear
our songs, or know our names.
Allahuddin, Mohammed, Mubarak, Bismillah.
Our names are prayers.
Someone must be saying them tonight
in the other country

Like a conversation, as if we were there.

JACKIE KAY

George Square

My seventy-seven-year-old father
put his reading glasses on
to help my mother do the buttons
on the back of her dress.
'What a pair the two of us are!'
my mother said, 'Me with my sore wrist,
you with your bad eyes, your soft thumbs!'

And off they went, my two parents
to march against the war in Iraq,
him with his plastic hips, her with her arthritis,
to congregate at George Square where the banners
waved at each other like old friends, flapping,
where they'd met for so many marches over their years,
for peace on earth, for pity's sake, for peace, for peace.

SUHAYL SAADI

from paradise gardens carpet

Glasgow: Mantle of the Green Hollow

One morning,
by the exquisite scent of sweet alyssum we were drawn
from the wild peacock reeds of the cold green river
to the centre of the City of the West Wind
to a caravanserai in a wall with no gate

From behind the Wall of Thenew came the ragim creaks of water-
      wheels
through its cracked substance fired shafts of white light

we, the shadow people of the borders,
each from another place
peered through many fissures,
separate niches, each
saw a different garden beyond the wall,
discussed, at length decided we
the gardens must be infinite

The garden was a robe with eight sides, many levels
the sky, a dome of blue and white flowers
petals, fluttering, changing in form
rolling into one another like cloud-banks
each bagh was four, seamed by
rivers of wine, honey, water, milk
flowing through the palms of water-wheels,
quadrants dividing again and again
into yet smaller squares, each
filled with the floating forms of cypresses ringed by citrus groves:
lime, orange, lemon
lime trees formed hijaabs, shading the fragile from the light, while
pungent lemon kept away stray vermin and
mihrab orange trees led to garden rooms and plaster courts
where on eight-sided tables, antique scrolls
wrote upon themselves in Kufic script with reed quills
and seeds burst joyously from the skins of pomegranates

Stone pavilions striped in ochre, black and terracotta sheltered
            beneath mulberry trees, rock and leaf
shadows, reflected in the uisge of tiny lochs,
danced in the House of Joy that was the garden
scent of Damask roses, heavy
of musk sweat, camphor wood and ginger plant, we smelled
and the white baadil of jasmine turned us
into night-dancers and weeping willows and laughing children

And as we were spun into beggars, falcons and pigeons,
so were the letters on the scrolls changed
into gazelles and lions, dragons and phoenixes
and at length there was no longer any sun and moon
but only the sides of a tambourine, dancing and swaying,

bells tinkling like the sound of water through stone
And all the music of the jannat:
the birdsong, the water, the emptiness
came to one, single note: Peace

At the centre of the chahar bagh, into which all streams flowed,
lay a basin built on the backs of twelve stone bulls
and from the basin came, not water merely, but
a giant, tortuous vine with branches bowing far into the sky
meandering foliage, ladders and wings, leaves split
by wondrous caterpillars weaving shimmering silken veils

As we shaded our eyes from the blinding noor,
we saw above the trees a gate, the shape of re-joined badams,
beyond this, a trellis bearing tiny blossoms around a giant, eight-
       petalled flower
four gates barring different layers of the garden
each bearing the petals of different flowers:
snowdrops, tulips, roses and gentian trumpets
On the lower branches of the vine tree, perched
two calligraphic birds and a silver fish, all gazing into
a spherical hanging glass in which burned a lamp

When we returned to our homes, everything had changed
The river, once-glaucous, flowed down from the mountains like
       liquid diamond,
the city had turned from frozen tomb to burning bedchamber,
rhythms of reel and iron flowed as blood through our veins
that which had enclosed the courtyard of our bodies was no longer
we were free, yet we were blind

In the centre of each house, a tall loom
across the floor, threads of many shades
we were blind yet
like worm, seed-hair and lustrous pashm,
we knew by touch and smell and taste the colour of every thread

We set to work, each on a different carpet, a separate loom
we strove to reproduce what we had seen
but wool, cotton and silk are not petals and streams and stars

our hands, human not divine, so
the beings emerging from the taut weft and weave
had not life, breath, words, but were merely simulacra
as music is to the whisper of the Friend's breath

We were stone blind, had no pattern,
only our memories, and the memories of those who had gone before
for this work spanned many generations, the pain of countless partings,
it moved with us
across darya, desert, moss and law

We wove herbaceous borders of irises, lilies and bluebells
planted polygons of tulips, hyacinths, guls
beneath the tips of our fingers, palm fronds became
vine leaves and lotus blossoms
fissures and tolls in stone opened
into window-frames and ladders and the kairi of ancient mango trees
the dun splendours of the city which we could never have had,
strutted and moaned as peacocks
ancient scrolls, which we could never have read,
we wrote as filigree silver and gold
dark places, into which by a thousand armies we were cast,
we fashioned as wild asses,
wings upon which we were denied flight,
we grew as almonds
Beinn Kaaf, up whose steep, horn sides we clambered,
the skin of our hands tearing from the bone,
we dreamed as a black pyramid
The Loved One, as a gazelle.

When the slowest carpet was finished,
the last trump fashioned,
the final hole cut in the shehnai reed of the unseen farishta,
we found that we did not know how to tie the end knot
left in that state, the carpets soon would unravel, their paths,
become lost in the furze and brash and musk of the green hollow
so we hauled the rugs into the courtyard by the unknown river
upon our hunched shoulders one, great loom
and using this frame, with our fingertips we sewed the ends of each
        carpet to

the beginnings of another,
so that the whole became one, great carpet with neither beginning
        nor end

And then we moved our homes to the rug,
and sat and lived and swam upon it as upon dark water,
and like the words on the scrolls in the pavilions,
it grew within us, and so
we began the weaving of an endless carpet, one
which can be added to by every guest who passes through our homes,
each traveller may leave their mark,
their vision of the gardens, become heart,
upon the green earth of our place
until eventually
the carpet will spread out and cover
the mountains, the lochs, the world
Our pain is turned to laughter, our blindness to light

IRFAN MERCHANT

Address Tae Chicken Tikka Masala

Fair fa' the nation's favourite dish
fulfilling everybody's wish,
great chieftain, O so very Scottish,
                the spice o life;
ye came and conquered the English,
                curing the strife.

Born in Glasgow's Shish Mahal
during Thatcher's iron rule
your origins stretch to the Mughals
                but when they tried
the chicken tikka the locals
                found it too dry.

And so the chef would open up
a can of Campbell's tomato soup,
add chilli, then colour with pap-
                                    -rika for zest,
and then, O what a glorious sup,
                                    simply the best.

As Scots we want the hottest thing
on the menu, a dish with zing:
haggis disnae mak us sing
                                    in the teenies;
the mince and tatties ye'll hae tae sling
                                    wi yer jeeli-piece.

Noo we export tae India
oor national dish, making it clear
that Scotland is a warld leader
                                    in aa the airts
fir chicken tikka masala
                                    ye've won oor hairts.

Lord Ganesha, tae please the Scots
remember whit they want is lots
o sauce and spices, very hot,
                                    but dinnae worry;
Ah've got the answer in ma pot –
                                    gie them a curry.

GERRY SINGH

India Gate

The noon sun over Delhi
Lit up the M8.

On my soft shoulder
Was a hard shoulder
Laying out a long carpet
To the pink city of Jaipur.

Looking towards the Lomonds
I saw a lama
On the cooling heights of Shimla
Walking on a cloud of dust.

And a small train
Rattling the iron gauges
Fuelling a trip to the Ganges.

Waiting on the platform
At Varanasi
I met so many strangers
Who had been here before.

Watched them
Bathing in the warm light
Where Emperors had stood
Not hearing the thundering clatter
Of the Raj.

And reflected in the churned
Up waters of the flood
Was a lovely child of both.

GERRY SINGH

Ladhar Bheinn

Little cairns mark the way like hill stations
For the independent minded.
Fifty years have passed
Since the Gandhis lived at number forty-seven.
Here, spiders do not hide in caves
Swinging away from the light
And waiting on a sign.

A colourful crowd head for the summit.
The rock stood up
Walled in a halted hardness
And all that is hidden
From the historian's little perch

Whose tiny trickle
Cannot disturb the continuing flow
Of water on stone.

The astonished stag freezes time,
His wait measured in breaths
Lost from way back then
When Bruce was bold.

Stepping in the rich chocolate peat
Travellers plod and mutter
Rinsing out the squelch of absenteeism
To welcome home to the fold
The leaky streets of Glasgow and Calcutta.

Nothing to crow about yet
While dressed up *spuggies*
Tell us tales that do not tally.

spuggies: sparrows

For ruler and ruled alike
The rock waits.
The path is clear,
Dry and dusty as an Asian mouth
Where colour, birth or better
Cannot fashion a sari from a fetter
Or lock horns with the king of the deer
Who waits for you to move.

VAHNI CAPILDEO

Shell

The sea needs no ornament.
She adorns herself with herself
and is herself our wreckage.
Unspontaneous as disbelief
the island combusting
– every sunset, despite the mist,
such mist, so very missed, chances
ourselves plunged in sunset
forever lying off the coast.
The railroad makes straight the house.
No names for you pass muster.
I wrote gods' names in the sand.

TARIQ LATIF

After Lights over Girvan

Drunk and bored the lads leap
off the sea wall and crush
the empty lager cans.

The sea waves do not break
but move as one, oblique
and silent. The oily
surfaces bear the burden
of granite-blue ribbons.
A navy mist erases
the horizon. Even
here, where the rust-clotted
railings under my hands
give way to the pitch-black
sea, the cries from the lads
reach us – muffled as if
they were drowning. And I
am troubled by the thought
of falling in fathom-
less black – fighting for breath
and light but finding just
slimy wetness and hard
pain – I inhale sharply
and stare at the sea-gulls
flying by in silence.

The dense mass of the sea
reflects the weightless sky.
An empty can drifts by.

BASHABI FRASER

Do' care

In a Paris hotel lounge on one occasion
My thirteen-year-old five-foot-five
Daughter glowed with the attention
Of three young men striving
To pigeon-hole her Scottishness
And break her brittle brusqueness
With their far-eastern finesse.

If Scotland played England
Whom would she support
– Sco'land – was the answer delivered
And if England played India
– India – she claimed with triumphant swagger.
If England played Germany
– Germany – was the response
From the unassailable position
Of a new-found nationalism.

And what if it were Scotland and India
One demanded with the diabolical confidence
Of an argument-winning lawyer –
She clamped down her glass, shrugged her bare
Shoulders, turned away saying – do' care.

BASHABI FRASER

Tartan & Turban

Give me your tartan
And I will imbue it with
The spirit of my race.
I can defend your borders
As I did the Punjab's
In long war-torn days.

I will wear your tartan
With the pride and strength
Of my history and tribe.
I will weave in its pattern
The breadth and length
Of five rivers that subscribed
To my wealth, which I will now
Lend to your tartan
And make it mine – this new
Singh tartan, willing to
Blend with my Sikh turban
At my journey's end.

GEORGE MUREVESI

Pleas

dreich you are callous
you inflict misery to these parts on impulse?
dear dreich, l beg you not to banish the sun from the Scottish skies
not to make this place a bore where, at your mention, everybody sighs
dreich, tone down these incessant torrents
or relocate to places with droughts
dreich, pacify the sky to allow the sun to smile on its canvas

GRACE NICHOLS

The Queen of Sheba replies to Kathleen Jamie

Scour Scotland for a Solomon...
FROM 'The Queen of Sheba' by Kathleen Jamie

Dear Kath, here I am lass,
penning these lapis lazuli lines
from the balcony of my spice kingdom,
pausing, every so often,
to watch the birds fly in,
(no longer bringing leaves of cinnamon)
so preoccupied are they these days
with dodging air pollution.

Well, girlfriend, I've just set
my Himyaritic seal of approval
upon your much-loved praise poem.
Indeed, the gorgeous 'hanging baskets'
of my breasts were fitted to a T
not to mention my head, still warm
with memories of the peat,
the bracken; the awestruck lads and lasses.

Having the keys to the National Library
bestowed upon me was such a pleasure
(My love is like a red red rose...)
The only wee regret, however,
was that time did not permit
the highland fling, as I've long
harboured a curiosity
about your menfolk's kilts.

But on to more prudent things.
It is with the most cordial
of intentions
for Sheba-Scottish relations,
that I presume to let

my queenly armour slip
revealing some of the nitty-grittier
aspects of my older trip.

Take the shindig in my courtyard
on the morning of our departure –
no less than a hundred cud-chewing
secretly incensed camels
predisposed to wreck a havoc on my buttocks,
simply because I had christened them;
'Ships of the desert'
(I was told this later by their cameleer)

The lavish gifts being loaded for Solomon –
not only gold, myrrh, frankincense,
but also the best of spices;
attendants running around to procure
last-minute dainties; honeycombs, figs, pomegranates.
All my garments perfumed by my favoured gabanum.
Then the great train moving off...
to the handbells of musicians.

As you rightly said;
The cool black skin of the bible
could not hold me.
Neither could the Red Sea –
Sand to the left of me; Sand to the right of me
Sand, countless scintillating miles
of it – ahead of me.
The lewd sun pouring down.

I will not go into the nights
of song and dance,
the emblemic music
that pervaded the slyly shifting sands.
Suffice to say
that I was burnished to my ultimate.
It was a fine and stately madness,
but girlgirlgirl Solomon was no mirage.

He was rich where it matters
(And I don't mean his jewelled robes and slippers)
With seven hundred wives –
Edomites, Ammonites, Moabites
(not to mention lovebites)
he would have to be –
behold the half was not told me!
his thighs alone like twin-trunks of the cedar tree.

Well, I came to prove and prove
him I did, with hard questions,
conversing into the most ungodly hours...
succumbing slowly to his musk
as he to my gabanum –
two sovereigns shivering
in the heat of love's passions.
So much for wisdom and trade relations.

Well, lass, I must not unbridle
too many memories upon you.
Don't get me wrong, of Solomon I am still fond,
in fact I wrote him many songs
(a bundle of myrrh is my beloved unto me)
but there was no way
I could leave my kingdom
to join a throng.

So our affair did fizzle out
the way these long distance lusts do
when unbacked by the currency
of warm flesh. yet I have no regrets –
ageless, raceless, classless as I am.
Qualities, which incidentally,
should stand us in good stead even as we gird
ourselves for the turbulent winds of the 21st century.

I will stop here. By order of my own royal command.
Regards to everyone in Scotland.
                         Yours as ever,
                              Makeda, Queen of Sheba,
                              High Priestess of Adventure.

SHAMPA RAY

My India

India has moved in next door
She had flown in from Heathrow
Landed here at Number Ten
I am number nine. She has brought with her only her custom
And pocket book to declare
There is stress, goody goody
Damn, as in damn right
Cleavage look! As in sexy
But still no translation
For privacy or eating alone no solitude or wow, exclamation

Me, I fly infrequently
In the back bedroom at night
Rest in yesterday's reservoir drop off the ballast of this pen
Curl up asleep on paper cuttings:
There words will join up in dreams

This Ikea lucky bamboo only 99p
Durga announces from her hallway
I smile and close my door
Seal a distant railway sound
And in this silent Scotland
I hear a language all my own.

TAWONA SITHOLE

climbing hills

like faces of the sun
black ice is invisible
unsteady feet
slurred speech
but no intoxication
just fresh air of winter
nae bother big man
cheers big man
thrown into slight confusion
but somehow feeling alright
alright, it gets soggy and smoggy
in these layered streets
but can't get drowned
in the hailstone sleet
got to look up
or miss the architecture
got to look up
or miss the mist

here comes another hill to climb
this one has a different slant
dark secrets glazed in skyline
past riches drawn in storyline
attraction
          extraction
                    expansion
                         extension

here comes another hill to climb
this one has another slant
tunnels unravel in parallel options
round and round in opposite directions
underground
              playground
                         break ground
                                   common ground

here comes another hill to climb
this one has another slant
happy hourglass steadily silting
hearty swigging and slowly sipping
soirée
      hooray
           holiday
                 hogmanay

here comes another hill to climb
this one has a different slant
odd friction caused by colour of skin
contradiction for the recycling bin
recycle
      full cycle
           spin cycle
                life cycle

here comes another hill to climb
this one has another slant
waterways and other ways
concrete shapes and open space
flowing
      going
           showing
                growing

here comes another hill to climb
this one has another slant
hectic heat cooled in rain shower
how slowly things move in rush hour
expect
      accept
           respect
                reflect

here comes another hill to climb
this one has a different slant
momentum lost, momentarily
firm footing found, eventually

reclaim

      regain

            retain

                  remain

like faces of the sun
black ice is invisible
unsteady feet
slurred speech
but no intoxication
just fresh air of winter
nae bother big man
cheers big man
thrown into slight confusion
but somehow feeling alright
alright, it gets soggy and smoggy
in these layered streets
but can't get drowned
in the hailstone sleet
got to look up
or miss the architecture
got to look up
or miss the mist

MAUD SULTER

Flight

To the frozen north I flee. Another country.

Well a hid tae get awae couldn'y staun the pressure
n a couldn'y face the reality o bein sae loved   So
here in the room o ma adolescence a'm awake again
before daylight filters perculated through bamboo
blinds   Fearful

Paint dapples the morning
I paint
to make this space a sanctuary
for us
so that somewhere we have security
knowing
that as soon as we do our own place
should follow.

n the poor n the needy n the spiritually
lost are still here n the city gets greyer
again   edges sharpened voices mair piercing in
desperation we try tae survive another winter here
in *thatchur's britain* wains wi runnin noses auld wimmin
wi nae enough money fur heatin n the cauld   the cauld seems
wirse than last year   aye the cauld seems wirse than last year
the seventies promise of a better future tastes bitter on ma
tongue nae mair   a wunder wit happened tae the semblance
o tolerance now replaced wi mair bigotry in the wake o
the anglo-irish agreement   graffiti reminds us that
the bitterness remains n tho it isn'y ma main
concern it's a shame fur the wains is it no
aye a shame fur the wains is it no?

JACKIE KAY

In my country

walking by the waters
down where an honest river
shakes hands with the sea,
a woman passed round me
in a slow watchful circle,
as if I were a superstition;

or the worst dregs of her imagination,
so when she finally spoke
her words spliced into bars
of an old wheel. A segment of air.
Where do you come from?
'Here,' I said, 'Here. These parts.'

IRFAN MERCHANT

The Indian Upon Scotland

Gin onybody unnerstuid a wird
Ah said then Ah'd speak Indian English
but it'd dae yer heid in, an this weird
has brocht me tae this alien language
throu whit Ah'm tryin tae transmit ma Zen
yet dis Scots hae a wird fir Reality?
There's ower twenty wirds fir 'cough' Ah ken
but wirds maun be importit, juist lik tea.
It seems tae me the Scottish Enlichtenment
husnae heppent. Nor dae the Elders o
the Kirk ken Truth, thon muckle disapyntment
which lea's ye lauchin: shunyata; zero.
Awaukenin is better syne than shrooms,
tae see Speerit cled in sindry costumes.

IMTIAZ DHARKER

How to cut a pomegranate

'Never,' said my father,
'Never cut a pomegranate
through the heart. It will weep blood.
Treat it delicately, with respect.

Just slit the upper skin across four quarters.
This is a magic fruit,
so when you split it open, be prepared
for the jewels of the world to tumble out,
more precious than garnets,
more lustrous than rubies,
lit as if from inside.
Each jewel contains a living seed.
Separate one crystal.
Hold it up to catch the light.
Inside is a whole universe.
No common jewel can give you this.'

Afterwards, I tried to make necklaces
of pomegranate seeds.
The juice spurted out, bright crimson,
and stained my fingers, then my mouth.

I didn't mind. The juice tasted of gardens
I had never seen, voluptuous
with myrtle, lemon, jasmine,
and alive with parrots' wings.

The pomegranate reminded me
that somewhere I had another home.

NORTH

FRED D'AGUIAR

from Sonnets from Whitley Bay

Troubled but not distressed
from a window in Durham cathedral

2

We always star in one another's dreams
In full technicolor and super sixteen.
We fall asleep like spoons and only turn
When one or the other decides to turn.
Morning is a silence that won't fracture.
An elbow-room closeness and the odd gesture
Confirms the other's thoughts in sea-air thick
With desire. We nod our approval at brick
In a city where I first said, I love you,
Climbing the cathedral's 325 steps to view
One shire shouldering the next, like molars,
As God would have it or Buddha, or some polar
Icecap and then the warming of the globe,
Exactly as the heat I feel when inside you.

4

My love you fill my head to distraction.
I am pacing a room you hardly looked into,
Furthest from the bedroom-cum-granary
Where we lived and loved and woke in an aviary
That quietened as the light intensified
And objects muddled by the dark, clarified.
All that night nothing could come between us,
A sliver of light or dark couldn't separate us.

By morning the bed had split into half –
Us in a dividing current on two rafts;
Us in our deep dreams, private and sweet.
How did we drift apart, even in sleep?
One look from you of panic, loss, love,
And I leapt from my raft to share yours.

6

This kind of loving wrecks the body,
Makes it impossible to function properly.
You wake up mid-morning feeling like the night before,
But to go back to bed would turn your head forever.

You stay on your feet and sway like a ship
Becalmed, waiting for anything to happen, to slip
Your world back into orbit, but nothing does,
Except the light slips and you register a dull pulse.

The ship is hers and the sea is hers, the light
You see the world by, hers; the loving that night
Was all hers; the feeling that you're wrecked, hers.

The love you think is a blessing is a curse,
A weakness, something not hers, but yours: stop,
Before you have no pulse, before you drop.

9

When I turn my back on this North of Norths
And I kiss you goodbye, how come it hurts?

When sea-lit winds loosen a stinging rain
On Whitley Bay, your tears drown out mine.

This curved beach of seaweed and stones
Shows from my wavy footprints I'm all alone.

The waves form an orderly queue to see
Who's the miserable man bringing misery.

When those waves wreck in despair on sandstone,
It's my back breaking with my need for home.

I give up town and sea for glass and concrete,
And a capital adding to itself,

House by red brick house on the *For Sale* shelf,
And new-post-code street by tarmacked street.

SHEREE MACK

Bonny Baby Contest

In the stuffy old village hall,
in a corner, jam-packed,
under the stairs are Geordie
mothers, smiling into the faces
of their babies or the camera.
My mum fixes the camera with
a weary stare.

Twenty eight years old
and newly married,
my sister sits on her knee,
with head turned around,
making sure mum's still
there, the touch of her knee
and hands not being enough.

Mum does not smile.
In her face, I see my sister
grown, and in my sister's face
I see her son grown.
Between their years
and their stories,
time is running by.

KAYO CHINGONYI

Baltic Mill

Though you maintain the elements
have conspired against us we still
inch the cobbled street past Castle
Keep down to the Quayside's rain
slick paving slabs all for the whim
of standing across from Baltic Mill
in a turbid mist lifted from the Tyne.

We planned to catch a talk at the Laing
or the Biscuit but, pushed for time,
plumped for a backstreet pizzeria, throw-
back to another world, a haberdasher's
maybe or greasy spoon for blackface
minstrels from Gateshead mines and
iron works. The North Sea wind-chill

bids us leave behind this city of faces
cast in stories passed down, vestige
of years when hundreds of miles stood
between us. The exact course that brought
us here is unimportant. It is that we met
like this river, drawn from two sources,
offered up our flaws, our sedimental selves.

GRACE NICHOLS

Angel of the North

Travelling on an InterCity to Newcastle
I spot you hovering somewhere over
Gateshead.

No cherubim or seraphim. No crossed swords
pointing to or from the great
northern forest

Just an angel emerging out of scrap metal
and the conscience
of coal

Just an angel framed by sky and wind
guarding with corrugated
wings

The dark light of a people's spirit.

CHERYL MARTIN

Driving Back from Durham
Bastille Day 1990

Suddenly it's summer in England.
Gilt sun on green water:
a yellow boat;
we four rowing raucously downriver.
We slip with the stream
under willow tress,
pulling leaves and laughing.

Our necks, backs, hands burned –
I wrung the water from my red dress
while my shoulders ached –
but the sun shone good,
and I was beginning
to look into your
sky eyes –
no, don't look, look down –
that was silly,
you'd think I was fourteen, not thirty –
but kindness is so seductive
and you are so kind.
I am beginning
as smiles tumble up streets,
we tumble up stairs
to tea and crumpets.
It could have been twee,
but not with these greedy people,
cramming down hot pie and cream.
The ride home was green,
and that hay on the side seemed
like blond blankets rolled –
God, it must be odd
to have gold hair.
I am beginning
for the first time in five years
to feel,
and fifty years on
I will close my eyes,
taste an apple pie,
a river,
cotton candy with flies,
and it will still be you.

KAYO CHINGONYI

Denouement

> ...*One afternoon at four o'clock, we separated,*
> *just for a week... Alas,*
> *that week became forever.*
>
> CAVAFY

I am afraid it will be too easy;
we'll meet in a restaurant made ours
by habit, reminisce about the cheesy
opener and petrol station flowers
that sent you tumbling on my first attempt.
You'll order a Prawn Korma with boiled rice,
a Pakora, jug of water, repent
before asking for a glass of house white.
And when the laden plates settle on the
cloth of our favourite table; the talk will
move to the hill-top castle at Bamburgh;
the buzz cut lawns we'll never walk. *Still*,
I'll say, *we could always go as just friends?*
The waiter, on cue, will come over to see
the food's to our taste, unsure what it portends
that we do not answer, just scrape cutlery.

JACK MAPANJE

The Seashells Of Bridlington North Beach
(for Mercy Angela)

She hated anything caged, fish particularly,
Fish caged in glass boxes, ponds, whatever;

'Reminds me of prisons and slavery,' she said;
So, when first she caught the vast green view

Of Bridlington North Beach shimmering that
English summer day, she greeted the sight like

A Sahara girl on parched feet, cupping, cupping
Cupping the water madly, laundering her palms,

Giggling and laughing. Then rubbing the hands
On her skirt, she threw her bottom on the sandy

Beach and let the sea breathe in and out on her
As she relaxed her crossed legs – 'Free at last!'

She announced to the beach crowds oblivious;
And as the seascape rallied and vanished at her

Feet, she mapped her world, 'The Netherlands
We visited must be here; Norway, Sweden there;

Beyond that Russia!' Then gathering more sea-
shells and selecting them one by one, she turned

To him, 'Do you remember eating porridge from
Beach shells once?' He nodded, smiling at another

Memory of the African lakes they were forced to
Abandon. 'Someday, perhaps I'll take that home

To celebrate!' She said, staring into the deep sea.
Today, her egg-like pebbles, her pearls of seashells

Still sparkle at the windowsill; her wishes still ring,
'Change regularly the water in the receptacles to

Keep the pebbles and seashells shining – you'll
See, it's a lot healthier than feeding caged fish!'

GRACE NICHOLS

Outward from Hull

The gulls of Hull
the train pulling out –
a metallic snake
along the estuary
leaving behind
the forceful ghost
of Wilberforce
the confluence
of the Hull and the Humber.
Brough, Selby, Doncaster.
How many times
have I sat this way
England, gazing out
at the leafless names
of trees; at cathedrals
I still haven't seen –
our inter-city boa
pushing through
the deepening night –
the wet black roots
of the country.
Suddenly, for some
unearthly reason,
it falters, then stops –
an inexplicable
paralysis of rhythm –
the brooch of a small
town gleaming

in the distance –
the eels and eels
of branching tracks.

O England –
hedge-bound as Larkin
omnivorous as Shakespeare.

LORNA GOODISON

At the Keswick Museum

Amidst the packhorse bells, cockfighting spurs,
the glass walls of stuffed birds, and a giant set
of cordierite impregnated stones which sound
to create an early form of xylophone, it stands.

The wooden chest you are asked to handle
with care, for it houses the 500-year-old cat.
Its concave eye sockets still scoop darkness.

In those days darkness was on the whole land:
take for example in the parish of Lamplugh
in 1658, the following deaths were recorded.

Three frightened to death by fairies.
Four perished from being bewitched.
One old woman put to death for maybe
bewitching the four just mentioned.
One poor soul led to unfortunate end
by a will o' the wisp carrying her wide.

In addition, educated people in Lamplugh
claimed their domiciles were inhabited
by bogies, spirits and dobbies (duppies).
A dobby or duppy, it seems, was or is
an household spirit which can get mean
and vicious if not hospitably received.

So there in the pastoral Lake District
the good people found it was necessary
to root frightspirit rowan trees by gates,
and to place oddly shaped, waterworn stones
(preferably those with a single eye-hole
representing the all-seeing adder) atop walls.

Eye of adders to ward off witches, bogeys,
dobbies, all categories of malevolent spirits,
including nightmares, which were steeds
ridden by witches like the one put to death
for taking the lives of those four souls. So when
they took her life, her cat gave up his ninth.
That's it there petrified in that wooden chest.
Cross yourself and just back away from it.

LORNA GOODISON

To Mr William Wordsworth, Distributor of Stamps for Westmoreland

The host of golden flowers at my feet
were common buttercups not daffodils,
they danced and swayed so in the breeze
though overseer thorns were planted among them.

Still, it was a remarkable show of sorts
which opened my eye, the inward one,
which once opened enabled me to see
the overflowing bounty of my peoples' poverty.

Sir, did you pass my great-grandmother?
Like you she lived in Westmoreland,
she rode upon a great gray mule,
she could not read or write, she did not buy stamps.

But great-grandmother was a poet
who wrote her lyrical ballads on air,
scripted them with her tongue
then summoned them to return to her book of memory.

She never did arrange them
the exact same way twice
but they were her powerful overflow
recollected in tranquility, sir, what she chanted was poetry.

Great-grandmother was Black Betty's daughter,
sister to fool fool Rose, distant cousin
to Betty Foy's idiot boy. Laughingstock
of the West Country, of no degree, she spoke funny.

But, sir, whenever she would sing
even the solitary reaper's voice was stilled
as her wild mystic chanting issued
over the cane brakes and hills. Only Keats's nightingale

could compete with her guinea griot style.
But she was not in any contest
for the fittest of the fit, she had just come
with her wild ways to enchant with her riddling lyrics.

Mr Wordsworth, I am not buying any stamp
to post a letter to my great-grandmother.
She is a denizen of the spirit world like you
so I am asking you when you pass her there, to tell her

that I collected up all her songs and poems
from where they fell on banana trash.
The binding ones on the star apple tree,
the ones hidden like pound notes under her coir mattress.

I rescued them, rat-cut Blue Mountain coffee,
the ratoon and dunder ones, refuse and trash
of the sugarcane, the ones they call broken
and indecent, patois, bungo, words for bondage and shame.

And I've written them down for her,
summoned them to stand, black-face type
against a light background, Mr Wordsworth.
Please tell Miss Leanna her poems are now written down.

JACKIE KAY

Windows, Lakes

I always wanted a house with a bay window, my mother said,
reading the estate agent's window in Kendal.
Imagine – sitting in the sun and reading a Simenon – heaven! –
in a cushioned bay window in an L-shaped room of a bungalow.
It took me back to the houses of my mother's imagination long ago:
turrets and wings and open-plan kitchens –
space for Aga – conservatories, entrance halls,
ground-floor cloakrooms, *ooh la*, three double bedrooms
(one en-suite), dining, drawing and reception rooms.
Double-fronted Georgian townhouses, shutters and sash windows.
The years of window-shopping dream houses.
She never moved from her 1950s semi-detached Wimpey.

Wouldn't you have just loved a conservatory? she said,
peering at another: *4 beds, 350 grand –*
grow cherry tomatoes, read the Sunday papers in the sun?
All landscapes exist in the imagination, Naipaul said:
My mother's best houses were in her head.

I picked her up at Oxenholme, that nostalgic station.
I saw her searching for me through the train window.
She climbed gingerly onto the old platform,
William Morris walking stick in one hand, suitcase in another.
The train she got off sped into the past.

                    *

I drove my mother the scenic route to Carlisle
Through Staveley, past Beatrix Potter's Troutbeck,
Over the Kirkstone Pass – Grizedale to the west,
Beda Fall to the east, past Patterdale,
the tail end of Ullswater, Place Fell, Matterdale End,
Little Mell Fell gently waving hello,
snaking and winding our way, singing
You take the high road and I'll take the low
drinking it all in, the plains and vistas:
beautiful, beautiful, my mother said,
I always wanted to see the Lakes,

Wordsworth and Coleridge, Grasmere and Windermere.
But nothing compares to our Campsie Glens, our Fintry Hills,
she said, kissing my cheeks at Carlisle,
pulling herself onto the train for Glasgow,
too busy finding her seat with her stick and her bag to wave
through the window. I stood watching the train gather speed
along the track, until just the lines were left,
the double lines of the old train track.

I drove down the M6 back to Manchester,
past Penrith, the turn off to Kendal and Windermere.
I gripped the wheel, stared through the car window,
remembering the imaginary houses years ago:
the big bay window, bay horse and Play-Doh,
a half-open baby grand playing *fah soh lah ti doh*.

E.A. MARKHAM

Epilogue

Here we are after all those funerals,
dressed in these clothes not meant for funerals
as we head to the house or pub relieved
that food and drink will comfort and divert us
for some time longer. But already

you've said all the things necessary
to this gathering, bringing our lives up to date,
like at the outing of the evening class,
halting over a Mediterranean feast
on a damp Yorkshire night, determined
to accept on your plate only such nouns
as pronounced to the satisfaction
of the waiter. But this, perhaps, isn't about food.

So we stand here, two men and a hundred years
in England between us, waiting
and not waiting to move on, balancing
fantasy of home and return against
return and home. This is not voiced, the men
have much in common; they've missed the dinner.

ANTHONY KELLMAN

Roofs of Yorkshire

What are those birds circling the roofs of Yorkshire?
Seagulls in for winter, frowning crows, two-hued magpies.
What are they thinking? What are they saying?
We reflect your beings, body and soul.
We mirror racial hatreds, racial hopes,
over Yorkshire, over deciduous birches plainly poised,
over rowans budding for spring,
over dry-stone walls.

For centuries, birds and walls course
through the hills of north of Leeds,
around unhurried villages where garlands
of millstones, spotted with moss,
whose grits once crushed corn to flour a village,
are precise as pyramids and as resolute.

One seeks to compose a verse so tightly packed,
so naturally united, out of one's own plainness:

long stretches of sandy beach,
rows of cane rustling with crows and cranes,
long runways of singing surf.

SENI SENEVIRATNE

Frame Yourself

When my mother said *Frame yourself*, my sister and I
would stare at each other, trying to keep our faces straight,
and draw a frame in mid-air. We pinned our mouths
shut to suppress the laughter as she hurried us into
sensible school shoes that were wide enough for our feet
because she knew what it was like to nurse corns and blisters.
The radio was always plating some sweet music and the numbers
on the front never made sense as the needle whizzed past them.
First a crackle, then a strong signal that brought clear sound
so we turned our ears towards it, and were still not ready.

SENI SENEVIRATNE

Yorkshire Childhood

Swings and roundabouts across the road,
at the end of a cobbled street, down steep
steps from a scullery, with a sink too high
and a bucket underneath. Out of a back room
with a shiny black fireplace filled with red hot –
Don't touch! Don't stand too near!
as I held the toasting fork to brown the pikelets.

My brown hands were stinging with the heat,
red face beaming as I waited for melting
butter over licking lips. I disappeared then

into a worn armchair, but never my Grandad's.
That waited empty, like his slippers, till he arrived
to eat his dinner, always ready on the table, and drink
his gravy from the plate – though we were never allowed.

My grandma taught me to make egg custard
tarts, very carefully. Said I had pastry fingers.
My brown hands dipped in and out of fatty flour
moulding, rolling – like her fingers that she
worked to the bone, so she wore a gap in the
gold of her ring (when I always thought
gold was too hard to wear out).

My grandma wore pink corsets, laughed at
her own long baggy knickers, let me snuggle up
to her bum in bed, told me I was important
and special; that no matter what anyone said
or teased, I had a right to be who I was, and
that I would be great, I would be wonderful,
I would show them all in the end just how good I was,
my brown hands reaching across the mound of her belly.

ANITA SIVAKUMARAN

Ice and Ice Age

Ice held this rock face, then slid, melting,
Moved half the hill, cleaved a valley,
Gave way to life.

Black and glassy sides, sheer drops,
Stacked slates and sediments – he points at them,
The Yorkshire man, and speaks their story.

Here a new age dawned from ice.
We walk along the stone wall,
Touching fingertips with history.

You nod. You contribute.
I'd like to say something, but my tongue slips
In my brain's crevices, cut by references that slid away before I existed.

Glacial ice only puts to mind the Himalayas,
Carrying cold on their shoulders,
As do the hills of this country,

Bearing up miraculous fish to an attainable heaven,
Moving an inch an age.
(Fish are sedimented in the rocks here too.)

But even the Himalayas are a distant reference,
A song on the radio, to us South Indians
Roasting on our coastal plains,

Where all history's ages were long and perishing hot,
And ice is what we crack out of the fridge
To suck whole on hot days.

R. PARTHASARATHY

A Northern City

Dressed in tweeds or grey flannel,
Its suburban pockets bursting
With immigrants – coloureds is what
They call us over there –
The city is no jewel, either. But ugly
And wet. Lanes, full of smoke and litter,

With puddles of unwashed English
Children. Unfriendly moors that I
Haunted, especially Ilkley
Or Kirkstall abbey – on a long
Afternoon in summer with notebook
And pencil – built of gritstone

In Norman style. And snow
In January that took away
The city's wrinkles and gout. It was
Like being on another planet. Now,
Five years later, I think of this
Northern city, affectionately.

JACK MAPANJE

After Celebrating Our Asylum Stories
At West Yorkshire Playhouse, Leeds

So, define her separately,
She's not just another
Castaway washed up your
Rough seas like driftwood,
It's the nameless battles
Your sages burdened her
People that broke her back;
Define him differently,
He's not another squirrel
Ousted from your poplars,
It's the endless cyclones,
Earthquakes, volcanoes,
Floods, mud and dust that
Drafted him here; define
Them warmly, how could
Your economic émigré queue
At your job centres day after
Day? If you must, define us
Gently, how do you hope
To see the tales we bear
When you refuse to hear
The whispers we share?

KHADIJAH IBRAHIIM

from **A Snapshot History of Leeds**

56 Cowper Street

As Grandma said,
New broom sweep clean
but the old one knows all the corners,
so brick by brick
I rebuild a house that once stood in Chapeltown,
56 Cowper Street,
a Victorian terrace with a green front door,
my grandparent's home,
where I slid down the staircase banister
into laughter and now in memory.

I try to remember all things special,
like the Canadian gift of an oil painted portrait
of my dad and Aunt Sylvia
hanging against midnight-blue
circle-print wallpaper in the lounge;
Grandma's rose-porcelain tea sets;
her crystal and dust-free silverware,
for viewing only.

This seven-bedroom house signified
Importance in the ready hands of my
Jamaican family, blood spiced with Africa
and something of the colonial past.

Grandma grew roses and dahlias
in the front garden, picked gooseberries
to make jam and wine; Grandad dug tuff dirt
in the back yard, planted potatoes and cabbage.
Their tea they sipped from ceramic mugs,
blue for Grandad, red for Grandma,
except on special occasions, when Granny liked
a teacup with saucer.
Every day full-cooked breakfast from the kitchen –

nutmeg spiced condensed milk,
smoothed cornmeal porridge,
salt fish and callaloo, fried dumplings –
filled hungry bellies;
and the ritual of meals
at the oak dining-room table
with family and familiar friends
each with a story from which lessons
were to be learnt, now brings smiles.

Homespun

My stays at Cowper Street were long –
sometimes up to a year of Grandma's 'kidnap' –
to compensate for my father being overseas,
so I was split between
my mother's looser apron strings
and Grandma homespun rules
of do's and don'ts and decency,
when chores were regular and never shirked
for skipping ropes, jacks and hot rice,
when skylarking carried the repercussion of:
Stand up straight, pull your socks up!
Never mind de playing outside wid dem
pickney. Dem favour leggo beast.
Go find a book and read.
At Cowper Street,
love's strict hand nurtured studies,
mental arithmetic and recitation on the spot,
but Grandma also styled party frocks
on the Singer in her bedroom
and quilted the foundations of our kinship
for generations; told me of her Welsh-blooded grandfather,
Jabez, who gambled away the family's Jamaican land,
and of her first and second husbands,
her six children: five names beginning with the letter 'D',
the first born with an 'S';
these stories stitched tightly to me.

Home Schooled

In my aunties' bedroom, the world moved
to the heartbeat of *I'm black and I'm proud*.
Aunty Dana and Dahlia wore natural hairstyles
cut pepper-grain short, combed smooth,
their stereo player played
soul melodies of Curtis Mayfield
We got to have peace,
and the reggae revolution of Steel Pulse
stirred their words.
Their bedroom walls carried through the atmosphere,
posters of Garvey, Ras Daniel Heartman's natty roots children,
and the Jackson Five, with their doctorates in Afros.

Combing through the thickness
of my little girl plaits, Aunty Dahlia tied satin ribbons,
left them long to dangle to my neck.
Aunty Dana spoke of ancestry,
African empires before Hawkins sailed in greed,
gave me the gift of their narratives
and books for my birthday –
on Harriet Tubman and her soldier stance –
books not seen in schools.
They educated me.

Grandad's Home Brew

In the front room, whether indigo skies
or a rainy grey covered the afternoons,
Grandad hammered bottle caps onto homemade brew,
welding metal caps onto brown glass bottles
as he listened to Beethoven's symphonies,
or sang folk songs with mento rhythms
like *River bank Coverly, River to the bank Coverly...*
paced to match the speed of his work.

The taste of beer already bottled
would wet the mouths of Will Ruddock,
Valentine and Winifred Daley

who synchronised visits to slam dominoes
to wood, and fire up games of Ludo.
And more big people brought talk,
not always for a child to hear,
their tongues navigating the West Indies,
stretching back to Paul Bogle's Jamaican revolt.

And within this room in Cowper Street
Grandad rallied the Brotherhood
like a rebel god, hungry to put
wrongs to right, reshape man's thinking.

Roots *on TV*

Oats porridge, hard-dough bread,
a snip of herb tea for breakfast:
I'd remember to wipe my mouth
at the bus stop on Roundhay Road
where I walked short Grace Jones Afro style,
black girl pride channelling my steps.
I rode two buses to Bramley Town End
just to get to school at Intake High.
During class registration
the teacher asked,
Who watched Roots *on TV?*
and me, the only black child in class,
screwed up my face,
kissed ma teeth at the classroom
laughter, cut my eye at
Janet Whitehouse sat next to me
scribbling National Front Party
on her desk; white girl pride.

At Intake School not one
hard-dough bread-eating kid in my class
just chips and beans
NF and British Movement followers
propelled spits, taunts in Yorkshire slang
slurred names: *Chocolate Drop,
Nig Nog, Sambo, Jungle Bunny,
Golly Wog, Kizzy go home.*

MICHELLE SCALLY-CLARKE

Granny Betty Scally Bates

to Michael, my dad, aunty Maureen and uncle Stephen Scally, thank-you

I know I was only seven
So it might be a dream, a sigh
But me granny loved me
So God much
That me honour her
Till me die
Truly it was my granny
Not in her blood or in paper
Rolled in her suet scones homebaked
In her tears showed she prayed
She loved me from inside
Her hair was white and grey and soft
Her eyes a twinkly hue
Her cuss or scorn could lay you dazed
Her love sweet mother's perfume
Now I could not own a mother
So young so confused
But I clung to granny Scally
Her pope and her disputes
She lived in Halton Moor
You see
Reigned by the working class few
Those who put all cost in children
Those who gave and grew
I'd sit on her gold buffet
I the princess she the queen
She'd poke the red hot coal fire
I awed by her speed
I loved her in her Sunday best
And at weddings and at gatherings
She would control the family with her laugh
As I came to us as blessings
I know I was only seven
So I could not tell no lie
I miss the way I shone for her
I could see it in her eyes

SENI SENEVIRATNE

A Wider View

From the backyard of his back-to-back,
my great-great-granddad searched for spaces
in the smoke-filled sky to stack his dreams,
high enough above the cholera to keep them
and his newborn safe from harm.

In eighteen sixty-nine, eyes dry with dust
from twelve hours combing flax beneath
the conicals of light in Marshall's Temple Mill,
he took the long way home because
he craved the comfort of a wider view.

As he passed the panelled gates of Tower Works,
the tall octagonal crown of Harding's chimney
drew his sights beyond the limits of his working life
drowned the din of engines, looms and shuttles
with imagined peals of ringing bells.

Today, my footsteps echo in the sodium gloom
of Neville Street's Dark Arches and the red-brick vaults
begin to moan as time, collapsing in the River Aire,
sweeps me out to meet him on the Wharf.

We stand now, timeless in the flux of time, anchored
only by the axis of our gaze – a ventilation shaft
with gilded tiles, and Giotto's geometric lines –
while the curve of past and future generations
arcs between us.

VAHNI CAPILDEO

from **Winter**

II *Harewood Estate*

The sudden shape of a tree in the water
into which he looked down, not expecting reflection –

He had looked away, not to see,
looked down, away from someone else.
The water having run high with winter
had stopped before it fledged a form of ice.
The sun westered. The woodland blushed
improbably, the woodland burned with liquid
sun, like the idea of strawberries, never good enough
till remembered, like the ripeness of strawberries and wine
in a wedding boat, on a southern river,
a river that cradled the most privileged drinkers,
the bride being toasted by the groom's old flames.

– The momentary shape made him pleased with his migrations.
The sweet anxiety of it all.

DREADLOCKALIEN

Fires burn in Bradford, Rockstone fling innah Oldham

I don't see no Asians on the football pitch,
A mus a dem turn fi seh 'Inglan is a bitch'
Fire burn a Bradford, Rockstone fling inna Oldham,
But a who dem a blame? the one Indian.

The one thing the camera never sees
Like a petrol to a match the b.n.p.
Gathering momentum and versatility

Propaganda leaves,
Brutality trunk tree,
Wolves in sheep's clothing
Hiding underground,
u.k. terrorist network,
man from out of town.

But a di Indian youth we see angry on t.v.
Kickin up a rumpus in their own high street
A gallery of brown faces, dem did get the blame
Can't speak our language Oh what a shame!

Remind me...
we must give them some money to enrich their community.
How many years to the next election, one two or three?
A few new parks... photographed... skylarks,
Between politicians and shop owners.

The same ones who disown us?

20 years time Asians may be partly accepted
Is then the Eastern Bloc migrants
will be targeted and rejected.

LINTON KWESI JOHNSON

It Dread Inna Inglan

(for George Lindo)

dem frame-up George Lindo
up in Bradford Toun
but di Bradford Blacks
dem a rally roun

mi seh dem frame-up George Lindo
up in Bradford Toun
but di Bradford Blacks
dem a rally roun...

Maggi Tatcha on di go
wid a racist show
but a she haffi go
kaw,
rite now,
African
Asian
West Indian
an' Black British
stan firm inna Inglan
inna disya time yah

far noh mattah wat dey say,
come wat may,
we are here to stay
inna Inglan,
inna disya time yah...

George Lindo
him is a working man
George Lindo
him is a family man
George Lindo
him nevah do no wrang
George Lindo
di innocent one
George Lindo
him noh carry no daggah
George Lindo
him is nat no rabbah
George Lindo
dem haffi let him go
George Lindo
dem bettah free him now!

TARIQ MEHMOOD

Mined Memories

Now:
I am stuck in a crawling line of traffic. I should turn left into Lumb Lane, drive through the town and leave this city. But the Lane is blocked by land mines of memories.

2006:
S says wiping his greying beard.
'The police broke down my door and stormed in. I was lying half asleep on the sofa.'

1981:
S comes to my flat around midnight. He has run away
from home. Again.

2006:
'They went into my mother's house at the same time. She pleaded with them "We are not terrorists. Don't break my door. I will open it." They smashed the door and burst in.'

1981:
'Make me tea and give us something to eat, yaar.' S asks.
'I am not your mother.'
'I don't know how to do this sort of a thing.'
'I have a kettle you can make some tea. I have eggs you can eat these. Or go hungry.'

2006:
'I went to Mancester Airport to collect A.H. my twenty-one year-old son, he was coming back after six months in Pakistan.'

1981:
S puts milk, tea, water, sugar and eggs into my kettle.

2006:
'At Manchester armed police surrounded the plane, took my son off. He has been charged as a terrorist.'

1981:
The egg explodes inside the kettle, and everything overflows.
'Can you not do anything right?' I swear.

2006:
They couldn't get me so have taken my son.

Now:
The little grass mound just past the traffic lights on the Lane, is unaware of its demolished ancestor in which I had dreamt of a world free of racism. In the damp grass, a little boy is searching for something.

TAJINDER SINGH HAYER

Holy Man

Forty years he's been walking these streets. Maybe more.
Sandals, cassock, satchel. A face that matches them. Looks like a monk. And some call him that. Others call him worse. I don't know if he listens. I've never met him.

Say he was a businessman. Went out walking one day. Didn't stop. Fell through a hole in his world. Kept using those gaps. Moves in the spaces we don't see. Sleeps where he can under the sky. Winter too. Relies on the charity of the elements.

Say he lost his love. A wife. Dead. Broke into a lifetime of   .
And buried the splinters on his way. The canal. The moors. The library. Pieces of his heart. Say he found God. On the underside of a sheet of paper. Raised his hand to stamp it. Stopped. And he was there. A moment. Clarity. The switch from this to that. That to this.

Say nothing. Then river beds just sang to him. Stars blinked. The sun laid down its head. And he knew.

Everyone has their tale. He waved when I saw him. 'He waves at everyone.' He swore at me. You deserved it. He's mad. So? I don't like him.

And he walks through them. They are cobwebs. A string of droplets on a summer's day.
We watch for them. Him. This city. Its living landmark.

TAJINDER SINGH HAYER

A Seasonal Picture

Imagine a city held by winter
– its people puckered into jackets,
their skin peeled,
wind-stripped of all feeling.

See them battle the morning,
shear frost from windshields
and tune out the icy fractals
forming on the glass.

Let them swap lives
with lateshifters
– everyone with their somewhere to go –
and see the sky sift darkness away
– the moon dissolve like a mint.

Then visit the municipals
where eruptions of ice
cover the ponds,
and moorhens mince
on transparent toffee.

There too
the archaeologies of ice
– branches, bottles and bread
embedded in the past.

Follow a stray cry
to the industrial estates
where every excuse for heat
cauliflowers into steam,
and the funnels stand there
like candyfloss sticks

Watch,
rise with the air
and realise
that only we
seem to move
through the stillness.

MERLE COLLINS

Visiting Yorkshire – Again

Yorkshire was not really as I remembered it
But then, the last time I visited
the Brontës had created for me a world
not so much of Black or white
as of indeterminate shades
of art
that had no colour
of pleasure that existed
for its artistic self

then I loved the cobbled streets
sometimes I even walked
the mystic moors

Yorkshire when I visited, later,
was not exactly as I remembered it
from then

Now people stared at a
Black
woman
walking the cobbled streets
alone
and art, for me
began to have a new colour

when I think of their Yorkshire now
I see the cobbled streets
the stark brown of distant trees
the cold silence of shuttered houses
the rolling landscape of the mystic moors
and what one never misses
in England
what one never sees while visiting
with the Brontës, from afar
the glances, the stares
the averted gaze
the quickened step

After the Brontës,
I decided not to visit with Keats
and Wordsworth
Discovered that art
in England
comes in Black and White
in rich and poor
that an art called Black
exists
for England
in some region called the Fringe

Yorkshire was not at all as I remembered it
But then, England is not as I remember it, either,
from the times when my dad smiled and sang
put on his ex-serviceman's uniform
went off whistling to celebrate the day that
WE
had victory in the war.

DALJIT NAGRA

Raju t'Wonder Dog!

First good penny I spent in 'uddersfield,
after t'shop, were on a sweet-as-ladoos
alsatian, against me wife, Sapna's wishes.
Reet from t'off there were grief cos Beena,
what's Sapna's friend, were visitin' –
showin' off her reet bonny aubergine sari
t'spit o' Meera Syal. Appen t'cage fer Raju
weren't locked... I were fettlin' stuff
on t'other aisle when I 'eard him skatin'
towards t'till fer Beena! I legged it to

'ead him off, 'cept I forgot about me new
pink wafer display – all t'tower, as I
lunged round t'corner, kem crashin'!
I lay ont' floor watchin' Raju anglin'
fer a kiss – Beena's mouth gaped wide
as t'Pennine Tunnel; a bob-haired lass went:
Tha gret wazzack! Rolled ont' floor
near me wi' laffin', got me laffin' too
and t'queue of 'ouse weefs near weein'.

Our Sapna could strangle that daft mutt
what's narked our few relations from visitin'
'cept Raju helps us deal wi' sorrows:
all t' 'arf-price 55lb sacks o' tatties
sold in t'world won't buy us a little 'un.
And t'IVFs keep failin'. She'll be seen
as havin' dodgy karma by t'community
fer 'er past-life sins made 'er barren.

From time ter time she'll say: *Get thee sen
a fresh bride who'll production line
fer you an heir! Who'll get our 'ard earned
dosh, eh? Raju?*
       By t'way 'soofna' means 'dream' –
a bit like Sapna in't it? That's why Raju
and me'll stoop and I'll say: *Sapna,*

you're me soofna. Why would I do
owt like to upset me soofna? Chucklin'
she'll add: *Aah Avtar, you're me avatar.*
T'customers'll coo or look reet confused.

In t'storeroom, as Raju kneels like 'e
were in t'temple, Sapna'll say that even if
t'price hungry customers turn their backs
cos they've bin teken by t'bright lights
o'Morrisons, we'll never be left looking
at our sens warped in t'shopliftin' mirrors
cashin' up at night wi' nowt in t'till
fer we've got Raju! And mebbe he's secretly
t'incarnation of some 'indu God ovvaseein'
we don't wake from t'fate of our soofna.

MERLE COLLINS

For the Lumb Bank Group, December 1991

Here in this misty valley
you have reminded me of the simple things
that a house is not a home
that warmth may not be a sunny beach
in summer

Here you have been the sand
and I have been the water
You have been the water
And I have been the sand

The cold is still a living force
but you remind me again that
Home is not a house
Happiness is not a heatwave
Warmth might just
sometimes
be found in misty cold.

MERLE COLLINS

The Lumb Bank Children

Today we walk here where once the miller walked
Imprisoned in time
Confined for a week to the beauty that is now

In the valley the mist hardly ever lifts
the hands that hold that white blanket down
are children's hands, they say
and that wail that wanders nightly
on this December wind
is not a christmas carol
but children howling an ancient hunger
around the mill-house
a gaunt memory of a living graveyard

Last night, while a child's mangled memory
moaned under the misty white
a ghost walked from ancient India's cotton-fields
moved tall and stately through this lonely valley house
connecting

Last night, while wailing carols wandered
in the whitening cold
a figure walked through time and space
from a water-mill somewhere near a Caribbean
cane-field
searching

The restless ghost-child sighed, sucked a thumb,
turned over in her valley bed, and slept.
Early this morning, the mist lifted slowly
And the waterfall shouted a story louder than its voice.

Today we walked where once the miller walked
Released in time
Surrounded for a week by the quiet beauty that is now.

JOHN LYONS

Weather Vane

I

Not easy to understand
the hard fettle of Hughes' poetry
distilled from the Calder Valley,
where the sun keeps its distance
and the sky is a puckered tissue
greying everything.

Sometimes there is a blessing
in perceiving language in landscape:
Autumn in mid-Winter
with its yellowing and reddening;
blue wood smoke rising
amidst scraggy sycamores
with their dark blooms of rooks' nests.

II

Quick as a thought
I find myself in a Walcott haunt,
Trinidad, where miles of coconut palms
crowd the beach towards Chacachacare
like Columbus's first Arawaks at Punta Arenal.

His poetry is the sea.
Stanzas like patterns of spume on sand,
endings enjambed, their meaning historic,
at on with the rhythm of the island.

Here the sun is gratuitous.
Here, his metaphors are thin disguises
for the island's life-lust.

Back in the Calder Valley
I see the seasons falter
and forsythia deceived into bloom,
I find a comforting rhythm:
the dactyl in Caribbean *cassia*.

JOHN AGARD

Caribbean Eye Over Yorkshire
(for John Lyons)

Eye
perched over
adopted Yorkshire.

Eye christened
in Caribbean blue
and Trinidad sunfire.

Eye tuned in
to the flame
tree's decibels

and the red
stereophonic bloom of immortelles.

Eye once a stranger
to silver birch and conifer
now on first-name terms

with beech and elm and alder.
Eye making an ally
of heather and lavender.

Eye of painter
eye of poet
eye of prankster

eye looking into linden
for ghost-traces
of silk-cotton

eye of crow
in carnival cape
seeing inward

eye of blackbird
casting
humming-bird shadow.

DALJIT NAGRA

Parade's End

Dad parked our Granada, champagne-gold
by our superstore on Blackstock Road,
my brother's eyes scanning the men
who scraped the pavement frost to the dole,
one 'got on his bike' over the hill
or the few who warmed us a thumbs-up
for the polished recovery of our re-sprayed car.

Council mums at our meat display
nestled against a pane with white trays
swilling kidneys, liver and a sandy block
of corned beef, loud enough about the way
darkies from down south *Come op ta
Yorksha, mekkin claaims on aut theh can
befoh buggrin off in theh flash caahs!*

At nine, we left the emptied till open,
clicked the dials of the safe. Bolted
two metal bars across the back door
(with a new lock). Spread trolleys
at ends of the darkened aisles. Then we pressed
the code for the caged alarm and rushed
the precinct to check it was throbbing red.

Thundering down the graffiti of shutters
against the valley of high-rise flats.
Ready for the getaway to our cul-de-sac'd
semi-detached, until we stood stock-still:

watching the car-skin pucker, bubbling smarts
of acid. In the unstoppable pub-roar
from the John O'Gaunt across the forecourt,
we returned up to the shop, lifted a shutter,
queued at the sink, walked down again.
Three of us, each carrying pans of cold water.
Then we swept away the bonnet-leaves
from gold to the brown of our former colour.

DALJIT NAGRA

Darling & Me!

Di barman's bell done dinging
        so I phone di dimply-mississ,
Putting some gas on cookah,
        bonus pay I bringin!

Downing drink, I giddily
        home for Pakeezah record
to which we go-go, tango,
        for roti – to kitchen – she rumba!

I tell her of poor Jimmy John,
        in apron his girlfriend
she bring to pub his plate of
        chicken pie and dry white

potato! Like Hilda Ogden,
        Heeya, eaht yor chuffy dinnaaah!
She huffing off di stage
        as he tinkle his glass of Guinness.

We say we could never eat
        in publicity like dat, if we did
wife advertisement may need
        of solo punch in di smack.

I pull her to me – my skating
        hands on her back are Bolero
by Torvill and Dean. Giggling
        with bhangra arms in air

she falling for lino, till I
        swing her up in forearm!
Darling is so pirouettey with us
        for whirlwind married month,

that every night, though by day
        we work factory-hard, she always
have disco of drumstick in pot.
        Hot. Waiting for me.

MARIE GUISE WILLIAMS

My Mother's Porch #1: First Love at 15

I once kissed the pastor's son
on the way home from some
conference in Sheffield

I wasn't being Jezebel or nothing

but the way he asked me
so gently in my ear
if I would
if I could, if she wasn't there, his girlfriend

as though his love was bulging
through some prison he couldn't escape

I just found my lips
moving closer to his,
for that split second
of saccharine situation
of briefly requited love

and for that moment
there was only two in that backseat
our lips slotting together
just perfectly
and I was nuzzling in his arms
till that hour of Snake Pass love
was through with me

and then plucked
from the safety of his arms
excited but unsure again

rooting around
on my mother's doorstep
for the keys

E. A MARKHAM

A Politically-Correct Marriage

Romance it was with that leap of the imagination in Sheffield
when her wave at the station added warmth to the day
that so far had been brightened only by snow; and he,
a man so robbed in confidence, hesitated before waving back;
so she greeted her friend instead, a woman wholesome as the fresh snow.
But here's a problem for a girl so caring, confusing a sad man in public:
don't be embarrassed, her quick smile said, don't be embarrassed
her bashful eyes said, as she rehearses the embrace with her friend.

Back then, the story had no shape; before the children came along,
so that now no one thinks of one partner without the other;
though, it must be said, there's sometimes pause for reflection, lacking in,
y'know, *Horse & Hound*. Or *Fox & Firkin*. Like checking the Solicitor's
between the butcher and the cake-shop. So they come in handy,
this couple, when we give up the other *items* that depress us;
on the rich north & poor south, on biblical fish & the ocean.
Palestine & Israel. Archbishop & Actress. Poet & poem.

E. A MARKHAM

To My Mother, the Art Critic

I

I put it down, I say, to my mother, my first art critic.
Back then, oh, in another country, a woman in her prime
nicely contained in that dress we know, its modesty protesting
those *The Lady at her Piano* snaps for the album. But that was Before –
yes, we've had too many images of After –
that was when, on a Sunday afternoon after church,
Anancyman came to the house and arranged a sitting:
In the drawing-room a detail of her dress is out of place.

II

No, of course, you do not understand. I come back to this scene
decades later on a day in Sheffield laid out to be painted.
I pause in mid-stride, the rinsed landscape too clean for February;
the bruised sky of yesterday clearing up, a scent of elsewhere drifting
indoors, from the garden. I think of men in berets and cravats
at the *salon* – of a provincial Degas whose aim was to trap you dancing.
Or an island Renoir with no fear and hatred of women.
Of your afterlife drawing suitors to worship Orsay and Marmottan.

III

So, yes, I'm thinking back to the small accident in the churchyard
(sermons do not prepare you for the dangers of uneven ground);
and then to your pampered ankle after lunch, caught on canvas,
along with the vicar and headmaster providing the conversation.
The boy with the made-up name was praised for the likeness
of the bandage on the lady's foot: he could have been a medic as well
as artist. Not bad, you said, the sternest judge. and then you asked:
But how are you going to paint my other shoe, over it?

DEBJANI CHATTERJEE

Reason for Coming

(for Nadia and Abdullah)

'We had to come to Britain for our son;
        more can be done for him here,'
you said. Your role was simply caring.

Now Sheffield holds his eight years' bones
        and you are still in thrall, grieving.

JOHN LYONS

Drinking up the Drizzle

What is there to be done
but stare astonished at the greyness
swallowing up a weaker relation
of my tropical sun!

I take the unbelievable stance:
stoic expressions,
– no efficacy in home-spun philosophy –
'my spirits must drink up the drizzle'.

But there is no obeahman here
to push the Pennines away,
or turn the wind about.

JACKIE KAY

85th Birthday Poem for Dad

Last night on the eve of my father's birthday
I watched, from the bench by the sea in Erin Bay,
a large red sun fall behind the cliff,
ever so slowly, like a ball in a penalty.
Later, the moon smashed into the clouds –
a goal from the past lobbed into the present.
I remembered how my father's only bugbear
with my mother, his wife of over fifty years,
was how she never watched him play football
years ago, when he was centre forward
in the South Island of New Zealand.

And with the red sun and the full moon
so close in time in the sky's great pitch,
I found myself thinking of the way
my father used to dance across the ballroom floor
like Fred Astaire, or how he climbed the Munros,
and of how time is so fast and so slow.
I raised my half-pint glass –
my half-full glass –
then my extra wee half in his honour
a nippy whisky, *a Port Ellen*, my mother's name.

A half and a half or a *hauf and a hauf*,
the best way on this night away
to toast his health. 'Happy Birthday,'
I say to John Robert Kay.
If he were here on the Isle of Man
he'd already be thinking associatively:
Thomas Paine, Rights of Man.
Nobility is not hereditary, aye.
But he is not here, and so I raise
my nearly-drained glass to the empty sky.

DOROTHEA SMARTT

Bringing It All Back Home

Here I lie. A hollow
Samboo. Filled with your tears

and regrets. The tick in the eye
of Lancaster pride. The stutter,

the pause, the dry cough, shifting
eyes that cannot meet a Black man's

gaze. Questions, questions from either
side that foul us for answers. The how

and the why ultimately defeating us
with shame, with anger, with the defensive

voices of those who lived and enjoyed
the benefits, who did not question too

deeply the source that enriched
alll of Lancaster life.

Who will heal and elevate to light
the souls of your ancestors if

you refuse to remember? If you
cover their incarnations with half-truths?

Grocer? You were a Slave Trader!
And everything has its price,

and denial is only debt
with interest to be paid.

DOROTHEA SMARTT

A Few Words for Samboo

Bilal, a Fulani son,
unwilling, unconsenting sacrifice
to Lancaster town's transformation from wood
to gleaming Georgian stone, Lancaster city,
each rising white house a gravestone,
with window eyes, half-closed
to the far-off shore of screams.

And their ships kept leaving for more.

DOROTHEA SMARTT

Today on Sunderland Point

The boy who looks out on Lune Estuary calls;
tradewinds moan through boughs of beached schooners,
sucked into tidal muds; both longing for a ship
to sail, heading with the reeling birds, home.

SUANDI

Sambo's Grave

Sometimes when the moon is full
He pushes the earth aside
Scattering the gifts, toys, tokens
And stands on the highest point
Tip toed to extend his boyish frame
And he looks out to sea
For now he can see beyond water and land
Right to the coast of Elimna
Through the Door of No Return
And into his village and his mother's arms
And he smiles once again

BERNARDINE EVARISTO

from Soul Tourists

What did they expect when Curtis wrapped
me in his arms on Blackpool Pleasure Beach 1959?

It were so windy he said I'd fall into the icy sea
if he didn't shelter me in his too-tight tweed jacket,

handed down at St Andrew's Home for Boys.
They'd never had a lad so tall until him,

son of a black GI, six foot three and broad of back.
And why didn't we go down to where the boats

were moored, he said, find an empty one, never
had a cuddle before. He were only fifteen,

but I could smell his manhood. You see the nuns
hadn't offered sex education classes –

got sent to the coal for touching a boy
let alone kissing if someone reported.

After I'd done what I wasn't really sure
I was doing with Curtis,
we had a go on the Grand National Roller Coaster,
but it was still hurting between my legs
in between my laughter, roaring
Isn't this fun! Isn't this great!

Wasn't that I *felt* unloved like other whingers
who had two parents, a brother and a sister,
a home, hearthside fire, Sunday roast,
birthday cards and a pet rabbit.
I *was* unloved, proven fact, no parents,
just a house full of frustrated elderly virgins
what hadn't a clue how to love the seventy-odd
waifs and sad strays at their mercy.

*

Come from a long line of fallen women, me,
so had to uphold the family tradition, didn't I?

No one had to tell me my mother was born
into stigma and got my own stigmata

'cos Terry was so stubborn he had me
screaming thirty-two hours, a scar across

my stomach when he should have slid out
in sixty minutes I were that young and wide of hip.

And when I held him for the first time I cried
at how my own mother could've dumped me.

Couldn't leave my Terry for a minute, breastfed him
till he was four years old. You see no one

taught me mothering. I wanted him by
my side all the time. But he never listened to me, my

Terry was a disobedient teenager, tall
like his dad, wanting to go out playing

all the time like he didn't have a family, like
he didn't have a home to go to, like

he didn't understand he was the first thing
that was all mine ever in my life.

                        *

Curtis was banished to a home in Birmingham,
me to a house for unwed mums in Nottingham.

My child up for a good Catholic home, they said.
Who me? My baby? Only thing I owned

wrenched out of my arms by blood-sucking bats?
I'd inherited something in my genes:

send a herd of elephants to stampede all over me
and I'll not be crushed. Maureen McCarthy

kindly took me in – St Ann's alumni,
cashier at Haycroft's Ironmongers,

in town while I looked after her kid and mine.
Once a month we went to the Mecca Ballroom

to hear Jimmy Saville spin the decks.
Then I discovered Ella Fitzgerald and started to mime.

NABILA JAMEEL

The Island in Preston

I remember this in the middle
of a busy junction, being breathless
as we ran up and down it
on our way to town.

The grass was like carpet –
we wondered if it was real.
The sun was warmer on our faces
at the top of this island.

We would talk about it
with our cousins in Pakistan.
They said to us 'but you live on an island;
England is a jazeera, an island!'

I see it now – levelled ground,
holding a Care Home. Through windows
I see sullen faces waiting for death,
that once smiled with young faces
at our innocence, when we plucked daisies
at the top of our island.

NABILA JAMEEL

A Book Closer to Home.

Every Saturday mum took us to the library.
We dispersed into different parts of the room,

craving this yellow smell of bound paper
and a peep into lives we did not live –
where tea was not chai, but dinner.

Mum sat in the Urdu section,
soon dissolving into a magazine
full of squiggles that only made sense to her.

Her large almond eyes smiled.
Her soft fingers turned the pages,
pausing while she glanced at us with motherly duty.

We sat with our books on the carpeted floor,
following the curves and lines of English
with our fingertips,

the red signs on the mahogany shelves
silencing our tongues.

LEMN SISSAY

This Train (sing along)

This train is bound for Wigan, this train
This train is bound for Wigan, this train
This train is bound for Wigan
Praise the lord 'cause it's a big 'un
This train is bound for Wigan, this train.

SUANDI

Bolton Safari

Some mornings
When October waves in November
The damp wraps itself about
Defying top level dial of central heating
Opening eyes still see the dark of night
And all that is winter clouds the mind

I know these streets
Bolton
Where no beast of four legs ever roamed
Around back yards where wild grasses
Never grew above 6 inches

Here I have never smelt ripe mango growing
Never plucked down a banana
They don't grow on lampposts anyhow
Never had red soil dust my feet

But still I remember
And on days when the wind is not chill
But warm and eager
I swear I can smell something familiar
Something not of Lancashire
And the grin on my face scares passing strangers

JOHN SIDDIQUE

A Map of Rochdale

We are not London or Germany.
The war barely touched us here. I am drained
by allusions and distances, signs to twin towns
hundreds of miles away, replicas of clock towers,
the clone shop confusion of every town high street.

Let us make our own map of the sprawl,
its life and ours, a bit unseemly and tough,
filled with early sexual adventures
stemming from boredom and flesh. Politics
grown from isolation and inverted snobbery.

We'll rename the streets after their real stories,
Smack Head Valley. Skinhead Avenue,
Race Riot Street. Touch Me There Road.
Drug Deal Walk. First Kiss Gardens.
Pissed-up Lane. Possibility Fields.

JOHN SIDDIQUE

Industrial Landscape

She stands reflecting herself in the placement
of chimneys. Hill of ash black.
Oldham smokes distance.

Lead me through streets, funnelling,

past a funeral. Black hat.
Black horses. No flowers.
Blocking the airway to whited-out Pennines.

Babies in prams, dogs and back yards, oblivious
as the porcelain heads mid-ground to reclamations
at the Catholic church.

Her mind rises with the gasometers,
over ship canal and dock, over Strangeways
and Manchester, rising on thermals of industry.

JEFF CAFFREY

A Brief History of Manny (2006)

Atomic? – Powered. Computer? – Generated. Red and Blue?
Globally venerated. Historic prowess, The Cock o'the North
Industrial? – Revolution. Attitude? – Of course. Pan-African
Congress, Peter's Fields Massacre; The home of the Socialist –
Parliament? – laughed at yer. Gunchester, Gaychester, Manchester;
How – Kids with guns, corporate bungs, IRA bombs – Now?
Soul…? Doubt For corporate clout. The uniquely cultured Oh,
completely vultured. Urban Entrepreneurs Brushed aside, Sneaky
Councillors On the snide. Hundred storeys high Scraping the sky

– Buy, buy, buy! – Oh, aye! Northern wages Council Tax raises;
Overspill Estates Not City Centre places. The longer you've
stayed The more you've paid, for Clearing the way For the
tourists to pay, more. Some of it's good, Some of it's great – sure;
Wicked new bars But you're mate can't get through the door!
Independent, unique, Corporate – Slut! It's one thing being sold
But give us a cut. Don't mean to complain (I'm used to the rain)
but, What good's a New City When all the doors are shut?

ROMESH GUNESEKERA

Turning Point

My host is a monk
from my grandfather's town,

exploring England
in a darkened age.

Stopped temporarily
in a shared room

we meet on my less
noble travels:

discover we are
exactly the same age.

At ten I knew
the world must change;

he, at ten,
also knew the same.

Twenty yards
of saffron robes

captured his boy's
imagination,

while mine slipped
on the slopes

of Tagaytay. He grew
decisive,

unencumbered
in a shaved head;

I became
progressively

less certain,
more curled.

Reaching our mid-thirties
– the age of enlightenment –

he speaks, I listen
only half understanding

this language from my past.
I have stumbled

off the path, tripped
by his inflections.

Once we had
in our Colombo house

a daylight alms-giving
feeding twenty monks.

We served, they ate.
This bright morning

at our breakfast
my laughing monk

serves me
his home-cooking,

turning the tables
in a Manchester flat.

LEMN SISSAY

Flags

These pavement cracks are the places
Where poets pack their warrior words,
Where insects have the Olympic races,
Where seeds slip from embittered birds,
Where vert valleys cling to ledges,
Where sliding silver rivers run.
These pavement cracks are the places
Where violent valleys swallow sun.

These pavement cracks are the places
Where shadows of moving bridges flow,
Where rain rushes rock faces,
Where heat crouches from the cold,
Where dying dust of dreams slide,
Where silt turns into food,
Where home truths confide,
And secret silent worries brood.

And perhaps these pavement cracks
Are the patterns of concrete butterflies
Where thoughts carefully cultivated
Wait to wake, grow wings and fly.
Perhaps these pavement cracks
Hold pieces of the Manchester myriad,
The people of a modern earth.
This world between the windswept flags.

LEMN SISSAY

Mill Town and Africa

How many fingernails of my own shall I pluck
till she sees that my blood is hers.
Revolutions have passed between us,
emperors dethroned, guns and red flags raised.
Churches have crumbled, stampeding our pathways.
Governments have collapsed.
We scattered on different sides of the debris.

While I wiped sweat and coaldust from my face,
wiping sweat and sanddust from her face
I saw her over the Lancashire Plain
fleeing Ethiopia with the remnants of a family.
She had washed into the hard Manchester rain
and I into the skating heatwave.

She became more to me than this
I would dream her, awake with a picture
see her on a London bus, unblinking.

RAMAN MUNDAIR

Name Journeys

Like Rama I have felt the wilderness
but I have not been blessed

with a companion as sweet as she,
Sita; loyal, pure and true of heart.

Like her I have been chastened
through trial by fire. Sita and I,

spiritual sari-sisters entwined
in an infinite silk that would swathe

Draupadi's blush. My name
a journey between rough and smooth,

an interlacing of banyan leaves with sugar
cane. Woven tapestries of journeys;

travelling from South
to North, where the Punjabi in my mouth

became dislodged as milk teeth fell
and hit infertile English soil.

My mouth toiled to accommodate
the rough musicality of Mancunian vowels

and my name became a stumble
that filled English mouths

with a discordant rhyme, and exotic
rhythm dulled, my voice a mystery

in the Anglo echo chamber –
void of history and memory.

SEGUN LEE-FRENCH

So many undone

Some words sound better
unsaid.
                              I don't know if I love you
the syllables stalled
between my lips.

& in piccadilly plaza,
        shoppers streaming like ghosts
        had more weight
than our last embrace.

SEGUN LEE-FRENCH

Rain

(for Aimé Césaire)

Rain, the sound of a distant drum,
earthsprung notes, a litany of
rain, black sand
& the screams
of gulls

. . . .

My mother had a magazine
I could not read. The pictures, backdrops
to recurring dreams: sepia ships,
like dried pomegranates, bodies
packed like seeds.

Roots haunted me & my sister. The stench.
And *Planet of the Apes*. No way to escape
the evil master race. Kunta Kinte's name became
playground abuse. I battered every week another boy,
until I learnt to turn away.

A song:

One nigger, two nigger, three nigger, four
Four dead niggers lying on the floor
Five nigger, six nigger, seven nigger, eight
Eight dead niggers served on a plate

My mum told us of countries, where they'd split us
apart, because she was white & we were
different shades.

She had a china ashtray she never used,
in blue, a picture of a black man's
head: *Toussaint L'Ouverture,*
she said, *he fought the French
& won freedom for all the slaves.*

Each day, Toussaint watched me stir
demerara sugar into my bowl
of Ready Brek & milk.

On the way to school, I hid beneath
my mother's coat & listened to the rain,
earthsprung notes, the darkness,
safe.

KEI MILLER

The only thing far away

In this country, Jamaica is not quite as far
as you might think. Walking through Peckham
in London, West Moss Road in Manchester,
you pass green and yellow shops
where tie-headwomen bargain over the price
of dasheen. And beside Jamaica is Spain
selling large yellow peppers, lemon to squeeze
onto chicken. Beside Spain is Pakistan, then Egypt,
Singapore, the world... here, strangers build home
together, flood the ports with curry and papayas;
in Peckham and on Moss Road, the place smells
of more than just patty or tandoori. It smells like
Mumbai, like the Castries, like Princess Street, Jamaica.
Sometimes in this country, the only thing far away
is this country.

SHAMSHAD KHAN

pot

so big – they said you shouldn't really be moved

so fragile you might break

you could be from anywhere pot

styles have travelled just like terracotta
you could almost be an english pot

but I know you're not.

I know half of the story pot
of where you come from
of how you got here

but I need you to tell me the rest pot

tell me

did they say you were bought pot
a looters deal done
the whole lot
sold to the gentleman in the grey hat

or
did they say you were lost pot
finders are keepers you know pot

or
did they say they didn't notice you pot
must have slipped onto the white sailing yacht

bound for england.

someone

somewhere

will have missed you pot
gone out looking for you pot

because
someone
somewhere
made you
fingernails
pressed
snake patterned you pot
washed you pot
used you pot
loved you pot

if I could shatter this glass
I would take you back myself pot.

you think they wouldn't recognise you pot

say diaspora
you left now
you're not really one of us.

pot I've been back to where my family's from
they were happy
to see me
laughed a lot
said I was more asian than the asians pot
I was pot

imagine.
the hot sun on your back

feel flies settle on your skin
warm grain poured inside

empty pot
growl if you can hear me

pot?

pot?

*Dedicated to a Nigerian pot currently incarcerated in the Manchester Museum
without charge or access to legal representation.*

CHERYL MARTIN

The Coffee Bearer

oil painting by John Frederick Lewis, 1805-1876

Some old white man painted her
in a citrus-coloured gown,
her black velvet jacket
embroidered with birds of paradise,
to be heaven for a washed-up European.

The scene wallows in evening sun,
as if everyone in this village
could spend her days
singing, bowing, serving:
showing how shit-work
transmutes to joy.

She will be a toy,
brightly head-wrapped,
carrying cut-crystal vases
as clear as this portrait's lies.

I'll never serve anyone
with that smile in my eyes.

('Painted after the artist's return from the Middle East, where he lived and
painted for many years, adopting native dress and customs.' – Manchester
Art Galleries)

PETE KALU

Manchester

Fire stokers, bridge builders, ball jugglers,
Weavers, tunnellers, atom chasers,
Guitar thrashers, geeks, sausage sizzlers,
Peaceniks, heretics, rebels, refugees,
Carnivalists, miserablists,
Swindlers, poisoners, punks, poets,
Centurions, slave barons,
Divas, Destroyers,
Rocket scientists, revolutionaries

All lived here.

PETE KALU

The Poet's Song

Some people talk about New York New York
The mangoes of sweet Trinidad, but me?

I love Moss Side.

Some people talk about trifle with double
Cream, waking up in waterbeds with their
toyboys/lovers, but me?

I love Moss Side.

Some people nibble ears, hold hands all
Day, give each other fluffy toys, steam
up car windows whispering sweet nothngs n stuff, but me?

I love Moss Side.

Some people go dippy at the sight of fresh pink flowers, some
spend their time dreaming of film stars,
some rave about Daleks, youtube and mtv, but me?

I love Moss Side

MAYA CHOWDHRY

My Eyes

I'm looking at the tower blocks of Hulme, holding up the sky,
and every 15 seconds the picture changes, smog catches
the back of my throat, coughing I look out at a Delhi skyline,
ragged and dusty, I have to shut my left eye to return to England.

My right eye composes Internet adverts that travel the Web, goes
dancing at the Hacienda, wears 10 denier, loves men.
My left eye drives a rickshaw, eats paan at 5am, loves women.
My right eye comes home to tortellini with spinach and ricotta, puts
on a CD of Portishead and crashes out in a crescendo of 70s revival.
My left eye objects, buys pani puri on the corner of Janpath Market,
while 'Chaltie, Chaltie' from Pakeezah blares out from a trashed
radio wedged between the boiling oil and a pan of chai.

I shut both eyes, wanting release, tired of reliving the collision
at Defence Colony between an auto-rickshaw driver
and a tourist's taxi going South.

D.S. MARRIOTT

The Day Ena Died

The words were often calibrated to hurt
all casings removed—
the eyes crimping—lightless—
at ease only when the wreckage burned.

The voice—corrugated, galvanised—
hard in its bleak certainly,
unhurried in its cobbled seething;
so thick dactyls could clog-hop on it

or haul hammers to the seams.
Even from this distance, I recall:
losing my grease-smeared grip
as the news reached me at the sink,

the mug breaking like wrecked walls
of that final dismal script,
the hole too big to be fitted or shaped,
as they hammered in the bolt, tolled the change.

Under the wreckage the immortal
grimace—how odd to believe it no
longer thickening or swathe? —and how Violet hated it:
The black hairnet shroud holding back the years.

TARIQ LATIF

MoonMen

We have travelled, up the Snake Pass, far enough
to lose the city lights and for the sky to change
into that clear endless dark. We gaze at the full
moon, wild goose moon, whose face appears strange
in the growing fuzz of shadow. The moon's dull
light drapes icily over the rough

Pennine moors. Slowly, visibly the umbra arc
creeps across the dazed orange moon. Another
car pulls up on the verge; a man and
a boy walk across the road then go further
into the moors. They stop and stare, hand in hand,
at the rusty moon which is now almost all dark

except for the thin lemon rind which becomes red
and then disappears, leaving us in total darkness.
The moon regains its vision of love and releases
intense heat, masses of heat, into the immenseness
of space. The thick dark fills the crevices
in our lonely, wounded hearts, that have bled

under the sharp swords of love.
How we dawdle like drunkards over the moors
over the moon dark moors, men made of moon,
men with broken hearts of moon, with stony doors
ajar on lost lives and love. How we spoon
the dust of our dreams to the emptiness above.

And no matter which way we turn, the charred moon
is always there huge and blood black;
even over the glass-spattered streets
of Salford where we leave Jon, then make tracks
for Withington through the sleepy streets
of Chorlton; to be home, home, home soon.

JOHN SIDDIQUE

Jali

FROM *A Seed to a Flower, the Simplest Thing*

Returning from the sun to return to his son.
Bouncing harp notes from the plate glass
of Superdrug.

Cutting the air with proud chin,
with cigarette smoke, with music passed
from his father's hands into his fingers.
Returning from Gambia to return to his son.

The kora is life. Life in Piccadilly Gardens
made clean and crystal, lifted spirit,
as we approach and leave.
Intersections of buses and trams;
Altrincham one way, Bury the other.
Cross cutting the notes of time and pitch
to hold his life together.

Humanity is different here, he says.
People don't know about each other.
Music penetrates us with imported humanity.
I don't play for money, I play for our souls.

There are bargains to be had in Superdrug,
two deodorants for the price of one.
Away down Market Street there are other musics,
the loop of a Romanian waltz played on accordion,
a French tango by the escalators near the shoe shops.

If you come here before the music starts,
you have to imagine the life of the city.
Jali with his kora, his amp and car battery
for power, riding in on the silver tram
as the shoppers gather. Chiming in the cold sun,
in the landscaped square where we pass by,
leaving our trails as music on the air

142

BENJAMIN ZEPHANIAH

Master, Master

Master master drank a toast
And dreamt of easy tea,
He gave you to a Holy Ghost,
    Come children see.

From Liverpool on sinking ships
Blessed by a monarchy,
To Africa the hyprocrites,
    Come children see.

Master master worked the slave
Who ran for liberty,
The master made us perm and shave,
    Come children see.

If slave drivers be men of words
We curse that poetry,
Its roots you'll find are so absurd,
    Come children see.

Master master's sons drill oil
It's all his legacy,
They put the devil in the soil,
    Come children see.

Fear not his science or his gun
Just know what you can be,
And children we shall overcome,
    Come children see.

Tis true that we have not now chains
Yet we were never free,
Still master's chains corrupt our brains,
    Come children see.

A word is slave for man is man
What's done is slavery,
The evils of the clan that can,
        Come children see.

Master master worked the slave
The upright sort was he,
That boy dug master master's grave
        Come children see.

Some now await a judgement day
To know his penalty,
It's blood and fire anyway,
        Come children see.

MONIZA ALVI

Arrival 1946

The boat docked in at Liverpool.
From the train Tariq stared
at an unbroken line of washing
from the North West to Euston.

These are strange people, he thought –
an Empire, and all this washing,
the underwear, the Englishman's garden.
It was Monday, and very sharp.

BERNARDINE EVARISTO

from **Lara**

Liverpool, England, 1949 –

TAIWO

OH MAMA! Your pride when I boarded the *Apapa*.
Your son, a man now, riding the whale to paradise!

Remember the man's voice from Broadcasting House
calling us over the air waves from England?

'London calling The Empire! Calling The Empire!
Come in Nigeria!' *I'm coming! I'm coming!*

I shouted at night into the warm winds on deck.
Mama, my dreams have been my fuel for years,

all those British films for sixpence at the movie house.
See London, then die! I was desperate to get here!

When I finally landed in Liverpool it was Heaven,
I had hoped for snow but it was just very cold.

These people run everywhere and wear mufflers.
Older cousin Sam came to greet me at the docks,

just as well because I thought the fast automobiles
would kill me. I asked Sam if many people are killed

by cars. He laughed, 'You will get used to life here.'
The Africans have European wives and sailor's children.

Sam has a house in Princess Park in Toxeth district,
his wife Maureen is Irish and their six-year-old

daughter is Beatrice. I said, 'Why a white wife, Sam?'
He replied, 'When in Rome do as the Romans do.'

Mama, I will write a letter soon. I promise you.

SAM SAYS this country is like fisherman's bait, Mama.
It attracts, you bite, then you are trapped. I told him

I'd be here five years, get my degree and leave.
Tomorrow I head for London. Centre of the Empire!

Sam drinks stout every night complaining that John Bull
only gives him work on the railways, and I've met elders

in the Yoruba Club in Croxteth Street who came
in the last century as stowaways or seamen,

fought in two world wars for Britain, but believe
back home is paradise. I argue Nigeria is small time.

Why eat rice and stew when you can taste Yorkshire
pud, meat and two veg. You can buy anything here,

there are so many shops, pubs on every street corner
and houses have all the modern conveniences.

Many people are respectful but some idiots shout
'Oi! Johnny! Sambo! Darkie! Nigger!' at us.

The elders tell us to take no nonsense from them,
so if I am abused I say quietly, 'Just call me Taiwo,'

and boof! I fight them. Even the West Indians say
'Do you people still live in trees in the bush?'

Mama, in this country I am coloured.
Back home I was just me.

JACK MAPANJE

The First Train to Liverpool
(Enfield: Liverpool 1, Stoke 0, 1972)
(A Letter for Angela)

No last minute haggling about prices
Of curry – chicken first at Balaka
No stinking Afro-wigs into your mouths
No leaping from bags of peanuts into
Baskets of tomato, cheerfully quarrelling
Nor finally sitting on half a buttock;
Euston Station contracts and dialogues
Through wires and innumerable papers
Only comfort welcomes abroad a sudden silence
That soon reigns, our eyes weighing and
Quickly avoiding each other between
The beverages and the local papers.

Runcorn Station welcomes aboard a haunting
Quiet where men obviously build more paper
Walls against other men. No curios, no mats,
No herbs sell through windows. No mothers
Suckle their crying babies. No jokes about
The rains held up by your charms this year!
At Lime Street itself, not even a drunk staggers
Out perhaps to announce his newly acquired
Cornerstones. Only recorded voices bid you
Come again before the engulfing impenetrable
Crowds. But the maddening quiet soon recedes
Locating a bright tarnished face once known.

LEVI TAFARI

Toxteth Where I Reside

Come with me yes I'll be your guide
to the city where I reside
let's take a walk
so we can talk
about Liverpool on Merseyside

In the sixties Liverpool
made its name
it went international
well crucial
admired at home and abroad
everybody wanted to speak scouse
Liverpool you're hard

But dread times came
and you lost your fame
pressure hit Liverpool

Now check out Toxteth my dwelling place
can you believe your eyes
there are beautiful houses on elegant streets
I bet you are surprised
because the media painted a picture
of us inna negative light
they magnify the rundown places
and ignore the ones which are out of sight

So forget the ghetto mentality
because we are not ghettoites
we are a talented people
with a lot to give
the oldest Black community in Europe
are we're positive

Now I admit in Toxteth
that things they can get rough
but if you lived down here you would understand
we just don't get enough
so we need a chance the opportunity
to make a positive contribution
so we can feel good in this neighbourhood
and improve our situation.

IMTIAZ DHARKER

Speech balloon

The Liverpool boss was pretty chuffed with himself,
said the news report, for being so tough
when he decided to snub the obvious choice
and go instead for the goal machine.
'I'm over the moon,' they said he said.
'I'm over the moon,' he said.

The Barnsley manager was lost for words
to describe his feelings when Chelsea fell
to the Tykes. 'We played fantastic.
I never thought we'd do it again
but we did, we did, and all I can say is
I'm over the moon,' they said he said.
'I'm over the moon,' he said.

The Hollywood mum was way beyond thrilled
according to friends, when she delivered
into the world, not one bouncing baby
but twins instead to the astonished dad.
'I'm over the moon,' they said she said.
'I'm over the moon,' she said.

Bollywood's hottest couple was proud to be blessed
by the jubilant father, the superstar.
'It's a match made in heaven,' he said to the press,

149

'Between two shooting stars with shining careers
and I'm over the moon, of course,' he said.
'I'm over the moon,' he said.

The Malaysian nation went mad with joy
on independence day in its fiftieth year
when a doctor-cum-part-time-model,
a local boy, went up into space in a Russian Soyuz.
'All of Malaysia over the moon,' they said on the news.
'Twenty-seven million people over the moon.'

You must have noticed, it's really quite clear,
this condition has spread, it's happening there,
it's happening here. It's full-blown, grown
beyond every border, to the furthest corner
of every country where English is spoken
or English is known.

There's no one just satisfied or mildly pleased
or chipper or chirpy, contented or cheerful,
no one glad or gratified, delighted or jubilant,
elated, ecstatic, joyful or gleeful.
All the happy people have left this world.
You won't come across them any time soon

and if it's happy sound-bytes you're looking for
you need to look way over your head
for the words in balloons

to the place where the cow keeps jumping
over and over
with all the footballers, team managers
and lottery winners, world superstars,
heroes and champions and legends and lovers
and proud mums and dads

and the whole of Malaysia
over the moon
over the moon
over the over the over the moon.

IMTIAZ DHARKER

Mersey Crossing

Small boy, red knees and nose,
sharp knuckles on the rail, you crossed

from Pierhead to New Brighton,
there and back and back again.

You folded up whole days
between two riverbanks,

half your mind on the rivermouth,
the north and west, the east and south,

the whole world wide for you
and out of breath.

Today, on the river
whose ships have sailed away,

grey waves sliding over darker grey,
you point to places I must see

when you are not there,
some other day.

The whole city, the grand sweep
of buildings from an earlier, confident time,

the lights just coming on,
the riverflow, the sky, all seem

to lean in towards you
as I do

to take warmth
from the shelter that you make

against a bitter wind.
It seems the natural way of things.

Some other day
I will unwrap your life to look

at what you have become,
far flung,

spread out to north and south,
beyond the rivermouth,

but blessed with a small boy's
stubbornness.

Between the riverbanks, obsessed
with finding,

always crossing, crossing,
crossing back again.

WALES

PATIENCE AGBABI

North(West)ern

I was twelve, as in the twelve-bar blues, sick
for the Southeast, marooned on the North Wales coast.
A crotchet, my tongue craving the music
of Welsh, Scouse or Manc. Entering the outpost
of Colwyn Bay pier, midsummer, noon,
nightclub for those of us with the deep ache
of adolescence, when I heard that tune,
named it in one. Soul. My heart was break

dancing on the road to Wigan Casino,
Northern Soul Mecca where transatlantic bass
beat blacker than blue in glittering mono.

Then back, via Southport, Rhyl, to the time, place,
I bit the Big Apple. Black, impatient, young.
A string of pips exploding on my tongue.

PATIENCE AGBABI

Postmod:

a snapshot. Monochrome. A woman
in a '60s rayon suit. A knee-length pencil
skirt and jacket with three-quarter sleeves.
Hot aqua and a mod original.
That shade translates to stylish grey. It's me.
And on the back, someone's scrawled in pencil
Brighton Beach, 1963

for fun because I wasn't even thought of
in 1963. Imagine Rhyl,
'82, where the image was conceived
by someone with good taste, bad handwriting
and lack of a camera. Yet that negative,
in our heads only, was as sharp and real
as the suit so out of fashion it was in.

ERIC NGALLE CHARLES

A Mountain and a Sea

A story from a distance.
They were my only witness,
A mountain and a sea
Whose lips engulfed the green sky,
A lasting kiss,
Washing her waves off-shore,
Leaving behind a boat.

That for my home-coming.

The mountain
Like a giant slate,
With trees keeping vigil
Like relatives awaiting
Their departed children.

Her giant gaze
Looking down at me
Like Yomadene,
The guardian,
The mountain
Where my grandmother
Lived after her death.
A mountain of broken hearts.

That for my homecoming.
A shining mountain
Where sheep grazed,
By which means
My heart rejoiced.

That for my homecoming.

On a wet journey to Llandudno
Washing away pain and longing,
A re-born voice crying
Between a mountain and a sea.

Where voices echoed
Across the town's horizon
And conversation on common things.
Wake me from my slumber
Then this poem
Will be over.

That for my homecoming,

Between a mountain
And a sea.

TARIQ LATIF

Trefor

Sunlight is cut by the blunt edges
Of the slate gutted mountains.

Tidal waves break
Through coves, crooks and corners.

Spume shoots up and then
Drops, like white pebbles,

In the receding swell
Casting lots of soluble rings.

The frontiers of the sea
And the land shifts

With the crisscross of tides.
I visualise the moon, beneath

My feet, through the many miles
Of earth and space, effecting

These waves, tracing out
Time curves along the shore.

'Look, look a boat,' shouts
My son of three. I barely

Make out the tiny white sail
Trembling on the thin edge.

JOHN SIDDIQUE

One New Year's Eve

I drove two hours alone to the sea.
Stood on the beach at midnight, screaming
in the rush, while the fireworks
went off in the Welsh towns nearby.

Drove home slow, left the radio off.
Not wanting to arrive, the heater matrix
barely working, damn that old Volkswagen,
a fleece blanket over my freezing knees.

No one else out until I get to the city,
I'm so glad to go home alone tonight.

AIMÉ KONGOLO

Non-toxic trust

a year has flown and passed
leaving its memories to last

each dawn is painted by holy skies
known as a contentment of flame
little is known that can't inflame
your goddess skin and cry

i see you in every breathing corner
plotting aloud to increase your
quantity of non-toxic trust
that I can't reduce to dust

like solid snow on Mount Snowdon
I approve my consent to sustain
every second to adore your lips
in years that will float us in the same adoring ship

MAGGIE HARRIS

Cwmpengraig, place of stones

Where yuh navel string bury is not necessarily home
Dis gurl gon walk my grandmother say
And walk I walk from Guyana to West Wales
And leave I leave that place of oceans and slave bones
For bruk down cottages and hills where people still pray

And come I come with my forked tongue split syntax
Of Hinglish and street Creole to wander lanes
With no names and no map where even
Sat-nav wuk hard to find being alimbo
Beyond satellite beyond stars

And stars and dreams of stars and songs
Called these Welsh from home
To cross oceans to a continent
Of the imagination

And is peel dis country peel like onion
Garden cups my cottage in its fists of seasons
Caring nothing for my ignorance
Of names, pronunciation, language

And History running in the stream right there
Beneath the stone: mill-worker foot-bottom still indent
Ghost voice talking story wild a catchafire
How he catching boat with intention get the hell outa dis place

It nat fuh him to know some gurl would bring his story
Right back here and tell him tales of sugarcane
And captains tracing latitude and longitude
With quadrant, quill and octopus ink

Is laugh he would laugh, true true
Whilst that stream keep gurgling,
Stones keep tumbling,
Underscore the footfall of my feet.

MAGGIE HARRIS

Llamas, Cwmpengraig

Oh you – coming to greet us over the farm-gate
Your camel-like heads elegant against this Welsh hilltop
Whose sheep graze like commoners beneath your gaze

Your heads turn as one,
Ears – inverted commas, sickles, sweet horns of plenty
Eyes languid behind fringed yashmak of lashes

Peru seems a long way off,
As does Guyana; but for a moment there we shared
An echo between us, of continents.

TINASHE MUSHAKAVANHU

The Green Man Festival

I

Three days we camped
Behind the Black Mountain's shadow
Sharing cigarettes & snide remarks
of rain pissing down, our spirits scalded
It was supposed to be a weekend of fun
but sitting on the damp grass i saw her
Make a quick farouche-eyed inventory
Of the crowded arena but she
Disappeared before i could even say 'hi'
No, i wasn't drunk. My minds clock
stuck backwards since i set eyes on her
the day before at three minutes to three

II

evenings on the FOLKEY DOKEY STAGE
a caul of coloured veined lights, tangled rods
we came for the night dance
it was Robert Plant's howl that sounded
the moments trumpet. I looked up.
There was a slight Welsh drizzle but
our bodies did not stop swaying to the
metallic rhythm of the night

III

from the Thai food stall
a sizzling goulash unsettled a smoky muck-off
the overworked waitress stubbornly astride
to serve the long hungry queue
her smithy and butcher's apron grimed
she paused. Long fingers on proud hips.
Was it my weak eyes? Or time's fading imprints?

MONIZA ALVI

Spring on the Hillside

You coax the flames, choosing
the logs thoughtfully.
You're happy
as if a bright ghost of yourself
moves through the openings
in your wigwam of sticks.

We stumble down the valley
to make phone calls.
The evening sun
wanders like torchlight
across the trees
the agate river.

I have never known wild flowers
live so long in a vase
as in the hills of Llandogo
where the sleet falls like blossom,
the stone path trails upwards
further than we know.

GRACE NICHOLS

Opening Your Book
(in memory of R.S. Thomas)

Why should departures of the flesh
still make us weep
when what we're left holding is
the bright indestructible spirit?

And yet it does, RS, the flesh.
This morning travelling by train
to Victoria, I open your book,
Laboratories of the Spirit –

Dipping into the well
of your conversations with God;
crunching through the communion
of your Welsh valleys –

Your Ash Wednesday falls
and Easter morning rises.
Filled with an overwhelming sense
of what it means to be human.

MONIZA ALVI

Luckbir

My Aunt Luckbir had full red lips,
sari borders broad like silver cities,
gold flock wallpaper in her sitting-room.
Purple curtains opened

on a small, square garden
where Uncle Anwar fed the birds
and photographed Aunt, her costume
draped over a kitchen stool,

the backdrop – a garden fence and roses.
Luckbir found her Cardiff neighbours
very kind – thanked them in a letter
to *Woman's Own*,

spoke to me warmly of Jane Austen
remembered from an overseas degree.
Aunt had no wish to go out, take a job,
an evening class.

162

Picking at rice on pyrex
she grew thin – thinner.
In my dreams she was robust,
had a Western hairstyle, stepped outside.

After she died young
Uncle tried everything –
astronomy, yoga, cookery.
His giant TV set flickers into life –

a video of the ice-skating championship.
Has he kept Aunt's clothes,
let their shimmer slip through his hands?

LEON CHARLES

'Tiger Bay' Heart of Wales

magic spawned etched by sea
islands to die for druidic prophecy
from far perfection necessity unites
brown sugars eclipsed race riots
gloved bare fist fights

multi ethnic paradise
from Merlin to Mabinogion tales
Taliesin forged the word
creating rainbow Wales
voices erupt down dank satanic mines
communities forged spirits soar
along ley lines

black gold drives nuclear fission
steam accelerated high tech vision
power proliferates paving the way
re-invent recycle sustain
welsh folk without delay

tourism flourishes blooms
world welcomed to glorious strata
visions of eternity beckon come along barter
cliffs morph into spectacular valleys
visit Glamorgan's vale traverse the heritage coast
alight at the captain's wife
enjoy fresh local fare with a favourable host

MARSDEN FALCON

'It's a big ask...'

It's a big ask,
I'm only 16 but I'm growing up fast,
But what's the point of asking if you don't ask big?
Celebrating the realness,
Tell me if you feel this,
This career is...
My Faith, My Dream, and as I reveal this,
Young boy, pretty insecure,
Paranoid yeah that's for sure,
But that's what makes me superior,
To yes everyone,
From my generation,
I was always taught to be patient,
'Cause good things come to those who wait,
If you rush around all it does is frustrate,
Plus it makes a lot more room for mistakes,
Mistakes that you can't afford to make,
On your way to the top,
No time to flop,
I used to put my dunks on, and tie them up tight,
Go for late walks in the middle of the night,
Sub-Urban Lurking, call it what you like,
I did it all day, but I never took a right... Turn,
Just stood there and watched my future burn,
Until I realised I was wasting my time,

Cleared my chest and spat out one big rhyme,
Used a pen and paper with all its might,
Then when I woke up in the middle of the night,
I didn't go for walks this time I'd write,
Get my feelings down onto the paper,
New work place, being my brain's narrator,
Then being my tongue's dictator,
Pulling away from the field of Cardiff,
I don't belong here my flow's too retarded,
Putting my little town Barry on the map,
No film... it really is Mar's Attacks.

TISHANI DOSHI

Memory of Wales

This is how it arrives, the memory
of Wales, on a day of scanty light.
I'm walking towards the playground.
I will never know newness like this,
or fear. I'm walking, and I'm eight.
I see a girl on the swing – my mother,

or at least, a version of my mother:
fair-haired, small. In the memory
of Wales it is often cold. I'm eight
and the cows are stalking light
like monsters in the playground.
I will never know newness like this.

I will never know a world like this.
This is my childhood and my mother's.
Everything begins in the playground:
beauty, decay, love, lilies. Memory
starts here on the stairs, in skylight.
Cows chew eternally. I'm eight

in this memory, I'm always eight.
There's a painting that speaks to this
malady of recurrence – an indigo twilight
of melting clocks, which shows Mother
Time as a kind of persistence, memory
and dream, coupling on the ground.

Everything we love returns to the ground.
Mother, father, childhood. When I'm eight
I know nothing of betrayal, but the memory
persists. Only once, is it different from this.
The playground is empty, and my mother,
no longer a girl, is walking a ridge of light.

Now she's at the wooden gate. Light
from Welsh stars tumbles to the ground.
Bronze cliffs in the distance sing. My mother
has met a man. She's going away. I'm eight,
but I've always known she'll leave all this.
Forsaking, after all, is a kind of memory.

My mother is eight and in Wales again.
She's in the playground of memory,
swinging towards light, towards this.

MAGGIE HARRIS

Montbretia, Wales

In search of poetry I wandered Ireland,
head full of myth and mist,
Boland, Heaney, Kennelly…
and girls with Cork and Kerry accents
slipping out of cars on narrow country roads
to tumble through hedgerows in search of wrecks.

Their laughter sliced the air like bees
and lens foreshortened squares of blue
over heads of corn through singing stable doors
askew with age and longing.
And there you were...
shot through with summer, rampant in the hedgerow

gold with song. And I sang, *Belong*.

I gathered up your name
and a miniature bouquet
to press between words as yet unsung.

And your name came back to me
when islands later on
I stumbled on this garden wild with sheaves
and *you* house-hunted *me*
your leaves precise as spears, your head aflame
with madness, wild, frantic, blazing poetry.

SADI HUSAIN

Not in India

'I want a proper bag,' I cried.
'But this is a proper bag.
In India we always took these to school.'
'We're not in India!'
'Go on, go to school, Craig is here,' ordered Mum.
Craig, his clean pink face beaming a smile,
had his bag across his back.
My satchel laboured at my hip,
constantly trying to get away.

We arrive in school, late for prayers again. Good.
Spelling test. Easy. Full marks.

'This boy came to Britain when he was six.
He couldn't speak English.
Now he's a better speller than all of you.'
Maths, just long division and fractions.
'Indians are always good at Maths,' Mum used to say.
Geography. Maps. Places I haven't seen.
'Sadi came to Wales two years ago and now he knows
all the countries in the world.'

Leaving school for another day.
A boy runs shouting 'Chocolate!'
Craig defends me, 'Then you're a Milky Bar!'
'But I'm not chocolate, I'm just like you!' I think.
'Home already?
In India we didn't come home till five,' said Mum.

'But we're not in India, are we?' I cried,
running upstairs and locking the door behind me.

RAMAN MUNDAIR

Welsh Postcard

In passing places
rain veils disappearing
seas in salty blurs.

Across the horizon, soft
focus humpback isles and tankers
heave with industrial poise.

LABI SIFFRE

An Alien in Cymru

Foreigner

'A refugee from the city?!' We rush
outside with ladder brush and bucket of paint
to change 'The Crown' on the creaking sign
to 'The Farmer's Laugh'   bitter
as the pint in his scarred hand

weathered outside as I am in
I won't be trouble won't be telling him
how he should be greener   twenty years on
his life is vital here and I'm just passing through

still losing the fight   insignificant   sure
but I'll never give in   never go back
though the voice inside says never say never
and fear shakes my beer hand spills
living liquid over dead skin

How's the shearing going?
I steady my glass with quivering lips
and drain life down in gulps   my eyes
on his answer   my mind far away
my head very nodding   my interest
will it be   convincing enough
to fool us both

Incoming calls

Thriving in the borders
we know we'll never be Welsh
but our children are   or will be
and we're happy to help

We're refugees from the cityscape
we came here to give them freedom
to grow
where the air won't line their lungs
with grey snow

Yes, some of us are ageing hippies
who art and craft and grow green vegetables
for seemingly little gain
but we add our incoming voices loud
to the chorus who want the village school to remain

We came here to join the community
though some fear we're taking over
'cause we want to protect what we came here for
when some who've been here for hundreds of years
want jobs no matter what the ecological discord

and some of your sons and daughters
can't live in the place they were born to
'cause some of us had loads of cash
from the sale of our city semi-detached

and we've forced the prices
beyond your dreams
and you don't see why *your* kids
have to leave

and it's happened before
It'll happen again
we can only try
to help our children be friends

'cause everyone wants a better life
and everyone fights to have it
and change is a river that flows on and on
no matter how much you damn it

Across the Great Divide

The postman's wife and the colonel's lady
don't bother with who isn't Welsh and who is

They roll up their sleeves and muck in, they're brisk
There's a job to be done it's no use complaining

There's raffles and fêtes, first aid, cakes and teas
Hospital visits and meals on wheels

One votes Conservative the other's *Old* Labour
They're not afraid to dirty their hands
and they don't ask for favours

They know they're a cliché but those who laugh
don't visit Mrs Morgan who broke her hip
and needs help in the bath

DEREK WALCOTT

from Midsummer

XXXV

Mud. Clods. The sucking heel of the rain-flinger.
Sometimes the gusts of rain veered like the sails
of dragon-beaked vessels dipping to Avalon
and mist. For hours, driving along
the skittering ridges of Wales, we carried the figure
of Langland's Ploughman on the rain-seeded glass,
matching the tires with his striding heels,
while splintered puddles dripped from the roadside grass.
Once, in the drizzle, a crouched, clay-covered ghost
rose in his pivot, and the turning disc of the fields
with their ploughed stanzas sang of a freshness lost.

Villages began. We had crossed into England –
the fields, not their names, were the same. We found a caff,
parked in a thin drizzle, then crammed into a pew
of red leatherette. Outside, with thumb and finger,
a careful sun was picking the lint from things.
The sun brightened like a sign, the world was new
while the cairns, the castled hillocks, the stony kings
were scabbarded in sleep, yet what made me think
that the crash of chivalry in a kitchen sink
was my own dispossession? I could sense, from calf
to flinging wrist, my veins ache in a knot.
There was mist on the window. I rubbed it and looked out
at the helmets of wet cars in the parking lot.

MIDLANDS

KIMBERLY TRUSTY

New Vic Theatre, Stoke-on-Trent, ring bell for service

box office laughter echoes
up into the restaurant
meshes with autumn sunshine
the clink of cutlery
and elevenses confessions

handing me an oatcake
Jean says
'It all happens here duck'

plans for golden anniversaries
holidays in Costa del Sol
dissolutions   resolutions
little earthquakes that
erupt over scones
pots of tea   and
coffee machine
cappuccinos

at noon
in the midst of coiffed ladies
drama students wound
in black and white keffiyehs
and dedicated labyrinth dwellers
the tin man emerges
from his woodland home
script in hand   running his lines

handing me a plate
of chicken madras and rice
Jean says,
'He was married once'
no surprise then
that he'll ask the wizard
for a heart

this may not be
a performance in the round
but it is around the clock
regular as the tides
the waning and waxing
of the moon

ROMESH GUNESEKERA

Frontliners

(for Shanthi)

House sparrows that shook our pink
blossom loose became enemy
aeroplanes in flight – targets
to the pellet-guns of my childhood.
The war of another age
Raged in the mid-afternoon lull
of our shaded veranda
as I culled an imperial culture
from a pile of tatty war-comics
and second-hand adventure stories.
In a post-colonial garden
I grew up
dreaming in English,
biting my tongue.
I made out a Sherwood Forest
of tropicalised longbows,
tommy-gun justice
and an ace James Bond. In those foreign
anachronistic battles
I sided with the language I knew best,
already marked
with a rolling stone's droll beliefs
and in love
with rock an' roll.

Now at the frontline for my new-born
I find myself fighting again –
this time in a language under stress.

D.S. MARRIOTT

The Ghost of Averages

1

hard work,
        hard even for a nigga, but not you.
The French grammar,
        lies open on a table
smeared with grease, oil, –
        unfettered by the chains
    opening the mind begins its flight
and maybe,...
        who knows....
the harvested cornfields are green, once again,
    a home for what can be reclaimed
                rather than loss, or delusion,
derided by you, Booker,
        as proof the ancient memories lie unredeemed.

2

There is hard work
        in the school yard.
I am Kunte Kinte on the hill,
the stars torn from the rolling dusk,
        I sit side by side
with the dark, the unwelcome brown.
Re-read says my father,
        the coal dust lining his eyes
the focus
        for the reprieve of time, the art of discovery,
                for the receipts
of less gnarled hands and feet.

He used to call me 'dee',
reminders too, of how missed letters
    are often the most permanent of things
when the tin can spills
onto the oilcloth near the unopened book
and he takes deep breaths
on his knees
    reading the seams of coal for 'this is not-me'.

3

I wrote his funeral program in *Word*.
    If one day,
    life rains on you
    a similar dereliction and collapse
        read that French grammar.
And the boy,
pitied for the ever patient, worn-out binding,
    the loneliness and levels of neglect,
gives tithes against his will:
    remember what is valued, the price it gives.
The privilege is reserved for us–
    Each letter blackened
because a wish to live is deeper
than seams to be mined,
    or eyes darkened by dust.

PANYA BANJOKO

Arriving

Six to a room, squeezed tightly,
seven years since the war
had made no impression
the colours no imprint
on dull winter grey.
England wasn't ready,
for white ankle-wrap wedged shoes

red dresses at Trent Bridge
where people gathered
to see amongst the colourless border
bizarre cocktails of yellows and greens
whispering loud and bright,
you wouldn't believe me if I told you
of things back then,
before the levels of frequency changed
and settled
to a hum,
an imitation stand back style
with conservative browns and bottle greens
that challenged the notion of home

MICHELLE HUBBARD

Take the girl out of Notts, but you can't take Notts out of the girl!

I'm of Nottingham, camouflaged in Robin Hood Green.
Making my way through the mighty Sherwood Forest,
Loving the smell of fresh pine needles.
Bow becomes paper, arrow becomes pen.

I am known as 'The Mother' –
Jamaican girl with Irish eyes.
I am the urban Maid Marian, waiting for a surprise,
Avoiding the sheriff and his axe:
I can't afford my council tax!

My house could never be Nottingham's castle
But I sit, happy, on my throne, without hassle.
Nottingham's night clubs, full of merry men
That become CCTV and *Crimewatch* legends

Nottingham flows through my veins and through my accent,
Like water down the murky blood of the River Trent,
Where fish are poisoned alongside the minds of school children,
Saturated by stories of that brave hoody: 'Robin of Nottingham'.

SANDEEP PARMAR

Archive for a Daughter

November 1972, Derby

A dance card embalmed in sweat.
Her ruthless curve of palm
mowing the carpet into sheaves before a gas fire.

Liquidescent virgin in a purple dress.
Oil paint, shaded avocado, umbrella sun-wings.

Box 2, folder 20, 'Early Married Life'

a single page:
recto
a fashionable centre-parting
verso
consonants: midnight affair nuclear affair bleach affair
watermark indecipherable

[But here we are jumping ahead]

The archivist notes that no exact birth date is known.
An already Western dressed 6-year-old reads the headlines
of English newspapers for party tricks.
Her black eyes are blunt and unequivocal like the prophecies of
pharaohs.
In a Punjabi village, she and her impeccable mother, gemstoned,
oracular,
princess a vernal causeway.

Box 1, folder 2, 'Emigration'

The BOAC stewardesses Max Factor crinkled baskets
of sweets to soothe the girl's swinging, impatient feet.
Aviation – a risky endeavour in 1963 – levels a curse at her progeny.
Aerophobia – her own daughter's –
fear of the air between home and exile collapsing.

Box 1, folder 7, 'Education'

Homelands Grammar School For Girls

Miss Moore leans across an oak sea and parquets a line of future mothers.
Her bovine sympathies, neatly pressed, tentacle
                             towards the only Indian in the class.
      The Georgian battlecross marking her forehead,
                         kindly and thoughtfully, segregates.

The girl bounds wildly through the Public Library –
Huxley to her 11-year-old mind suggests individuality –
                but the Savage's feet recommend no one specific exit.

    folders 8-17

Unbound Notebook, mostly unreadable:

*I thought I could become a doctor and asking found I could not think to ask
to become anything*

The archivist notes that these pages are not continuous.
Refer to Box 2, folder 10, 'Correspondence'.
A photograph of a prospective husband and several handwritten credentials.

Box 3, folder 1, 'Notes on Motherhood'

Nursery – pram – groceries – pram – doctor's visit –
                            cucumbers in half lengths –
– over each shoulder some conspicuous intellect –

Husband-academic, wife-typist
      She door-to-doors Hoovers, Avon, thick rosaries of factory lace,
while her children pop tic-tacs for invented ailments in plastic houses.

Nottingham hurls snowballs at her black turbaned gentleman.

      Soaked typescript, fair copy of a life –

When she asked her parents for a spare suitcase for an exodus,
      they replied, my child, *nothing is ever spare*

Box 4, folder 1, 'Exile'

1985, Vancouver – ablaze with cherry blossoms from here to the kindergarten.
We arrived with one steel pot, a bag of lentils and an onion.

folder 2

1987, North Hollywood – submarine fences root Thanksgiving potatoes,
one a piece. My daughter reads Laura Ingalls Wilder to her menagerie
of dolls. Raft sails calmly on.

folder 3

1989, Oxnard – Gifted children are pursestrings. We mind their collegiate
years with interest. El Rio wizens to a stockpile of citrus and rental agreements.

folder 4

1995, Ventura – Bibled to real estate, gold blazers cinch round a wade of
blonde, leathered adulterers. The neighbours tend their god-plots of lawn
and hedge.

Box 5, folder 1, 'Drs Parmar'

She saunas with the ladies of the Gold Coast –
    one Japanese ex-comfort woman, one savvy señora
    goldbuckled and multifranchised.

    Stanford, Northwestern, Harvard, London, Cambridge –
    and when my husband's sisters wept because I had no sons,
    I said I have two doctors (one of body, the other of mind)
    and sent my uterus via Federal Express to the village,
    with my compliments!

On the verso, written in ink, is a page from Box 1, folder 8
[misplaced]

I remember clearly when I knew that I would one day die.
I was on the toilet and I was 11.
The bathroom was white and oblivious.

ROMMI SMITH

Night River

> *The moving waters at their priestlike task*
> JOHN KEATS, 'Bright Star'

III

I want to talk with you about tonight

the field a page of green and you, a gift
in wait, just by the sentence of the stream
my open mouth, my tongue, the dew of words
that only this place, and your hands will know
the deepening sky unfolds it is our book
our fingers trace each wave of cloud, those far-
off oyster planets, and each drought of light,
we read them for the clues to find your star;
we can't, the wide unknown before us will
not spell its secrets out and we must cross
its river, there's no map, or moon, to guide.

Except, one word, like soft and tender rain,
the healing one and it means – everything.

HAZEL MALCOLM

Blues in the Black Country

In the heat and the sweat and the blackness
Swirling shades of ebony embroil together in the ruby shadows
Smelting fragments of molten desire
Slag oozes from the dandy and infuses
With the sweet orange blossom and ginger
Embers of gilded women line the wall
Red ribbon glares rave across the room
The track fades
Only cinders of the moment remain
In the heat and the sweat and the blackness.

MARTIN GLYNN

Highfields Style

De Highfields style
Iz de Brixton style
Iz de Handsworth style
Iz de Moss Side Style
Where pepul a survive
An' de mind run wild.

GHETTOLOGY
Iz de name of de game
Psychological destrucshan
Inflict de pain
Dat run doun yuh life
An' tun yuh insane
Tun yuh inside out
An' empty out yuh brain
Ghettology style
Ghettology style.

It mash up yuh 'ead
destroyin evry cell
where de life yuh live
iz one pure hell
where dere's too much noize
an nasty smell
where de crime rates high
prostitushan az well
Psychological destrucshan
is lickin evry man
de life dem a live
dem nuh mek nuh plan
dem mind get unbalanced
dem dash dem inna van
guh tek dem mental hospital
go gi dem a brain scan.
PSYCHOLOGICAL DESTRUCTION
PSYCHOLOGICAL DESTRUCTION.

De concrete life
iz one rat-race
where social security pay de rent
an council gi de place
a likkle time lata
it tun inna disgrace
cause evry bit a livin'
de hustla dem a chase
de blackman run de area
a own dem corna shap
de man dem jus a hustle
to mek rent trouble stop
de woman dem a push pram
until dem legs waan drop
society's created anotha human flop
but dem nu bizniss

Once again itz been ignored
dem push it to one side
like a cancer in we body
sumting to hide
but a likkle understandin'
is sumting to be tried
because de people in dem area
still av dem pride
if yuh feel seh dem life easy
yuh waan guh pon dem side
an wen it get ruff
yuh yeye dem open wide.

Because de Highfields style
iz de Brixton style
iz de Handsworth style
iz de Moss Side Style
iz de St Paul's style
iz de Chapeltown style
iz de St Ann's style

ITZ WHAT WE AZ GHETTO PEPUL CALL

GHETTOSTYLE!

CAROL LEEMING

Highfields Fantasia

In,
Highfields terraced houses
concertinaed off street
or pallisaded,
all night wrapped
agent orange haloed
with furtive stars
at play behind
patinas of trees
curlicues of muezzin calls
loop into august bells
neither smother dismal djinns
false light gods pulsing
behind filigree netted windows

There,
huddled in dank kitchens
forked brows lines straighten
dwellers disrobe disillusions
to invoke a seething alchemy
brief escape to play here
from blaring fluorescent tubes
fatigued sombre living rooms
all blipping wiis and gameboys

They.
conjure up black skillets of,
hearty soulful seasonings
tiny geysers of rice pots
fuming so expectantly,
while joyfully clapping their lids
for sizzles of garlic
bangles of onions
swathes of spinach

Magic.

CAROL LEEMING

Valley Dreamers

On London Road
fly eyed to view
Old John's ruins
distant in braggy peak
below, a city
glowers on with neon
prickly pollen beams
awhirl, in gasps of traffic
no one will swallow
Lestar's rising glossolalia
hamper its wild gesticulations
neither temper, its rude music
a worlds' there
ready to launch
its valley dreamers
long sunk deep
in a curve of earth
unbound from 'middle lands'.

ROSHAN DOUG

Flash of Independence

We cram a photo booth at Digbeth
one Sunday afternoon in '89
waiting for the National Express.
We smile at Khalistan's Bhupendra Wala,
Bobby Sands and Blair Peach, indifferent
now to the violence and assimilation,
forgetting the rain outside, the clouds,
forgetting the fragility of our world,
the instability of our amphoteric lives
as British immigrants in an English universe
– while Gandhi weeps alone in the distance.

In a momentary flash we're a whole
a unit captured in time, not even
razor-sharp death can separate us.
Yet not a word or deed or countenance
can justify us completely. Like Mountbatten,
Macaulay's Union Jack and the scholarly
on Shakespeare works secure in the British Library,
we're a living irony detached and static,
moving like a spinning wheel of '47,
a symbol of India made in Lancashire
– while Gandhi weeps alone in the distance.

ROSHAN DOUG

Sound Bites

News reel; chimney smoke; narrative:

it was the coldest February on record, the day her brother died
near the DAC furnace in Smethwick, living like the rats in Deshnok
and suffering from alop-

his last meal (packed in a cellophane bag) was that morning's *roti*
with *achár*, which he ate with a friend from his village.
And on his death hardly a word was said

just a cautious crew from *Nationwide* who recorded 'Life
at the Foundry': a long shot; a close up. Interception
with a tooth-eyed Brummie, a union man

who said what a tragedy it was and mispronounced
his name, in an accent that was indiscernible,
clashing with the received pronunciation of the narrator –

his media looks, education and formal words, and then
back to Frank Bough in the studio. Signature tune;
fade out; cut to *Top of the Pops* and *Mind Your Language*.

In the background we heard the women wailing next door.
Sound bites.

SUE BROWN

Birmingham

(this settlement has always been a city of many trades
Industry Manufacturing and Engineering
In the heart the country the revolution made its mark
With the canals system flowing with rich and varied cargoes
commerce was destined to flourish profitably)

From dawn to twinned city
From Beorma to Birmingham
From the outskirts to the Inner Circle
From Bourneville to The Bullring
This has always been a city of great diligence
From auction blocks to the first bank
From historical canals to Spaghetti Junction
From small arms manufacturing to the Thinktank
From The Museum & Art Galleries to Chinatown
This has always been a city of great and major influence
From Joseph Sturge to Jamaica
From the MAC to the riots
From Pirate Radio stations to Marcus Garvey Day
From enthused settlers to Poet Laureate – Dr Roi Kwabena
This has always been a city of great demonstration
From Lee Bank to Attwood Green
From the Grand Junction Railways to Fircroft College
From The Lunar Society to Birmingham University
From musical innovators to The Harriet Tubman Bookshop
This has always been a city of great progress
From Bingley Hall to the ICC
From The Cave to The Drum
From woodland clearing to urban villages
From Back-to-Backs to Leisure and Tourism
This has always been a city of great change
From Soho House to Symphony Hall
From Edgbaston Cricket Ground to Carnival
From The River Rea to SeaWorld
From The Town Hall to Spring Hill Library
This has always been a city of great admiration

From Aston Villa to the International Book Festival
From the Shubeens to Broad Street
From the Balti Triangle to the Birmingham Royal Ballet
From the Evening Mail to visiting Heads of State
This has always been a city of great success
From Matthew Boulton to Jasmine Johnson
From John Cadbury to Willard Wigan
From Olaudah Equiano to Benjamin Zephaniah
From Oscar Deutsch to Vanley Burke
This has been a city of great and creative minds
From Herbert Austin to the Jewellery Quarters
From the Rotunda to the Peace Pagoda
From the Botanical Gardens to the Mailbox
From master builder masons to the naturally gifted
This has always been a city of great involvement
From British Nationals to refugees
From yesterdays generation to tomorrows people
From history makers to story tellers
From a city of many cultures to a Star City
This has always been a city of great heritage

MOQAPI SELASSIE

Tellin de stori

Rule Britannia
Britannia rules
Di waves
Dem tek InI
Black people
Here innah Inglan
Fi wuk wi as slave
Again?
Natty Dread
wi livin

innah concrete jungle
Natty Dread
wi livin
innah concrete jungle
'igh rise ghettoes
houses in di skies
no one cyan tell I
dat dis is paradise
mi get up in di marnin
wot ah bam bam
guh fi ketch a lif
di lif outtah hackshan
di way dem bill deze
playsiz
its like a pris'n
Coz Natty
Handsworth
Aston
Ladywood
Edgbaston
Kings Heath
Balsall Heath
Sparkbrook
Small Heath
Evvryweh Iman guh
All Isee is concrete
Cum mek wi step it
Uppah freeman street

Coz Natty

ROI KWABENA

from Location:Re

illegal skateboarding 'round
chamberlain's fountain
perhaps
these
bangladeshi, sudanese, caribbean,
irish, vietnamese, somalian english children
be among
future proprietors

as love day
summer lane
city inn, washington wharf's
residents
conducting
business

on calthorpe or colmore
row. May-
-be no more
land mines
will ever be

proudly manufactured
here again. Forward

again

fifty-two degrees north
create proudly

Be
Birmingham

ROY McFARLANE

I found my father's love letters

I found my father's love letters
in strange and obscure places
often hidden in dark secret spaces,
where memories had closed the doors.

I found blank letters, with matching cards and envelopes.
A small drawer filled with letters unfinished,
crossed through, curling at the edges,
turning in the colour of time.

There was one in Marquez's *Love in the Time of Cholera*
sandwiched somewhere between
Fermina's rejection of Floretina
and a lifetime of loving, waiting for true love.

I found some penned in a note pad, half-written, half-thought,
scribbled to capture fleeting thoughts,
earnest in writing the emotional overflow
that time edits into streams flowing over with love.

I found one folded
lost in the attic
an elegy to love
that time had forgotten.

I searched to find the true name to those letters entitled *my love*.
A secret lover? Distant lover? First time lover?
or even my mother of whom you gave a thousand names
but I never heard you call her *my love*.

I wonder if they ever received their letters,
an amended version, a completed version
refined and acceptable, filled with rose petals,
signed and sealed with your love.

BENJAMIN ZEPHANIAH

The Big Bang

I was born where the Beorma people made home,
Handsworth, in Brummagem.
For many of my early years
I thought of this town to be a cold suburb
Of Kingston, Jamaica.
My then girlfriend Jasvinder Basra
Thought it to be a cold suburb of Jullunder, India,
And we were both right.
We, in our puppy love innocence
Knew that it was only a matter of time and space,
We Dark Matter grew up holding hands
Listening to Reggae and Bhangra
Eating channa and ackee,
And playing doctors and nurses somewhere in the future.

Handsworth does that to you,
Historic and progressive,
It wakes but never sleeps
Concrete with a heartbeat.
A private space for all its children
That is full of stars and it keeps expanding,
It is where voices from the past speak to us
Every day, lived in voices
Of working-class heroes reminding
Us that we are all Brummies,
But me and Jasvinder knew this anyway.

I saw riots in Handsworth,
I saw revolution loitering on the streets
Where money had been thrown down drains
In front of people who were needy,
But I also saw energy laden creators
Bringing hope,
And building sites of new galaxies
In Brummagem, the centre of it all.

This is where I discovered the natures of the universe,
This is where I realised
That The Theory of Everything leaves a lot to be desired,
This is where
The postman taught me everything needs poetry,
And that it is not gravity that gives us roots
But the things we do to ourselves.
But it was me that said relativity needs to relate,
Space stops everything happening to you,
And in my humble opinion
Faith and tradition will live next to progress
For as long as it takes.

Cosmology?

Well that's all about me and Jasvinder.
It all started with us
In Handsworth in Brummagem,
Where the philosophers of Grove Lane
And the great thinkers of Soho Road
Now recite Alpha and Omega continually.

Astrophysics?

That's about the nature of our celestial bodies
The application of our physical policies
And the intensity of our cultural intercourse,
It's about the way we greet when we meet
And the exploration of possibilities,
And it must be known
That all scientific studies have shown that
Brummies are at home with new horizons
And a multi-layered concept of place.

Time?
Space?

Time invented itself to stop everything
Happening at once.
Space was grateful
It had been given room to manoeuvre.
They remain good friends.

BENJAMIN ZEPHANIAH

Knowing Me

According to de experts
I'm letting my side down,
Not playing the alienation game,
It seems I am too unfrustrated.
I have refused all counselling
I refuse to appear on daytime television
On night-time documentaries,
I'm not longing and yearning.
I don't have an identity crisis.

As I drive on poetic missions
On roads past midnight
I am regularly stopped by officers of the law
Who ask me to identify myself.
At times like these I always look into the mirror
Point
And politely assure them that
What I see is me.
I don't have an identity crisis.

I have never found the need
To workshop dis matter,
Or sit with fellow poets exorcising ghosts
Whilst searching for soulmates.
I don't wonder what will become of me
If I don't eat reggae food or dance to mango tunes,
Or think of myself as a victim of circumstance.
I'm the dark man, black man
With a brown dad, black man
Mommy is a red skin, black woman,
She don't have an identity crisis.

Being black somewhere else
Is just being black everywhere,
I don't have an identity crisis.

At least once a week I watch television
With my Jamaican hand on my Ethiopian heart
The African heart deep in my Brummie chest,
And I chant, Aston Villa, Aston Villa, Aston Villa,
Believe me I know my stuff.
I am not wandering drunk into the rootless future
Nor am I going back in time to find somewhere to live.
I just don't want to live in a field with my past
Looking at blades of grass that look just like me, near a relic like me
Where the thunder is just like me, talking to someone just like me,
I don't just want to love me and only me; diversity is my pornography,
I want to make politically aware love with the rainbow.
Check dis Workshop Facilitator
Dis is me.
I don't have an identity crisis.

I have reached the stage where I can recognise my shadow.
I'm quite pleased with myself.
When I'm sunbathing in Wales
I can see myself in India
As clearly as I see myself in Mexico.
I have now reached the stage
Where I am sick of people asking me if I feel British or West Indian,
African or Black, Dark and Lonely, Confused or Patriotic.
The thing is I don't feel lost,
I didn't even begin to look for myself until I met a social worker
And a writer looking for a subject
Nor do I write to impress poets.
Dis is not an emergency
I'm as kool as my imagination, I'm care more than your foreign policy.
I don't have an identity crisis.

I don't need an identity crisis to be creative,
I don't need an identity crisis to be oppressed.
I need love warriors and free minds wherever they are,
I need go getters and wide awakers for rising and shining,
I need to know that I can walk into any temple
Rave at any rave
Or get the kind of justice that my folk can see is just.

I am not half a poet shivering in the cold
Waiting for a culture shock to warm my long lost drum rhythm,
I am here and now, I am all that Britain is about
I'm happening as we speak.
Honestly,
I don't have an identity crisis.

KIMBERLY TRUSTY

Alcester Road, Moseley, 50 Bus

that violet commuter
haze has me staring
blind out the #50
window
chip shops ladbrooks mosques
blur in a mess of patterns
and colours like early
experimental films
to which my heartbeat
provides the soundtrack

I think of unpaid visa bills
my nana's sad
smile and profiteroles
everything and nothing
all at once   on the 50
through commuter haze
I dream in twilight
cause daylight's
too harsh exposes cracks
my imagination can't fill

ROSHAN DOUG

Slow Motion

There's a patch where we kissed
underneath an elm on Malvern Hills
my mind reminiscing.
Thoughts come flooding; your silken touch
and your lips lingering over me.

There's a dream I've dreamt upon our bed
through the breeze
blowing softly from the East.
The *diva* flickers, it speaks
but only your touch can awaken me.

And I've lost a year, a second, a lifetime
moving and playing
the same reel of life, tormented,
like a piano out of tune and wondered
what hissing serpent of fate intervened between us.

DEREK WALCOTT

from Tiepolo's Hound

Real counties opened from that small blue book
I cherished: *The English Topographical Draughtsmen,*

turning page after page, now I would look
at what my father never saw, craftsmen

made real by names and counties, high clouds
over the counties, the copses and meadows

with posing cows, the illustrations closed
and camphored in the bookcase of our house.

I watched the mist with an old innocence
of wonder as he did, both island boys,

when steam smothered the small streets of Louveciennes
and seized Pontoise; cannon smoke without noise.

Fog I first learnt in Sussex, where it hovered
over the dissolving Downs, thickening the yard

through which trees peered and hedges were covered
by the smoking county, until its cataract barred

vision entirely. I knew its history here,
in films and novels, opaque conspirator.

On the ancient road we had startled a hare
who melted in it, a raindrop in water.

In the shrouded distance the barking of a dog
would carry over the shrouding copses, over

old words emerging from their roots, fen, bog,
and weald, but no fox leapt from cover,

no scarlet hunters vaulting from a pub print
over bowed hedges, a brass horn hallooing;

England became its art, no different,
except for the hound. I was the one pursuing.

Where a grassed hillock surged towards a copse,
the word 'broom' brandished itself, and there

an orotund oak, majestic in collapse,
exhausted that old metaphor of empire,

but I claimed nothing. Not from this landscape,
the ragged hedges opening Warwickshire,

not in my father's name, those fields of rape,
not even that blue patch where the sun was higher

over the sodden fields. Nothing ancestral
that I could see, nothing from the spire

of piercing Coventry. I heard the small
echoes in the skull's nave, an island choir,

responses carried in the polite noise
of rain beading the windows of the car,

as it this was the drizzle of Pontoise –
wires of rain encaging the familiar.

Nothing blood-recollected in the soil
of watercolour country, slopes with cows,

a broken castle, unlike his: an oil
of silvery willows on the flashing Oise.

DEREK WALCOTT

from **Midsummer**

XXIII

With the stampeding hiss and scurry of green lemmings,
midsummer's leaves race to extinction like the roar
of a Brixton riot tunnelled by water hoses;
they seethe toward autumn's fire – it is in their nature,
being men as well as leaves, to die for the sun.
The leaf stems tug at their chains, the branches bending
like Boer cattle under Tory whips that drag every wagon
nearer to apartheid. And, for me, that closes
the child's fairy tale of an antic England – fairy rings,
thatched cottages fenced with dog roses,
a green gale lifting the hair of Warwickshire.
I was there to add some colour to the British theatre.
'But the blacks can't do Shakespeare, they have no experience.'
This was true. Their thick skulls bled with rancour
when the riot police and the skinheads exchanged quips
you could trace to the Sonnets, of the Moor's eclipse.
Praise had bled my lines white of any more anger,
and snow had inducted me into white fellowships,
while Calibans howled down the barred streets of an empire
that began with Caedmon's raceless dew, and is ending
in the alleys of Brixton, burning like Turner's ships.

XXXVI

The oak inns creak in their joints as light declines
from the ale-coloured skies of Warwickshire.
Autumn has blown the froth from the foaming orchards,
so white-haired regulars draw chairs nearer the grate
to spit on logs that crackle into leaves of fire.
But they grow deafer, not sure if what they hear
is the drone of the abbeys from matins to compline,
or the hornet's nest of a chain saw working late
on the knoll up there back of the Norman chapel.
Evening loosens the moth, the owl shifts its weight,

a fish-mouthed moon swims up from wavering elms,
but four old men are out on the garden benches,
talking of the bows they have drawn, their strings of wenches,
their coined eyes shrewdly glittering like the Thames'
estuaries. I heard their old talk carried
through cables laid across the Atlantic bed,
their gossip rustles like an apple orchard's
in my own head, and I can drop their names
like familiars – those bastard grandsires
whose maker granted them a primal pardon –
because the worm that cores the rotting apple
of the world and the hornet's chain saw cannot touch the words
of Shallow or Silence in their fading garden.

L

I once gave my daughters, separately, two conch shells
that were dived from the reef, or sold on the beach, I forget.
They use them as doorstops or bookends, but their wet
pink palates are the soundless singing of angels.
I once wrote a poem called 'The Yellow Cemetery',
when I was nineteen. Lizzie's age. I'm fifty-three.
These poems I heaved aren't linked to any tradition
like a mossed cairn; each goes down like a stone
to the seabed, settling, but let them, with luck, lie
where stones are deep, in the sea's memory.
Let them be, in water, as my father, who did watercolours,
entered his work. He became one of his shadows,
wavering and faint in the midsummer sunlight.
His name was Warwick Walcott. I sometimes believe
that his father, in love or bitter benediction,
named him for Warwickshire. Ironies
are moving. Now, when I rewrite a line,
or sketch on the fast-drying paper the coconut fronds
that he did so faintly, my daughters' hands move in mine.
Conches move over the sea-floor. I used move
my father's grave from the blackened Anglican headstones
in Castries to where I could love both at once –
the sea and his absence. Youth is stronger than fiction.

203

MAHENDRA SOLANKI

In a Jar

I collect you in a jar.

I always imagined it would be ornamental,
                                    like a trophy.
It is plastic and weighs more than
its square shape suggests.

I lower you gently into the boot of the car, you in
a plastic jar propped against plastic bags full of offerings.

I have a thud in my head *Shri Ram jaya Ram*
as dull as the brown of the jar.
Shri Ram jaya Ram jaya jaya Ram.
I am driven to discard your remains in running water.

> *I imagine all your hardened*
> *edges made smooth;*
> *a life-time's harshness*
> *burnt clean by fire.*

I take off my shoes and in socks
                        on the Severn's edge
float a clay pot and *paan* leaves.

                        I plop balls of flour –
there are so many they begin to gather around my feet;
landlocked by flowers, rice, cotton threads and god knows what.
Worried that all this will not move
                        (I am aware of people staring),
I almost topple into the river as I aim
throws as far as my stiff neck allows.

I hold you squat in my hands,
open the cap and spill you out.

Solemnly at first, then with a final gush
I swill you out with the water;
muttering a request for peace *Om Shantih Shantih Shantih!*
as you go with the river
                    pulled down into the sea.

Shri Ram jaya Ram: a popular mantra in praise of Rama.
paan: betel leaf.
Om: the primal sound.
Shantih: peace.

DAVID DABYDEEN

Coolie Odyssey
(for Ma, d. 1985)

Now that peasantry is in vogue,
Poetry bubbles from peat bogs,
People strain for the old folk's fatal gobs
Coughed up in grates North or North East
'Tween bouts o' living dialect,
It should be time to hymn your own wreck,
Your house the source of ancient song:
Dry coconut shells crackling in the fireside
Smoking up our children's eyes and lungs,
Plantains spitting oil from a clay pot,
Thick sugary black tea gulped down.

The calves hustle to suck,
Bawling on their rope but are beaten back
Until the cow is milked.
Frantic children call to be fed.
Roopram the Idiot goes to graze his father's goats backdam
Dreaming that the twig he chews so viciously in his mouth
Is not a twig.

In the winter of England's scorn
We huddle together memories, hoard them from
The opulence of our masters.

You were always back home, forever
As canefield and whiplash, unchanging
As the tombstones in the old Dutch plot
Which the boys used for wickets playing ball.

Over here Harilall who regularly dodged his duties at the marketstall
To spin bowl for us in the style of Ramadhin
And afterwards took his beatings from you heroically
In the style of England losing
Is now known as the local Paki
Doing slow trade in his Balham cornershop.
Is it because his heart is not in business
But in the tumble of wickets long ago
To the roar of wayward boys?
Or is it because he spends too much time
Being chirpy with his customers, greeting
The tight-wrapped pensioners stalking the snow
With tropical smile, jolly small chat, credit?
They like Harilall, these muted claws of Empire,
They feel privileged by his grinning service,
They hear steelband in his voice
And the freeness of the sea.
The sun beams from his teeth.

Heaped up beside you Old Dabydeen
Who on Albion Estate clean dawn
Washed obsessively by the canal bank,
Spread flowers on the snake-infested water,
Fed the gods the food that Chandra cooked,
Bathed his tongue of the creole
Babbled by low-caste infected coolies.
His Hindi chants terrorised the watertoads
Flopping to the protection of bush.
He called upon Lord Krishna to preserve
The virginity of his daughters
From the Negroes,

Prayed that the white man would honour
The end-of-season bonus to Poonai
The canecutter, his strong, only son:
Chandra's womb being cursed by deities
Like the blasted land
Unconquerable jungle or weed
That dragged the might of years from a man.
Chandra like a deaf-mute moved about the house
To his command,
A fearful bride barely come-of-age
Year upon year swelling with female child.
Guilt clenched her mouth
Smothered the cry of bursting apart:
Wrapped hurriedly in a bundle of midwife's cloth
The burden was removed to her mother's safekeeping.
He stamped and cursed and beat until he turned old
With the labour of chopping tree, minding cow, building fence
And the expense of his daughters' dowries.
Dreaming of India
He drank rum
Till he dropped dead
And was buried to the singing of Scottish Presbyterian hymns
And a hell-fire sermon from a pop-eyed bawling catechist,
By Poonai, lately baptised, like half the village.

Ever so old,
Dabydeen's wife,
Hobbling her way to fowl-pen,
Cussing low, chewing her cud, and lapsed in dream,
Sprinkling rice from her shrivelled hand.
Ever so old and bountiful,
Past where Dabydeen lazed in his mudgrave,
Idle as usual in the sun,
Who would dip his hand in a bowl of dhall and rice –
Nasty man, squelching and swallowing like a low-caste sow –
The bitch dead now!

The first boat chugged to the muddy port
Of King George's Town. Coolies come to rest
In El Dorado,

Their faces and best saris black with soot.
The men smelt of saltwater mixed with rum.
The odyssey was plank between river and land,
Mere yards but months of plotting
In the packed bowel of a white man's boat
The years of promise, years of expanse.

At first the gleam of the green land and the white folk and the Negroes,
The earth streaked with colour like a toucan's beak,
Kiskidees flame across a fortunate sky,
Canefields ripening in the sun
Wait to be gathered in armfuls of gold.

I have come back late and missed the funeral.
You will understand the connections were difficult.
Three airplanes boarded and many changes
Of machines and landscapes like reincarnations
To bring me to this library of graves,
This small clearing of scrubland.
There are no headstones, epitaphs, dates.
The ancestors curl and dry to scrolls of parchment.
They lie like texts
Waiting to be writer by the children
For whom they hacked and ploughed and saved
To send to faraway schools.
Is foolishness fill your head.
Me dead.
Dog-bone and dry-well
Got no story to tell.
Just how me born stupid is so me gone.
Still we persist before the grave
Seeking fables.
We plunder for the maps of El Dorado
To make bountiful our minds in an England
Starved of gold.

Albion village sleep, hacked
Out between bush and spiteful lip of river.
Folk that know bone
Fatten themselves on dreams

For the survival of days.
Mosquitoes sing at the nipple of blood.
A green-eyed moon watches
The rheumatic agony of houses crutched up on stilts
Pecked about by huge beaks of wind,
That bear the scars of ancient storms.
Crappeau clear their throats in hideous serenade,
Candleflies burst into suicidal flame.
In a green night with promise of rain
You die.

We mark your memory in songs
Fleshed in the emptiness of folk,
Poems that scrape bowl and bone
In English basements far from home,
Or confess the lust of beasts
In rare conceits
To congregations of the educated
Sipping wine, attentive between courses –
See the applause fluttering from their fair hands
Like so many messy table napkins.

JEAN 'BINTA' BREEZE

Mi Duck

I know I know I know mi duck
I know mi duck I know
I know how England breaks your heart
how summer ends before it starts
I know mi duck I know
I know how cold can shut you in
the blows you've taken on the chin
I know mi duck I know
I know how your lover just walked away
never answered your calls night or day

I know mi duck i know
I know how much you needed love
longed for blue skies up above
for a friend to offer a cup of tea
to sit through the night writing poetry
I know how you long for a child to rock
how you count the ticks on your bodies clock
I know how evening cradles your tears
and how your wrinkles mark the years
I know I know I know mi duck
I know mi duck I know
I know how England breaks your heart
how summer ends before it starts
I know mi duck I know.

BENJAMIN ZEPHANIAH

I Have a Scheme

I am here today my friends to tell you there is hope
As high as that mountain may seem
I must tell you
I have a dream
And my friends
There is a tunnel at the end of the light.
And beyond that tunnel I see a future
I see a time
When angry white men
Will sit down with angry black women
And talk about the weather,
Black employers will display notice-boards proclaiming,
'Me nu care wea yu come from yu know
So long as yu can do a good day's work, dat cool wid me.'

I see a time
When words like affirmative action
Will have sexual connotations

And black people all over this blessed country of ours
Will play golf,
Yes my friends that time is coming
And in that time
Afro-Caribbean and Asian youth
Will spend big money on English takeaways
And all police officers will be armed
With a dumplin,
I see a time
A time when the President of the United States of America will
        stand up and say,
'I inhaled
And it did kinda nice
So rewind and cum again.'
Immigration officers will just check that you are all right
And all black people will speak Welsh.

I may not get there my friends
But I have seen that time
I see thousands of muscular black men on Hampstead Heath
        walking their poodles
And hundreds of black female Formula 1 drivers
Racing around Birmingham in pursuit of a truly British way of life.
I have a dream
That one day from all the churches of this land we will hear
    the sound of that great old English spiritual,
Here we go, Here we go, Here we go.
One day all great songs will be made that way.

I am here today my friends to tell you
That the time is coming
When all people, regardless of colour or class, will have at least
        one Barry Manilow record
And vending-machines throughout the continent of Europe
Will flow with sour sap and sugarcane juice,
For it is written in the great book of multiculturalism
That the curry will blend with the shepherd's pie and the Afro
        hairstyle will return.

Let me hear you say

Multiculture
Amen
Let me hear you say
Roti, Roti
A women.

The time is coming
I may not get there with you
But I have seen that time
And as an Equal Opportunities poet
It pleases me
To give you this opportunity
To share my vision of hope
And I just hope you can cope
With a future as black as this.

SOUTH

MONIZA ALVI

Rural Scene

The luminous Norfolk skies,
the tractors, the gunshots,
the still ponds, the darting rabbits,
cow parsley by the field gates –

all are re-imagining themselves
because Tariq walks in his village,
part of the scene, yet conspicuous,
as if he is walking a tiger.

JUDITH LAL

Kestrel

Finally becoming tired of everything
looking like something else
and after two glasses of red,

it's time to take each other
down to the undressed water
showing fallow curves in March.

Every river is sacred from East Anglia to
East Asia. *One river, one mu-ther*,
how the world looks different in the air.
how water takes ashes and pollen as its brocade

and everything looks like something
else in this dusky puzzle. You decide
on it being a dung heap with a kestrel on,
then I, an uprooted tree with a kestrel on.

A kestrel for sure,
stoking pebbles in her breast
or laundering a kill,
readying feathers

that we are not yet close
enough to get under
before well executed flight.

JUDITH LAL

Swallowtail Day

Kerchiefs pulled one by one from the
east sleeve of this island, wet silk in
a slow breeze over fens. A swallowtail
skips either side of the solstice,
interrupted only by a wolf spider,
whose web is like the sugared string
of a musical instrument come loose as
day is played over half way through.
Brings down lucky coloured plectrum
to sleep lightly in a thin hammock.
It doesn't know what to do with
the pompadour boutique eyes
brightly brushed with red shadows,
the war make-up of a Hindi Goddess
that stares out dreams, or its tail like an
inked comma that comes after the word death.

VAHNI CAPILDEO

Monolithicity
(for Blofield Church, Norfolk)

Knapped flint shines black. Flint's kind.
Flint digged from gravel pits
where flint has neighboured iron may
show   red   seepage.
Flint sourced from near the sea is grey.
Like   all   flint   knapped
it shines black. Hand over hand over
hand   over
a hundred feet   pre-electronic labour
placed
(not meaning to expose)   this basic
grimness   faced
the rough sides with strips of knapped
and   shining   flintwork.
The tower in a century neared
completion.
Now is the tower of six hundred years
ago.
You could see it as one. It rocks. The
bellringers
knees over head   scapulas over head   all
hands
over ropes in a lifethreatening lightening
feel   this
as charted colour   number   sequence   as
pulled   peal
and in the sway of stone in wind. The
tower   rocks.
Do you think it was meant to? While the
marguerites
make the white-capped ocean graveyard
meadow to mast?

DEBJANI CHATTERJEE

Visiting E.M. Forster

'But Forster doesn't live here any more.'
I knew that of course. He died the year before
– before my passage. I told 'Raised Eyebrows'
that I only wanted...to see his room,
to see the view. Why else would I have come?
'But this is not a museum, you know.'
(Cambridge, not a museum?) I nodded.
'An ordinary room.' Ordinary
is what it takes. I remembered my coach
journey from Canterbury. 'I have come
all the way from India. He was my friend.'
It worked. The brows subsided, defeated.

A bemused stranger occupied the place
– half apologised for everything changed.
The room was functional, anonymous:
he could not have lived here long. 'I'm afraid
even the furniture is not the same.'
What did I care, standing at the window.
Olive groves beside the forget-me-not
Mediterranean rolled below, with
a dust haze veiling the Marabar curves.
'It is the same,' I said, 'nothing has changed.'

HANNAH LOWE

Sausages

They hang from the washing line
between the tea towels and bleached sheets.
He has pegged them in neat clusters,
dark fingers of blood and gristle
with twisted ends and oily skins.
They flame against the trees.

She smells them from the backdoor –
ginger, clove and fennel. The house is quiet.
He is hiding from her. Her mother told her
not to marry a foreigner. *You always wanted
to be different* she hissed. *Now this. He's black
and old enough to be your father.*

The sausages are Chinese dragon red,
the red of a chilli or a shamed face.
They gather fire, drying on her line.
This is Ilford, Essex, 1965.
The neighbours eat mince and cabbage
and talk about her.

She asked him not to do it
but they taste like home to him
and he is like good food to her.
Tonight they will eat sausages together
and she will lick the oil and spice
from his hands.

MONIZA ALVI

Go Back to England

Model Town, Lahore.
I was born there, lived there

briefly.
What was it like?

Nothing like the houses I built
from Lego. Not a bit like

Welwyn Garden City.
But perhaps the houses *were*

spaced out and the gardens tended.
Lemon trees. Not apple trees.

                    *

In Model Town, the story goes,
to save money,

my mother made my father's
handkerchiefs from his shirt tails.

My mother, newly married
and wrapped in her Englishness,

tried to make herself at home
in her husband's Pakistan.

Cycled along the sweltering lane
to play Mrs Plover's piano.

Sometimes, at night,
the buffaloes wandered in

and grazed on the lawn.

What a noise they made!

She hardly missed Hatfield at all.

*

At least, not until 1954.
What happened then?

Well, I was born –
and the seismic happening

the birth of a child, rocked
everything.

The flat-roofed house trembled,
the grey-green trees shook,

and the ground beneath
my mother's feet gaped.

Kicking above the cracks
was a baby, who wailed,

who detested the heat
and the cold.

It was as if the solid house
had collapsed.

But the earth couldn't swallow up
the baby clinics

because there weren't any,
couldn't swallow up the wise advice

because there wasn't any.
And where was a set of scales

to weigh a baby?

*

So there was my mother – suddenly
thousands of miles from home.

Her phrase book instructed
You must water the plants

while I am away in the hills.
But that was no use at all.

And the lemon trees
were no use at all.

*

Go back to England
said the doctor.

Go back to England
said the stones and boulders.

Go back to England
urged the dusty grass.

*

July gasped in the heat
the day we left Model Town.

My mother hoped to be
a different mother.

The ocean knew
I would be translated

into an English girl.

PATIENCE AGBABI

Weights and Measures and Finding a Rhyme for Orange

In 1996 American sculptor and concrete poet, Carl Andre, exhibited
Sand-Lime Instar, a reincarnation of his controversial 'Tate Bricks',
at the Museum of Modern Art, Oxford. I ran three poetry workshops
during the museum's Family Day. This poem is dedicated to Carl
Andre and my workshop participants.

1983

Oxford is tinted with early Autumn's ginger
as I approach Pembroke Street and change
from Benin Bronze to fresher. Three fat layers,
vest, blouse, home-made sweater and the weight
of a Sainsbury's bag. Tea. Coffee. Poetry.
I'm learning to mark up poetry that rhymes
and discovering a family of feminine half-rhymes:
The Museum of Modern Art (MOMA), pizza and ginger
wine hangover. The symmetry of poetry.
In my mirror I sense the shadows change.
Formal dinner. Late-night bar. The dull weight
of a blackout. Its impenetrable layers.

1987

Poets are similar to bricklayers
except we repeat rhythms or rhymes
instead of bricks, and houses still carry more weight
than poems. I am still attempting to rhyme   orange
with something. Please could you coin some change?
I'm measuring women for M&S. Still write poetry.
An expert on the female form. I figure poetry
is the image of my old college room through two layers
of glass as women strip down to the epidermis. Times change
but if we wait long enough, everything echoes, rhymes.
Winter, Spring. Tangerine, orange.
I am recording data, beginning with height and weight.

222

FAMOUS	BRICKS	RETAIN	IRONIC	WEIGHT
OXFORD	MUSEUM	HOUSES	FORMAL	POETRY
COILED	RIBBON	SHINES	BRIGHT	BRONZE
CHALKY	BRICKS	SPROUT	DOUBLE	LAYERS
MAKING	SUBTLE	SILENT	VISUAL	RHYMES
SPIRAL	QUEUES	DONATE	SILVER	CHANGE
POETIC	ARTIST	SENSES	PUBLIC	CHANGE
SHARED	WISDOM	AROUND	POETIC	WEIGHT
FAMILY	GROUPS	SCULPT	DOUBLE	RHYMES
CEMENT	SPRUNG	RHYTHM	SENARY	POETRY
WHILST	OXFORD	SUMMER	SPURNS	LAYERS
BEHIND	MIRROR	SHADES	ADORES	BRONZE

On Pembroke Street we change bricks into poetry,
measure women who wear their weight in bulimic layers,
write poetry that rhymes orange with bronze and ginger.

CHRISTIAN CAMPBELL

Ballad of Oxfraud

I

Bright barefoot boy from Marsh Harbour,
Abaco; Abaco that wish to remain with the Crown
when the country wanted free. Abaco
of the Conchie Joe bosses, the subtle suck-teeth
of black Bahamians and the rising tide of Haitians.
Pigeon Pea, Sand Banks, The Mud, barefoot black
boy who did want to follow the footpaths of T.S. Eliot.
Green Turtle Cay, Coopers Town, No Name Cay,
Man-o-War Cay, Marsh Harbour, Cherokee Sound,
seventeen-year-old boy with sharkskin tough foot-bottom
at the base of a candy-cane lighthouse reciting

'Hollow Men'. Island boy who dared to apply
to Merton College, Oxford and get a turn-up nose,
but slip into Oxford Brookes Uni. nearby, good enough
to sneak a glance at Merton some days and listen
to the recording of 'The Wasteland', practising
that deadpan, faux English accent.
Island colonial with good practice already.

II

Up the road at Univ. College, poor Vidia
Naipaul, decades before, sleeping with the heat
turn all the way up, waking up in a sweat,
swamp-wet nightmare that he was back
in Trinidad. Just the other day the headline
of *The Sun* was, WOULD YOU LET THIS MAN
NEAR YOUR DAUGHTER? Why yes, they were referring
to Benjamin Zephaniah, Rasta poet, nominated
for Oxford Professor of Poetry. T.S. Eliot
was who this rockfoot man wish to be
and since he could not, why not beat Oxford
dons at they own game? Why not flam the spires
and go back home to a country that reward
the best flam, the best sham? Why not earn
a Master's in Tingumology, an LLB
in Dis 'n Dat, a PhD in Flamology? He trod
all over Europe and America swinging whitefolk
with his black Eliot jig. He wear ascots
and bowties, long Merton College scarves
and rolled his *R's* like thunder. Everyone
at Oxford was a fraud, and he could outdon
the dons, Oxford Professor of Flam,
chickcharney of chicanery, of dupery,
bamboozlement, hoodwink, hustle, baloney;
of banana oil, Abaco hogwash, skulduggery,
swindle, fourberie, skunk, fix, shuffle, hoax.

III

City of dreaming spires

City of beaming liars

City of screaming fires

Tweed jacket never washed

Tweed jacket never washed

P.I. Bridge is falling down

falling down falling down

Fancy dancer Junkanoo

Fancy dancer Junkanoo

IV

Back to The Bahamas, a red carpet rolled
for him, hardfoot Abaco man, dancing
in the road for our Oxbridge don.
All the fraud had make his hair fall out, had colour
his teeth a yellow English shade, had fatten
him like a Christmas feast hog, stuffed as a straw
doll, full full of hot air, he was bald and plump
as a West Indian M.P., fat men playing God.
He wear 3-piece suits every Jesus Christ day
in Nassau bushfire heat. He fight the Anglican
priests and the lawyers that article locally
for the best Oxbridge clip and tone. His mug
grace the papers every other day, resident expert
on the economy, politics, history, philosophy and,
most importantly, Dis 'n Dat.

VAHNI CAPILDEO

Night in the Gardens
(for Sarah Simblet)

I *Oxford and Port of Spain*

The river murmurs.
On the instant all is flattened.
Nightfall conjures up the flood it is not.
Riding high   best survivors   the glass houses
somewhere to the east   containing reptile climates
floating leaves great as gongs able to support
one who'd wish to stand on water
if he's one of the cloud-skinned casually destructive kind
spinning a discus on one finger   stepping even
lighter than
lightly
illuminated you.
Rising high   buildings anxious as with knowledge
of new gravity   weigh light's felt outlines
as anxiety sharpens   even as sweat softens
the same set of features.
Known paths crackle towards some untoward paradise.
Buildings staying switched on yet not the destination
yellow   carries day unhurried nonetheless   inscapes
solar prolongation.
Dusken stone through inwardness knows itself awkward
as if larger   not yet spacious.
Nightfall conjures up its bluish straits   less than generous.
Refoliation murmurs all in all creating
two true weathers
one for fall watch one for storm alert.

To bring a leaf of darkness
To bring a dusken leaf
The game how not to say it
Becoming not enough

Its back is ridged ensilvered
Its back is channelled code
For how it lived by moisture
And trembles with your blood

To hand it is to tear it
To hand one leaf is still
To scroll an ardent garden
Into your hand, I feel –

VAHNI CAPILDEO

La Poetessa

Liberal the college. Fair the lawn. Pontificating by the fountain in the middle of the quad: La Poetessa. Who wishes to hear? She cares not. Slight breezes blow in circles, catching on her words. Waxwings. English her name, English her language, English her absobloomburylutely witty garments. Yet in her arcane brainpan shudder puddles that are forever Europe. Ewig. Earwig. The bookworm tunnels erotically, spiralling through the silver marshes rife with synaptic missed connexions. Severed segments call out to one another, mateless, growing (with resignation) a head at either end. Don't think she can't take a joke...The crane perches on one leg. Hunch. Balance. Symbol of the self-regarding mystic: but who's oriental here? Derivations, derivations. Keep her roots derived. All she wants is a hooch-coochy poem edited inside...

SARADHA SOOBRAYEN

On the water meadows

I blame the twilight for coming too soon,
not allowing enough time for you
to drown without dying. And now
the water boatmen skate on the skin
of water, we should have practised
how to breathe. Instead we undressed
each other slowly: middle names, first
loves, spiders, toads and newts. Taking our
time to visit every corner, all the while
knowing we would soon run out of self.
I want to ignore the silver scar
on your left retina: the imprint of an iceberg.
Those places you were yearning for: Bermuda,
Pacific, Icelandic waters. Confident diver
that you are, land was never your best side.
What remains is the space around
your hands, their quietness, and at the tips
of fingers the fain hum of blue.

SHANTA ACHARYA

The Vulnerable Plot of Green

Under our very different sun
there are no illusions
about the sacred realm of art,
the shaping power of the imagination,
nor, for that matter, the imperial self.

No longer sacrosanct
the vulnerable plot of green,
begging 'Please, keep off the grass,'
on rusting metal plates.

It is now criss-crossed
by the paths of haunted minds
frantic to defend
their humanity through art,
by means of a means,
the green season of the mind.

SHANTA ACHARYA

Aspects of Westonbirt Arboretum

If you can discover the first leaves of the honeysuckle unfolding
and fly fearless on the magic carpet of the snowdrops in spring,

If you can rejoice in the flowering cherries in April,
tall columns of mahogany-red bark crowned by clouds
of blush white blossom, fragrant brides against the sky;

If you can be startled by clumps of primroses in bloom,
by bluebells waist-high, a purple haze on the woodland's floor,
by orchids, wild garlic, and dandelions, you will encounter
the spirit of the arboretum exuding from each leaf and bower.

If you can watch the bumble bee tumble out of a foxglove's throat
and hear the laughter of Silk Wood ringing through The Link,

If you can rest in the venerable oak's dappled shade
in the tranquillity of filigreed foliage,
mosaics of maples in bronze, copper and ochre,
a thousand and one shades of newly born green,
you will have a vision of heaven with all its munificence;
rhododendrons and azaleas, camellias and magnolias,
clusters of pink and red, mauve and purple, white and yellow:

If you can sit under the autumnal canopy on a mattress of leaves
as the afternoon sun refracts the rich, kaleidoscopic colours
and hear the excited voices of children blend in the breeze,

If you can listen to the sound of acorns falling,
worship the Japanese maples in crimson, gold and ruby,
flaming lanterns against the sombre yew at dusk,
you will be one with the universe, free.

FRED D'AGUIAR

At the Grave of the Unknown African

1

Two round, cocoa faces, carved on whitewashed headstone
protect your grave against hellfire and brimstone.

Those cherubs with puffed cheeks, as if chewing gum,
signal how you got here and where you came from.

More than two and a half centuries after your death,
the barefaced fact that you're unnamed feels like defeat.

I got here via White Ladies Road and Black Boy's Hill,
clues lost in these lopsided stones that Henbury's vandal

helps to the ground and Henbury's conservationist
tries to rectify, cleaning the vandal's pissy love-nest.

African slave without a name, I'd call this home
by now. Would you? Your unknown soldier's tomb

stands for shipload after shipload that docked,
unloaded, watered, scrubbed, exercised and restocked

thousands more souls for sale in Bristol's port;
cab drivers speak of it all with yesterday's hurt.

The good conservationist calls it her three hundred year war;
those raids, deals, deceit and capture (a sore still raw).

St Paul's, Toxteth, Brixton, Tiger Bay and Handsworth:
petrol bombs flower in the middle of roads, a sudden growth

at the feet of police lines longer than any cricket pitch.
African slave, your namelessness is the wick and petrol mix.

Each generation catches the one fever love can't appease;
nor Molotov cocktails, nor when they embrace in a peace

far from that three-named, two-bit vandal and conservationist
binning beer cans, condoms and headstones in big puzzle-pieces.

2

Stop there black Englishman before you tell a bigger lie.
You mean me well by what you say but I can't stand idly by.

The vandal who keeps coming and does what he calls fucks
on the cool gravestones, also pillages and wrecks.

If he knew not so much my name but what happened to Africans,
he'd maybe put in an hour or two collecting his Heinekens;

like the good old conservationist, who's earned her column
inch, who you knock, who I love without knowing her name.

The dead can't write, nor can we sing (nor can most living).
Our ears (if you can call them ears) make no good listening.

Say what happened to me and countless like me, all anon.
Say it urgently. Mean times may bring back the water cannon.

I died young, but to age as a slave would have been worse.
What can you call me? Mohammed. Homer. Hannibal. Jesus.

Would it be too much to have them all? What are couples up to
when one reclines on the stone and is ridden by the other?

Will our talk excite the vandal? He woz ere, *like you are now,*
armed with a knife, I could see trouble on his creased brow,

love-trouble, not for some girl but for this village.
I share his love and would have let him spoil my image,

if it wasn't for his blade in the shadow of the church wall
taking me back to my capture and long sail to Bristol,

then my sale on Black Boy's Hill and disease ending my days:
I sent a rumble up to his sole; he scooted, shocked and dazed.

Here the sentence is the wait and the weight is the sentence.
I've had enough of a parish where the congregation can't sing.

Take me where the hymns sound like a fountain-washed canary,
and the beer-swilling, condom wielding vandal of Henbury,

reclines on the stones and the conservationist mounts him,
and in my crumbly ears there's only the sound of them sinning.

KWAME DAWES

Bristol

I leave the cold wet of Bristol. A city of dull
spires and the ostentatious slave money
of the *nouveau riche* who built grand estates
and created a stained empire. The city
is changing. Old hints of glory are relics
and the water in the gorge crawls brown,
its concrete lips darkened by rain,
cracked in long fissures. Above is the Clifton
Bridge – that useless act of genius: Egyptian
anchors, towers on two sides, the gorge
below. The marvel of it, the absolute
hubris of it! This slave money makes you
think of empire in all things: Ah grandeur!

I limp along the country lanes. The fat
has been falling away each day. Stress
and the sorrow of a life shattered all eat

at the sullied flesh. My calf is strained
by cold and weight. I have lived in a red
call box, making petitions across the Atlantic
each morning before light; an onlooker
would call it love though it feels like pain
here in Bristol on these long gloomy days.

How easy it is to find nothing in poetry
in a week of patterns: the hills, the castles,
the mansions, the bums, the drunken
students, the moribund theatre, the bland
food, such dull simplicity. I leave quietly
at dawn, mutter polite farewells
to the inquisitive landlady who stands
there smiling as if on the verge of thought,
but so nervous, waiting to be mugged or hugged.

I say goodbye to her cheapness,
and think of the furnace I have kept
burning day after night despite the rules;
the dingy room a sauna – her sheets soaked
in my sweat, and smelling of my tears,
from my long nights haunted by dead slaves,
their unsettled shadows drifting
across Clifton Bridge.

RALPH HOYTE

Chew Stoke

Girdled by the ramparts of Dundry, the hip-swell of the Mendips
to the south, dreaming in lake-drawn veils of mist, Chew Stoke
murmurs to herself in the gloaming. 'Ketchly weather, John.'
'Aye, terrible ketchly.' Your gaze lifts, soars – then gets firmly
pinned back down to pocket handkerchief fields by folk what
burbles on about 'tumps', 'batches' and 'emmity butts'. Ghostly
farmers' daughters who *would* go out at night and get their-selves
drownded glide soundlessly across the Blue Bowl's dining room.
The great fat fox strolls across the bottom of the field and helps
himself to Joanna's chickens. 'Of Chew Stoke, Norton Malreward
and Nempnett Thrubwell' – that's the rector. The names demand
a precise enunciation, like a catechism of yeomanry, a world away
from and yet so near to the bluntness of 'Bristol'. 'When I come
over the top and see the valley spread out before me, the line of
clouds stretching out over the Mendips, the mist rising up from
the lake I always feel a surge of thankfulness.' Yes.

DEREK WALCOTT

from Midsummer

XXXIX

The grey English road hissed emptily under the tires
since the woods still drizzled. The sound was like foam
mixed with island rain, but the rain was Berkshire's.
He said the white hare would startle itself like a tuft
on the road's bare scalp. But, wherever it came from,
the old word 'hare' shivered like 'weald' or 'croft'
or the peeled white trunk with a wound in 'atheling'.
I hated fables. The wheezing beeches were fables,
and the wild, wet mustard. As for the mist, gathering

from the mulch of black leaves in which the hare hid
in clenched concentration – muttering prayers, bead-eyed,
haunch-deep in nettles – the sooner it disappeared
the better. Something branched in that countryside
losing ground to the mist, its old roads brown as blood.
The white hare had all of England on which to brood
with its curled paws – from the age of skins and woad,
from Saxon settlements fenced with stakes, and thick
fires of peat smoke, down to thin country traffic.
He turned on the fog lights. It was on this road,
on this ridge of earth long since swept bare
of his mud prints, that my bastard ancestor swayed
transfixed by the trembling, trembling thing that stood
its ground, ears pronged, nibbling him into a hare.

CLAUDE MCKAY

London

The fog prevails above all in my mind,
Wrapping around me like a cold gray sheet,
And shutting out the city, which oppressed
My spirit even like Teutonic art in stone.
A city without light and without heat,
Whose color was like iron in my breast
And freezing through my body to the bone:
Oh blessed was the fog that veiled me blind!

But how could I, tropical African,
Who claim the sun as my authentic sire,
Find beauty in that chilling atmosphere?
Ancestral intellect could help me bear
A little while, but surely not admire
The civilisation of the Englishman.

UNA MARSON

from **Spring in England**

Trees with trunks turned black
With London's soot and grime
Have robed themselves anew
In daintiest shades of green
That ever eye could see;
And like little black children
In flimsy summer frocks
Dance on the green and laugh and shout.
Trees of all ages and sizes
Bask in the warm Spring sunshine
And their robes are blown about
By the gentle breezes that whisper,
Ever whisper of Spring.

GEORGE LAMMING

Swans

By no other name are these
The imperturbable birds more beautiful,
No likelier image for the summer's curl
Of white light caught from the sea's
Arterial cells; or the moon's wry
Face carved on the curved aristocratic sky.

Sailing the solitude of their customary waters
Dark and dimpled in the windy morning,
Instinct prompts a ritual preening
The rude arrangement of their feathers,
And leaping with the leaping light of dawn
They crown the river with a white perfection.

Later the circus arrives
With its ready-made apparatus of pleasures,
Dogs and women and the dutiful masters
Of small boats swimming their lives
Through charted water
And chuckled warnings of the wind's laughter.

The birds thoughtful, decorous, austere,
Retreat to a far side of the river,
Their eyes held in a puzzled stare
Measure their recently arrived spectator.
Some cluster to a deep deliberation
Or ponder in amazement their own reflection.

Leisurely the evening ambles,
Through the stained air, on torn leaves,
Over the lame, dry grasses,
Sadly, silently the late light falls,
And the waving curl of water dies
Where the winged white quietude at anchor lies.

Now blank desertion fills the senses,
Over the howling city
Louder than the cry of industry,
The moon sheds a contagion of madness,
And water fills the eyes of the visitor
Entering the legend of this historic river.

London 1950

WOLE SOYINKA

Telephone Conversation

The price seemed reasonable, location
Indifferent. The landlady swore she lived
Off premises. Nothing remained
But self-confession. 'Madam,' I warned,
'I hate a wasted journey – I am African.'
Silence. Silenced transmission of
Pressurised good-breeding. Voice, when it came,
Lipstick coated, long gold-rolled
Cigarette-holder pipped. Caught I was, foully.
'HOW DARK?'... I had not misheard... 'ARE YOU LIGHT
OR VERY DARK?' Button B. Button A. Stench
Of rancid breath of public hide-and-speak.
Red booth. Red pillar-box. Red double-tiered
Omnibus squelching tar. It *was* real! Shamed
By ill-mannered silence, surrender
Pushed dumbfoundment to beg simplification.
Considerate she was, varying the emphasis –
'ARE YOU DARK? OR VERY LIGHT?' Revelation came.
'You mean – like plain or milk chocolate?'
Her assent was clinical, crushing in its light
Impersonality. Rapidly, wave-length adjusted,
I chose. 'West African sepia' – and as afterthought,
'Down in my passport.' Silence for spectroscopic
Flight of fancy, till truthfulness clanged her accent
Hard on the mouthpiece. 'WHAT'S THAT?' conceding
'DON'T KNOW WHAT THAT IS.' 'Like brunette.'
'THAT'S DARK, ISN'T IT?' 'Not altogether.
Facially I am brunette, but, madam, you should see
The rest of me. Palm of my hand, soles of my feet
Are a peroxide blond. Friction, caused –
Foolishly, madam – by sitting down, has turned
My bottom raven black – One moment, madam!' – sensing
Her receiver rearing on the thunderclap
About my ears – 'Madam,' I pleaded, 'wouldn't you rather
See for yourself?'

KAMAU BRATHWAITE

from The Emigrants

1

So you have seen them
with their cardboard grips,
felt hats, rain-
cloaks, the women
with their plain
or purple-tinted
coats hiding their fatten-
ed hips

These are The Emigrants.
On sea-port quays
at air-ports
anywhere where there is ship
or train, swift
motor car, or jet
to travel faster than the breeze
you see them gathered:
passports stamped
their travel papers wrapped
in old disused news-
papers: lining their patient queues.

Where to?
They do not know.
Canada, the Panama
Canal, the Miss-
issippi painfields, Florida?
Or on to dock
at hissing smoke locked
Glasgow?

Why do they go?
They do not know.
Seeking a job

they settle for the very best
the agent has to offer:
jabbing a neighbour
out of work for four bob
less a week.

What do they hope for
what find there
these New World mariners
Columbus coursing kaffirs

What Cathay shores
for them are gleaming golden
what magic keys they carry to unlock
what gold endragoned doors?

   2

Columbus from his after-
deck watched stars, absorbed in water,
melt in liquid amber drifting

through my summer air.
Now with morning, shadows lifting,
beaches stretched before him cold and clear.

Birds circled flapping flag and mizzen
mast: birds harshly hawking, without fear.
Discovery he sailed for was so near.

Columbus from his after-
deck watched heights he hoped for,
rocks he dreamed, rise solid from my simple water.

Parrots screamed. Soon he would touch
our land, his charted mind's desire.
The blue sky blessed the morning with its fire.

But did his vision
fashion, as he watched the shore,
the slaughter that his soldiers

furthered here? Pike
point and musket butt,
hot splintered courage, bones

cracked with bullet shot,
tipped black boot in my belly, the
whip's uncurled desire?

Columbus from his after-
deck saw bearded fig trees, yellow pouis
blazed like pollen and thin

waterfalls suspended in the green
as his eyes climbed towards the highest ridges
where our farms were hidden.

Now he was sure
he heard soft voices mocking in the leaves.
What did this journey mean, this

new world mean: dis-
covery? Or a return to terrors
he had sailed from, known before?

I watched him pause.

Then he was splashing silence.
Crabs snapped their claws
and scattered as he walked towards our shore.

   3
But now the claws are iron: mouldy
dredges do not care what we discover here:
the Mississippi mud is sticky:

men die there
and bouquets of stench lie
all night long along the river bank.

In London, Undergrounds are cold.
The train rolls in from darkness
with our fears

and leaves a lonely soft metallic clanking
in our ears.
In New York

nights are hot
in Harlem, Brooklyn,
along Long Island Sound

This city is so vast
its ears have ceased to know
a simple human sound

Police cars wail
like babies
an ambulance erupts

like breaking glass
an elevator sighs
like Jews in Europe's gases

then slides us swiftly
down the ropes to hell.
Where is the bell

that used to warn us,
playing cricket on the beach,
that it was mid-day: sun too hot

for heads. And evening's
angelus of fish soup,
prayers, bed?

MERLE COLLINS

Soon Come

Like I said before
Having a wonder-
full time
Told you also
Will write soon

Well child,
today
soon has come

So let me tell you about this England
and why soon come today

Today someone asked
again
if I write for Black people
Today I smiled
again
at a
Black
face
which alone understands my story here

Today I visited a
Black group
in a Black area
to hear Black history

Child, Soon come today
because it was just one day
too many
of getting through the Blackness
just to Be

Soon come today
because today was
just like
Yesterday
when I watched
a Black film
and the day before
when I saw
a Black play

Soon come today
because this was just
an ordinary day
being
Black
in London

Sister
In this place
so really full of wonder
so many wonders go unseen

A lot more to say
But
this subject makes me tired
So
Goodbye
for now
from your

friend
in London

P.S: I went to see Keats' house
        and where the Brontë sisters lived.

P.P.S: Do you still teach the

        writers
        Milton and Wordsworth?

ROGER ROBINSON

Parallel

And there under the plastic film of Gramps' album,
a picture of her in Demerara sugar sepia. 1974-short hair,
a brown dress with a thin red belt cinching waist to hips.
Her hand on curves – nearly defiant. Standing behind her

my father, grandmother and grandfather.
I was only four but I remember the clothes they wore:
It was in London and everywhere we ate Gramps
had his own pepper sauce the colour of Trinidad's dawn.

I look at the picture: the car our family car; the clothes,
the ones that would hang on the door of our small flat.
It's a mirror image of a picture in *our* album, but in ours
my mother stands right where *she* is. I look at her close –

she could pass for his sister, the spectre behind my father's
unaccountable time. The *I have to get to a meeting*,
the *I've got cricket practice*, the *I'm not made of money*,
the *I fell asleep in the car*, the sudden anger. All my life

my mother told me she dreamt my father had other children.
Repeatedly, friends have told me that they've seen my Dad's
car parked in front of a house miles away from ours,
doing weekly shopping in supermarkets in a different town.

As Gramps falls asleep, I slide the picture out and head home.
I get scissors and snip around her slim legs, carefully around
her short afro and long neck, and stick the picture on the fridge
– leaving a white space between my father and his parents.

FRED D'AGUIAR

Home

These days whenever I stay away too long,
anything I happen to clap eyes on,
(that red telephone box) somehow makes me
miss here more than anything I can name.

My heart performs a jazzy drum solo
when the crow's feet on the 747
scrape down at Heathrow. H.M. Customs...
I resign to the usual inquisition,

telling me with Surrey loam caked
on the tongue, home is always elsewhere.
I take it like an English middleweight
with a questionable chin, knowing

my passport photo's too open-faced,
haircut wrong (an afro) for the decade;
the stamp, British Citizen not bold enough
for my liking and too much for theirs.

The cockney cab driver begins chirpily
but can't or won't steer clear of race,
so rounds on Asians. I lock eyes with him
in the rearview when I say I live with one.

He settles at the wheel grudgingly,
in a huffed silence. Cha! Drive man!
I have legal tender burning in my pocket
to move on, like a cross in Transylvania.

At my front door, why doesn't the lock
recognise me and budge? I give an extra
twist and fall forward over the threshold
piled with the felicitations of junk mail,

into a cool reception in the hall.
Grey light and close skies I love you.
chokey streets, roundabouts and streetlamps
with tyres chucked round them, I love you

Police officer, your boots need re-heeling.
Robin Redbreast, special request – a burst
of song so the worm can wind to the surface.
We must all sing for our suppers or else.

FRED D'AGUIAR

Domestic Flight

I heard what I took for wind chimes
3000 feet above London's lights,
each light a small sound.

The pearl necklaces of traffic
break, trying to get round
my neck of the woods.

The Thames ribbed and corseted
by traffic despite its peregrinations
in a black wetsuit.

Occasionally real diamonds startle
at high points in the city.
Gold is on the horizon, a rim.

Some distance below us an insect
with a compound look and rotating wings
hightails it home with bare ski feet.

The river is sanskrit in black ink
scribbling away into the dark,
turning over with each tide.

GABRIELA PEARSE

Grenada... Heathrow... London

Sun dance
sun dial
around
the cloister
of a distance
too great.

A culture
a class
away
a warmth
a world
away.

Half smile
ginger cat
sneeks
across face
across place
of longing.

Silence filled
with words
with each
with you.

Unknowing
unsure
unnerving
a laugh
echoes.

Trip wire
around
barbed comment
keeps you
off balance.

Wanting home
enveloping
in cotton wool
the ache and need.

The dampened dance of time will take its toll

RAJAT KUMAR BISWAS

Cambridge

(in memory of David Rushton)

Seventh of January, 'fifty-three,
was a white letter day for me
because it was then that I learnt to hitchhike,
a word hitherto unknown in
my dictionary; my pal Cambridge,
cap-a-pie, wrapping himself with
his old college scarf, led me
as the lighted first tube train
disgorged us at daybreak in Hendon.

'That side is Wales and all the world
beyond, this side is England,' my comrade
opined; a shudder went down my spine
as, priest-like in my Pa's nineteen
twenty-nine style topcoat, I stood
with rubber-soled Dolcis
shoes, upon the pristine snow,
in a totally unused, Bengali way.

We hitched, thumbed and thumbed
as, slowly, my toes got numb:
'Biswas, say some Bengali slang!'
At the acme of exasperation,
a new red Austin gave a lift.
Icicles hung on the trees, the wind
swished over the cables, crows flapped
their black wings.

At last the hitching succeeded, this time
a truck-driver reduced speed, stopped.
My friend asked me to squeeze in
between his spread-eagled thighs,
leaving room for the driver's mate.
To break the ice, the driver
asked, 'what work do you
do?' Although a library student,
my pal said, 'I am a librarian';
for my private ear he said,
'otherwise these people would not
understand, I had to say so'.
At a transport café (loud
with a juke-box – a novelty)
where the driver parked,
my colleague warned, 'Don't give
to the lift-giver any baksheesh,
it isn't done by the English.'

ZHANA

Apartheid Britain 1985 (Or Kenwood Ladies' Pond)

This pond is for ladies,
    so they say.
We don't have nannies to look after our babies
So I guess we should stay away.

A carpet of white bodies
Covers the lawn.
Why should we want to come here?
We don't need any sun.
We're already brown enough.
And it's not much fun
    when the ladies decide to get tough.

The water's beautiful,
But if we were to use it,
We'd only pollute it,
        so they say.
After all, dogs are dirty,
So are our husbands,
And so are we.

I'm surprised 100 trendy white girls
Can stand the smells
        our two bodies give off.
Our white co-workers
Know we don't *have* husbands,
But they lie still and say nothing,
Part of the carpet.

ASHNA SARKAR

99 Flakes and The End of Something

Puddles of taffeta, weeping ice cream and
Melting eyeliner cried from my aviators;
I was rendered far too dramatic a figure for my liking.
Yesterday, our kisses scribbled plans for forest raves
And decadent fields, mapped contour lines
With bare hands. Only the highlands and rolling meadows.
Valleys and floodplains would have just been a bit slaggy.

A wink of sleep later
and I'm on the heath,
playing out the death
of a romance that lasted
as long as a reel of celluloid.

Office workers had shed their costumes, luxuriating
In the debris of shirts and ties and sunshine and us.
They stared as my rage played up to itself and almost
Made you cry. We acted our parts beautifully; gasps

Gossiped across the cityscape as I flung my bag
Over the grass and my jacket to the floor. An old lady
Forgot herself and started clapping as I stormed off,
Leaving a small trail of stylish destruction in my wake.

If it had been a film, that's when the strings would come in,
I wouldn't have had to go back to get my stuff and make my
Precarious way home.

Or else I would have stacked in my stilettos,
We'd have laughed and made up.
I'd have said
Something profound, rather than cursing that you couldn't
Just chuck me by text like normal people.
I ached for my mum and chocolate, to do away with spectators,
A squishy sofa, pyjamas. Flat shoes.

Every kiss since feels like punctuation
On pages of empty script. Xs mark spots
Where you're not and nothing feels quite as fabulous
As that time I bitch-slapped you on Hampstead Heath.

GOPI WARRIER

Cricket at Lords

Living behind Lords
I don't have to be
at the grounds or watch TV
to know the score.

Each time there is grand
applause England has scored a four.
Polite applause is the opposition's
six. A deafening roar that shakes
the house is an Aussie wicket
or the LBW of Tendulkar.
Pin-drop silence means England
wickets are falling like ninepins.

Last summer, by the lake in Regents Park
birds singing, world bright
and cheery I pass
a short, balding man in a fading three piece,
barrister's brief case underarm.
Perhaps an old Harrovian cricket fan.
He walks slowly, 'a schoolboy with his satchel'
and a heavy heart.

On his boyish face is gloom.
The bright day
cannot touch his heart normally languid in the sun.
Obviously England has lost the Match.
Sadly I let him pass knowing his grief
but still long to commiserate
him for a sunny day
when all was perfect
except the score.

DALJIT NAGRA

Our Town with the Whole of India!

Our town in England with the whole of India sundering
out of its temples, mandirs and mosques for the customised
streets. Our parade, clad in cloak-orange with banners
and tridents, chanting from station to station for Vasaikhi
over Easter. Our full-moon madness for Eidh with free
pavement tandooris and legless dancing to boostered
cars. Our Guy Fawkes' Diwali – a kingdom of rockets
for the Odysseus-trials of Rama who arrowed the jungle
foe to re-palace the Penelope-faith of his Sita.

Our Sunrise Radio with its lip sync of Bollywood lovers
pumping through the rows of emporium cubby holes
whilst bhangra beats slam where the hagglers roar
at the pulled-up back-of-the-lorry cut-price stalls.

Sitar shimmerings drip down the furbishly columned
gold store. Askance is the peaceful Pizza Hut...
A Somali cab joint, been there for ever, with smiley
guitar licks where reggae played before Caribbeans
disappeared, where years before Teddy Boys jived.

Our cafés with the brickwork trays of saffron sweets,
brass woks frying flamingo-pink syrup-tunnelled
jalebis networking crustily into their familied clumps.
Reveries of incense scent the beefless counter where
bloodied men sling out skinned legs and breasts
into thin bags topped with the proof of giblets.
Stepped road displays – chock-full of ripe karela,
okra, aubergine – sunshined with mango, pineapple,
lychee. Factory walkers prayer-toss the river of

sponging swans with chapattis. A posse brightens
on park-shots of Bacardi – waxing for the bronze
eyeful of girls. The girls slim their skirts after college
blowing dreams into pink bubble gums at neck-
descending and tight-neck sari-mannequins. Their grannies
point for poled yards of silk for own-made styles.
The mother of the runaway daughter, in the marriage
bureau, weeps over the plush-back catalogues glossed
with tuxedo-boys from the whole of our India!

DALJIT NAGRA

University

On the settling of birds, this man blesses

                                         his daughter.

She'll split fast for Paddington, then slide

                                         east

which may as well be the black beyond

                                         of Calcutta.

The low long curving train opening its

        mouth

gulps from his hands her bags to a far-side

        seat.

He gawps from his thin-rivered, working

        town.

The train roars, the tracks beyond humped

        with light.

The rucksack'd man with whom her eyes

        meet...

Five birds pluck their wings off the train

        and fly.

E.A. MARKHAM

Ladbroke Grove, '58

And we laughed at it, C.J. Harris' joke to us
on the jetty before sailing for the province,
that some habits over there would not be acceptable
to the Children of the House of Stapleton
abandoned now to the slow fate of ruin:
we must recall that even a great governor, back then
with his Latin, couldn't convince barbarians to the peace of Rome.
Ah, what sorts of questions will turn up now?

Tonight, Calgacus' speech to the Caledonians:
When I consider the motives we have for fighting...
I have a strongfeeling that the united front you're showing
will mean the dawn of liberty for all of Britain.
And two boys whom we knew came by and said
the natives were getting restless at Notting Hill.

ANDREW SALKEY

Notting Hill Carnival, 1975

Souse, fried fish and mauby,
magical pan, band and float,
costume, swagger and jump-up:
Carnival can't leap the Gulf!

Pick up the Port of Spain display,
complete in the head of the mas,
throw it straight across the water
and watch it drop flat and splayed
like a two-day anniversary drunk,
tricked and freaked out as we are,
stepping high, all over the Grove!

Look at the frantic stamp-and-go,
the tugging muddle in the mind,
the heavy hesitation over play,
the forced glinting tone-and-flash,
the tepid menace of the masquerade,
as losers trip and fake bacchanal,
stumbling, up and down the Grove!

Forget the slide of immigration;
simply mime the dreams of exile;
dress the naked pain with images
of history texts, sea and planets
and cross the road with metaphor,
knowing how short ten years are
to squeeze home, into the Grove!

Souse, fried fish and mauby,
magical pan, band and float,
costume, swagger and jump-up:
Carnival can't leap the Gulf!

BENJAMIN ZEPHANIAH

Call It What You Like!

Friday the 29th June, 1979,
temperature quite warm.
Need to rock a while,
things were looking calm,
so to myself I say, where should I have a ball?
and then the time out tell me the scene is Acklam Hall,
live groups beggar, samaritans, resistance.

And so I took my friends to Acklam Hall with me,
we didn't have to pay, they let us in for free,
it was good for them,
and it was good in there,
I saw white men dancing cool, and Black men dancing cool,
so we dip with the beat,
and we turn and repeat,
and we dip with the beat,
yes everybody rocking cool,
it's really beautiful,
it's really good to see how everyone was free.

The samaritans are getting ready to play their little rocking reggae.
Tuning up.

And everybody dancing to the sound system,
some even romancing where the lights were dim.

I decided to take a walk to meet some friends,
I was standing at the door, I was talking to a girl,
I told her that I write,
she said I must recite,
and then I saw a fight.
There was many, they looked like skinheads,
they were shouting 'National Front, National Front',
they were shouting kill a, kill a, kill a blackman,
they were shouting kill a blackman lover.

In their hands they had sticks, they had bottles, they had bricks,

they were hitting with the sticks, and the bottles, and the bricks,
a nightmare.

A nightmare, a nightmare I thought it was a nightmare,
people falling down everywhere,
and one little exit door,
all the people heading for the exit door,
only one little exit door.

Hysterical, it was terrible,
Hitler's pledge in progress,
women cried in Acklam Hall,
and the Racist beating all.

I made a little step and went into a room,
I saw six men standing over one man,
one man lying on the ground, complete with blood and splinter,
glass splinter and tears,
and he didn't want Charity, no ambulance,
St John's man talks in vain,
blood hides the cut from the eye,
glass splinter caused him pain,
not one policeman came.

And then a shout the Punks came about,
in cloths of plastic and coloured hair,
they were fighting for the black man,
defending the black child.

O punk, O punk the fight was not for long,
but you battle well.
I saw a punk holding a baby,
The black child was crying,
The punks were fighting back, it was the best form of attack.

And to myself I say, 'The Nazis are commercial',
And to myself I say, 'This should be controversial',

Me and my friends headed for the exit,
the place was just mad, hysterical,
no good.

I had to leave the scene.

O punk, O punk the fight was not for long,
but you battle well...

*A tribute to the Punks, Anti-Nazi Campaigners, and all who battled on
29th June, when the National Front invaded a dance at Acklam Hall.*

CRESWELL DURRANT

Colours
for the Notting Hill riots

                    bang
            saw them
graffiti confetti and perhaps a touch of frangipani
but nothing could stop them until the blood flowed
            not even the metropolitan.
  At the end of it
            when it was temporarily settled
        colours melted into one another again.
                    I saw it.
Saw once the silence of the street
            converge impolitely at five in the borough council morning
                on two crossing sweepers black and white
                    filling their brotherhood at a milk machine.

NII AYIKWEI PARKES

A Familiar Voice at the V&A Museum

The music of my footsteps shadows me
in the high ceiling of the entry hall.
I remember the movement being louder,
delivered with greater forte
by the staccato
        fingers of my infant legs.

Down the hall the enchantment remains,
but the awe of my flitting eyes is gone;
for in my journey, tales of the supernatural
have become natural, so I see the battles,
the blood, the women wooed, the men
double-crossed for a runaway place in
history that ripples in ever widening circles.

Yet nothing changes; each shiny surface
reflects the same me – alone this time –
taller, but bearing fossilised gestures,
hearing the Morse code of high heels
criss-crossing over a carbon cacophony
twenty-four years earlier – faint but surefooted
alongside the voices trapped in these walls like relics.

I can even hear my father's speech, bowel-
transmitted and comforting, obeying
the laws of physics – fading infinitesimally
but never dying – in this place he showed me;
joining the thunderous chorus of the dead
and living that only griots applaud; labelled insane
because they have found the logic of science.

So historians change everything,
remould the stories of this museum
to fit the code of the day as the previous
conjurers become fodder for plants
and nature wins. For flora script history better than men –
unhindered by prejudice, inspired only by an insatiable
desire for sunlight.

Nothing changes after all, though surfaces
are polished daily; these swords, shields
bowls and manuscripts are but matter
moved and moulded, and this hall
is the same, although I have lost
the warmth of a hand and the colour
of my father's speech to history.

NII AYIKWEI PARKES

Common/wealth

at the Commonwealth Institute, London

Without wheels their boy bodies are eloquent
in the cool air, tightly coiled springs
that jump and whirl and oscillate effortlessly

the same way boasts slip off
the roofs of their mouths like clay shingles.
Each move is demonstrated

with familiar ease, every element of motion
executed like a locksmith decodes
a knot, then the ringing chatter settles

like a dropped coin,

the expectant clatter of skateboards
rises then turns to air, flared jeans
lift, then fall, as though for a second

they had lungs, and the boys are mounted.
The first boy's feet propel him
towards idle boasts and after graceful

coasting, he launches himself, a raised flag;
his flight is jerky yet hopeful, like a plea
in a tongue he hasn't mastered the rolling of.

JOHN FIGUEROA

Hartlands/Heartlands

The flash of sound across
The city streets, the train
Shunting miles away –

Shoulder against the warm wall
I dreamt of trains that crossed
Our little country:
        Bushy Park
        Grange Lane
        Hartlands
                Spanish Town
                Olden Harbour
        May Pen
        Four Paths
                Kendal...

After that, the summer stop
For Spauldings,
The stations are not so
Easily recalled
But certainly there
Were also
        Frankfield
        Siloh
            Mount Pellier
                Cambridge
                MoBay

The screech the flash
The whistle would wake me

Then I'd recall the Summers
at Mrs Caine's oblivious of the others
In the heat and confusion of Kingston.

Now and again in strange cities
The sudden release of steam
The rush of the horn
Recalls it all

        Bushy Park
        Grange Lane
        Hartlands
                Heartlands
                Heartlands

Spanish Town
Port O' Spain
Port au Prince
Point à Pitre

    Grange Lane
    Bushy Park
Hartlands
    Heartlands
        Heartlands

King's Cross St Pancras
Gare St Lazare
Gare du Nord
Gare de Lyons
    Zaragoza
    Port Bou
    Port Bou
        Narbonne

Gare Mont Parnasse
    Dieppe/Newhaven
    Dieppe/Newhaven
    Dieppe/Newhaven
Victoria Victoria Victoria
King's Cross St Pancras
Gare St Lazare
Gare du Nord
Gare de Lyons
    Zaragoza
    PortBou
    Port Bou
        Narbonne

Gare Mont Parnasse
    Dieppe/Newhaven
    Dieppe/Newhaven
    Dieppe/Newhaven
Victoria Victoria Victoria

                    Bushy Park
                   Grange Lane
                    Hartlands
                   Spanish Town
                    Olden Harbour
                    Olden Harbour
                     Hartlands

          Heartlands Heartlands
                   Heartlands

JOHN LYONS

Home is Weyever Yuh Is

Well, ah lan up in Englan,
Victoria Station, London.
D I S M A L !
Ah didn't hear no,
'Wahappenin dey, man',
no huggin, no kissin,
no glad-glad cryin.

Englan shockin, *oui*:
sun here ehn no blazin fire
like back home
strong enough to bun people;
here dey so white-white,

an meh skin so black,
black like coocoo pot bun-bun,
still smouldering
wid sunfire dey cole looks
cahn douse down.

Ah feel so homesick, brodda,
yuh ehn goin believe dis:
Di good Laard come to meh,
an He point to de groun an say,

'Dirt same colour as Trinidad dirt,
it mek same grave fuh white man
as it mek fuh Black man.'

Well, ah tellin yuh, at dis point
ah kneel doun an ah kiss de dirt,
an ah shout out:
'Mamma eart, protek meh,
home is weyever yuh is.'

JOY RUSSELL

On the Tube

Walthamstow Central
Victoria line
& I'm scurrying
to Vidal Sassoon's Creative Hair Salon
to get all my nappy hair cut off

On the tube:
a young black girl
two exploding pigtails tied
symmetrical with red happy faces
Red T-shirt
On bottom red trousers
high top sneakers
pretty little frilly red gingham socks peeking out
& she writes
left-handed the scribble of the stops.
Her family:
attending brother

grandmother, dignified, holding baby
Directly across,
closed-eye mother leaning away in corner
& sweet new-born
fast asleep
in the stroller

Now,
all attention is turned
to Left-Handed-Young-Sister Red
   T-o-t-t-e-n-h-a-m H-a-l-e
Brother-Overseer beckons
   Have you done it yet?
Young-Sister Red,
   Yeah, man.
Brother-Overseer,
   Next.

& grandmother tickles baby
while bored Brother-Overseer sends
paper airplanes landing on
the runways of people's feet

   E-u-s-t-o-n

& a blue-jean-cowrie-shell-wearing man
Right on the Beat
squeezes lips
to cop a glance
at the fine sistah
bedecked
in a positively surreal red shiny jacket
dazzling orange trousers, smoky almond
eyes, raspberry mouth, & most
pleasing cleavage
Nods
Nods
Nods
   Yes,
   looking good
   looking good

& grandmother
smiles & cuddles smiles & cuddles
smiles & cuddles & pats & strokes
& squashes nose to kiss
baby & sweet new-born
fast asleep
in the stroller

& another brother
sporting X
on a black baseball cap
& tiny
shiny silver earrings
that adorn
each individual
beautiful black ear
& elbow

elegantly poised
at the thigh joint
leaving wrist
& hand
to hang
silent
like a tear-drop
&

Left-Handed–Young-Sister Red
spelling out
the stops

   O-x-f-o-r-d C-i-r-c-u-s

Heh, that's my stop!

& I'm
outta here
scurrying
to Vidal Sassoon's Creative Hair Salon
to get all my nappy hair cut off.

LOUISE BENNETT

De Victory Parade

Red wite an blue! Red wite an blue!
All London eena gog!
De street dem string wid Union Jack
An bans more pretty flag
De park got more pretty-pretty light!
De fountains luminate
Lamp post dem got awn silver paint
De road dem got big gate!

De bus an train dem pack up
Massa, Missis, servant, maid,
All London gwine out fe see
All great Victory Parade.
Right fronten Buck'nam Palace
Jus as yuh cross de street,
Pon de Victoria Memorial,
Das weh me tek me seat!

Me se soljas ride up pon horse
An form up eena row,
Me hear sweet music start fe play
He hear a bugle blow,
An de small fly dem start buzz-buzz
An de big bug dem start hum
Dem dah-pass de wud roun sey de
Royal fambily dah-come!

De buggy wid de big wite horse dem
Trot up eena view
Wid de King an Queen an Princess dem
Dah sidung two be two.
De King bow an de Queen smile,
As dem ketch eena de clearin'
An de buzzing an de hummin'
Tun eena uproarious cheerin'!

De carriage never got no top,
It pass so near to me
Dat ah coulda stretch me han an touch
De Royal Fambily.
Me watch de buggy gallop galang
Galang till it fade,
An dat was de beginnin o'
De great Victory Parade.

De car dem an de ambulance
De van dem, law missis!
More tank, an jeep an lorry
Dan me ever know exis!
Kitchen, restaurant and laundry!
Wash yuh clothes an have yuh meal!
Radio Station, Cable Office
All dem tings dah-run pon wheel!

Pump an ladder, truck an tractor,
Weasels, trailer meck de grade,
Down to ordinary street bus, was
Eena Victory Parade!
Everything what help fe win de war
Wat de dem lickle bit
Every soul who gi dem lickle chenks
A help was eena it.

De marching start wid 'Merica
An dem sweet ban a-play,
Den de balance of de Allies dem
Come marching on de way.
Some wid gun over dem shoulda
Some wid flag eena dem han
Jusa lef-right, lef-right, lef-right,
In tune wid de music ban.

An de army an de navy an de airforce
Of every lan',
Jusa lef-right, lef in unison
Lawd missis, it was gran!
An de crowd meck noise an halla out

Tree cheers fe Victory
Fe Monty wid him beret
An fe Churchill wid him 'V'.

De skirt dem an de trousers an de
Hats wat dem had awn!
Me never se more different uniform
From ah was born!
Red an black, wite, gole an yellow,
Green an blue in every shade,
Jus a-blen an shine an pretty up
De VICTORY Parade!

JAMES BERRY

Beginning in a City, 1948

Stirred by restlessness, pushed by history,
I found myself in the centre of Empire.
Those first few hours, with those packed impressions
I never looked at in all these years.

I knew no room. I knew no Londoner.
I searched without knowing.
I dropped off my grip at the 'left luggage'.
A smart policeman told me a house to try.

In dim-lit streets, war-tired people moved slowly
like dark-coated bears in a snowy region.
I in my Caribbean gear
was a half-finished shack in the cold winds.
In November, the town was a frosty field.
I walked fantastic stone streets in a dream.

A man on duty took my ten-shilling note
for a bed for four nights.
Inflated with happiness I followed him.

I was left in a close-walled room,
left with a dying shadeless bulb,
a pillowless bed and a smelly army blanket –
all the comfort I had paid for.

Curtainless in morning light, I crawled out of bed
onto wooden legs and stiff-armed body,
with a frosty-board face that I patted
with icy water at the lavatory tap.

Then I came to fellow-inmates in a crowded room.
A rage of combined smells attacked me,
clogging my nostrils –
and new charges of other smells merely
increased the stench. I was alone.
I alone was nauseated and choked in deadly air.

One-legged people stood around a wall of hot plates
prodding sizzled bacon and kippers.
Sore-legged and bandaged people poured tea.
Weather-cracked faces, hairy and hairless, were chewing.
No woman smiled. No man chuckled.
Words pressed through gums and gaps of rusty teeth.

Grimy bundles and bags were pets
beside grimy bulges of people, bowed, and in little clusters.
Though ever so gullible I knew – this was a dosshouse.
I collected back seven shillings and sixpence.
I left the place and its smells, their taste still with me
and again instinct directed me.

I walked without map, without knowledge
from Victoria to Brixton. On Coldharbour Lane
I saw a queue of men – some black –
and stopped. I stood by one man in the queue.
'Wha happenin brodda? Wha happenin here?'

Looking at me he said 'You mus be a jus-come?
You did hear about Labour Exchange?' 'Yes – I hear.'
'Well, you at it! But, you need a place whey you live.'
He pointed. 'Go over dere and get a room.'
So, I had begun – begun in London.

JAMES BERRY

Wanting to Hear Big Ben

Another traveller said: Man,
me, miself, I wahn go to Englan
specially – fi stan up unda Big Ben

and hear Big Ben a-strike
and feel it there, how
it did echo roun the Whole Worl

and have me rememba, how
when I was a boy passin a radio
playin in a shop, and a-hear

Big Ben a-strike the time,
gongin and vibratin, like it travel
unda centre of earth

or unda the sea
or fram deep-deep sky
and I did kinda feel strange, that

somehow, this mighty echo come fram
a mystery place call centre of mi worl
which I could not imagine at all.

Now – when I get to Landan
I jus wahn to stan-up
unda that striking Big Ben

an man, jus test out
how that vibration work – inside-a-me.

JAMES BERRY

Roomseeker in London

I saw him rapping her door
Field man of old empire stood
    with that era he brought

She knew a man from sunny skies
She knew a bundle in arms
    that walked with a hopeful mind

This then was the trial

Sugar man sighed
    on outrage the lady effused
    and she quickly bolted in

His knocks hurt both ways
Can two poles consummate
    sky and earth and blood?

The man wondered
How many more doors
    would his gesture take?

JAMES BERRY

Migrant in London

Sand under we feet long time.
Sea divided for we, you know,
how we turned stragglers to the Mecca.

An' in mi hangin' drape style
I cross worl' centre street, man.
An' busy traffic hoot horns.

I see Big Ben strike
the mark of my king town.
Pigeons come perch on mi shoulder,
roun' great Nelson feet.

I stan' in the roar, man,
in a dream of wheels
a-vibrate shadows.
I feel how wheels hurry in wheels.

I whisper, man you mek it.
You arrive.
Then sudden like, quite loud I say,
'Then whey you goin' sleep tonight?'

KWAME DAWES

Umpire at the Portrait Gallery

At the Portrait Gallery near Trafalgar Square
I am searched by an ancient umpire
who mumbles his request with marbles or loose
dentures in his mouth. I see my first
portrait: the blotched bony fingers, the warts,
the clumsy overlarge gold ring loosely turning
like it will when he is entombed for good;
that look of boredom around the eyes
he masks with considered politeness
like a drunk man's careful compensations
and this self-important thinning of lips;
the nose, the greenish veins, the cliché
of a mole on his brow. It is too dark here
to study him well, besides he has found nothing
and the natives are restless at my back.

I am looking for the faces of this country;
the rustic, the jaundiced, the worn,
sharp tight snaps so close the pores talk;
faces caught in unaware blankness,
the rituals of rocking to numb silence
on the trains; dirty light, the thin
mist of darkness in the underground
making the faces collectors' bits,
keepables of a post-nuclear tribe.

I find only the posed stateliness
of another time – the courtly manners,
the clean colours staring from the palette
masking the stench and filth of older ways –
nothing to write about, really, nothing.

I am back in the lobby staring at the native,
his Adam's apple bobbing, his fingers,
the thick blackened nails, the stale suit,
the cap, the poem he is – the simple grammar
of another time – the years of the bombs
falling; he must have seen broken bodies
too. Now he fingers my underthings
searching for what I may have taken.
He finds nothing, nods me along.
Still, the globular ring keeps me
from forgetting him altogether,
that and the absence of stories to tell.
It is brilliant outside. A black-faced
bobby points me the way to the Southern
Bank where the river reeks of history
and word-weavers converge in snotty halls
to flaunt their musings to the world.
Here we are in the carcass of empire
searching in vain for sweetest honey.

KWAME DAWES

Birthright

I

The narrative is a myth, not history, not in the blood:
the cricket, the books, the poems, the stories,
the lovers, (such unfaithfulness), the instinctive
charm, long letters, the tongue of seduction,
all of these as if the blood carries sin
from generation to generation. But it is all myth,
an inheritance stolen one careless night
in Mandeville. A man dying. A son caught
in the slow-moving air; a mother hymning
this deathwatch. It is as if something
is being passed. The thing is, I was there,
and no one else made it, and I took what I could
in that hour of lamentation. There in that night,
the green city so dark it turned everything
into a deep moving space, I looked again
at that photo and accepted the imputed glory.

Now, nearly twenty years later, I return to that photo
of two men walking along the Thames,
somewhere near a chapel, the BBC behind them,
its dark cold studios where in that hour
at the microphone they smelt the humid
saltiness of their island. For that quiet hour
they deposited love in the cadence of their island
talk. Then it turned into painful nostalgia
and longing in the sudden blast of the air off the river,
the stench of history and dog shit on the long street
beside the ornate chapel (grey and stolid against a pewter
sky); beside the statue of horses with bursting muscles
and grimaces; beside this place spared by the Luftwaffe;
the geriatric empire whose doddering they called
a well-preserved swagger (they were still believers).

The two men are walking towards the camera
with the wind flapping their baggy trousers
around their thin legs. On the left is our father –
so odd that he is younger than I am now,
so odd the way I want to mistake him
for me. But sandals, worn corduroys
and the dust and bush landscape were my youth,
and besides, he is thin (*these minor famines*,
says Swanzy, the kind BBC chap), which makes him
fit-looking. Hunger is a constant condition,
uniform of the desperate artist like the narrow tie,
the billowing slacks, the tweed jacket
with leather elbow patches, the empty pipe.
His eyes, his scraggly beard, his bright gaze
are thirsty for a pint and carefree laughter.

II

I see you, Mastermind, and not me in him. He was
twenty-five and could still not boast a convincing
beard, and you, at thirty, are still cultivating,
shaving and then watching to see if it will
come to full chin-cover. Your hair, too, is receding,
the strong thin legs, the look, bright with longing –
all you, not me as I have always wanted to imagine.
You wash-bellies, you are constantly assured
of your genius, yet never certain of when it will
be fulfilled. But mothers always believe; mothers –
yours and his – always hold that truth deep in them.

III

This is *your* heritage. I have stolen
much, first the photo, and then the idea
of the photo, as if that was me by the Thames.
But what is fe yuh cyaan un-fe-yuh.
I am the counterfeit inheritor, fortunate
to have been at the right place when these things
were given out. Ask Jacob. It was never
diabolic and he, like me, had God to blame.
But I am the wrong corpus for the melancholic
blue notes of a heart so broken, so hidden –
the language you understand so well.

And this was his vernacular, the complex
in those eyes, beady and bright against the grey
of London. Me, I am the caretaker, the keeper
of secrets, the one who borrowed his wisdom
and art and wore it well. These things I have taken
as if they were mine. I can't be blamed.
Even *he* thought me the heir; even *he* longed
to make me the next chapter. We arranged it,
the cricket, the school, the English Literature,
the big talk of Oxford because we all believed.

But tipsy with your insanities, you have known
it all along, though for years stayed silent
until that dark shed with the lizards
and the haunting broke something in you.
It is the way of narratives of blood
that are untidily ribboned in old myths.
It is the way of stolen birthrights, the messy
contracts we made with blood legacies.

MONIZA ALVI

The Double City

I live in one city,
but then it becomes another.
The point where they mesh –
I call it mine.

Dacoits creep from caves
in the banks of the Indus.

One of them is displaced.
From Trafalgar Square
he dominates London, his face
masked by scarves and sunglasses.

He draws towards him all the conflict
of the metropolis – his speech
a barrage of grenades, rocket-launchers.

He marks time with his digital watch.
The pigeons get under his feet.

In the double city the beggar's cry
travels from one region to the next.

Under sapphire skies
or muscular clouds
there are fluid streets
and solid streets.
On some it is safe to walk.

The women of Southall
champion the release
of the battered Kiranjit
who killed her husband.
Lord Taylor, free her now!
Their saris billow in a storm of chants.

ANTHONY JOSEPH

Who passed on Haymarket, winter night?

Who passed on Haymarket, winter night?
With the bush bug scent that sent me back
to nights in the Lopinot valley?
To the hoot of the flying frogs
        on the muddy leaf
– two lungs deep.
To the blue black stains on the cockroach back.
In hurricane light.
To an old woman sewing her slipper – no
        – she swings it –
till rubber splats the gland across the wall.

She also roasts
      scorpions
– that burning insect bone –
with poison rolling around its cryptic spine.
(limb by limb is antidote
      against its sting)

Who passed bearing these tones?
      Haymarket, January.

ANTHONY JOSEPH

Blues for Brother Curtis

When I see Curtis last August
that yellowbone day after the rain in Five Rivers,
leaning against his blue bottom door
an he show me he sore foot how it ban' up.
An he say how it pain him like hell, an he creak the hinge
so ah peep how the bandage was leaking.
And how foot fly does zoot there so
in his earthern room – linoleum and smoke –
I never did know—that 2 month later I be getting this
      message
            in winter
When breeze have teeth.
An it choke me right here so an a couldn't even bring
one word to speak.

In New Street, Tunapuna, by the ravine
Curtis say 'Fellas, leh we go an get some dead'
Them days 'dead' was in chicken fried
an we walk all up Indian farmland.
But was take Curtis take we to some backyard slaughtery
to buy up a few bag a frozen fowl.
An he laugh like echo chamber.

Wood lice was rot from his room that August day.
An burnt milk was blowing from his pitch oil stove.
An I wondered then, 'But you foot mister man,
     like it weeping black rain?' An when sorefoot bleedin so
     it doh heal.

And when I get the news I put on my winter coat
     and went out into the night   to teach.

CLAUDE McKAY

La Paloma in London

About Soho we went before the light;
We went, unresting six, craving new fun,
New scenes, new raptures, for the fevered night
Of rollicking laughter, drink and song, was done.
The vault was void, but for the dawn's great star
That shed upon our path its silver flame,
When La Paloma on a low guitar
Abruptly from a darkened casement came –
Harlem! All else shut out I saw the hall,
And you in your red shoulder sash come dancing
With Val against me languid by the wall,
Your burning coffee-colored eyes keen glancing
Aslant at mine, proud in your golden glory!
I loved you, Cuban girl, fond sweet Diory.

KAYO CHINGONYI

Andrew's Corner

I

Where an old man comes, to practise
standing still, tutting
that the street he fought to keep is gone
and, sixty years on, he doesn't belong
to this world of bass, blasting out of
passing cars, and earshot, at the speed
of an age when pubs close down
overnight; are mounds of rubble in a week.

II

Where flowers moulder in memory of Tash,
fifteen, her twenty-something boyfriend
too drunk to swerve and miss the tree,
girls own their grown woman outfits,
smile at boys who smell of weed and too much
CK One. Pel, who can get served, stands in line.
Outside his friends play the transatlantic
dozens; the correct answer is *always your mum*.

III

Where alleys wake to condom wrappers,
kebab meat, a ballet pump, last week
a van pulled up and it was blood. Today:
joggers dodge a dead pigeon, offer wordless
greeting to the night bus's army of sanguine-
eyed ravers, nursing bad skin and tinnitus.
Goaded by the light, past the same house on repeat,
they think of taking off their shoes; inviolable sleep.

KAYO CHINGONYI

Berwick Street

In the heart of London's record-collecting district, more and more small shops are pulling down their shutters for the last time.

ROBERT PLUMMER, BBC News, 7 June 2007

We schlep the quiet length of Poland Street
past the house where a blue plaque tells us
Shelley lived and diffident women who sulk,
Soho-bound, from a day shift of shop fronts

to a night made for those who will chase the
dark to its slow death in search of nothing
more than laughter; the glamour a certain
light gives to last night's half eaten kebabs

left, for someone else to clean up, just
metres from the nearest bin. As we stand
at the top of Berwick Street, wait for cars
to let us cross, I think of those who came,

some from as far as Japan, with song names
misspelled on bits of paper. All for the half
smile of one who knows the tune; that it was
recorded in a shack on a shoestring. Soon

no one will know of these gutted shops.
This street's been reduced to a thoroughfare,
there's no placard here to mark the loss,
only those passing through; going elsewhere.

LORNA GOODISON

Bam Chi Chi La La: London, 1969

I

Calm as a Coromantyn warrior baring his chest
to the branding iron, this man was standing outside
a corner Lyons in January, wearing a thin floral shirt.
One helluvabitch cold tore at the hibiscus over his heart.
So he unbuttoned button after button until almost
barechested, he stood calm as a Coromantyn warrior
giving it up dry-eyed to the white-hot branding iron.

II

In Jamaica she was teacher. Here, she is charwoman
at night in the West End. She eats a cold midnight meal
carried from home and is careful to expunge her spice
trail with Dettol. She sings 'Jerusalem' to herself and
recites the Romantic poets as she mops hallways and
scours toilets, dreaming the while of her retirement
mansion in Mandeville she is building brick by brick.

MAHMOOD JAMAL

from Two Women

I

Pearl Sravanmutta
is over ninety now.
She prefers to cook her own meals
'Indian curries, not what they dish out
on meals on wheels.'
She has no doctor
And feels dizzy crossing streets.
Her wiry hands wave about like sticks.
She dresses in a sari for the camera and smiles

She wants people to know she still has style.
Opening an old fridge she complains
'The rich are getting richer
and the poor poorer, Mrs Thatcher
has ruined this country.'
She finds it hard to do things on her own.
The lads from the betting shop are nice;
They send someone to help her place her bets,
though her TV is going up the creek.
She likes to take a chance now and then
on an old horse, she says
there's nowhere these days to go for a dance.
Her photograph, taken years ago
in a Bond Street studio
her prize possession
faded now and grown old.
She loves hot Biryanis,
I'm told.

JAY BERNARD

F12

I have pared around your wrists with light.
I will always have the deep crease in your thumb
your cupped & faceless hands around
my limbless waist. My green skin against
your blue skin

transposed & re-hung. You with your eyes closed on the Circle
Line into you with the deep crease around your mouth into you
with the shadow of St Paul's obscuring you into a woman sipping
into a woman stepping from a bus into the wine-chalk street.

Twice; I am behind a lens, behind an eye; again, behind a skull,
behind a brain, behind a mind; my view is ragged. The frame is
torn. All those people who made the world magic are gone.
Grown. I'm not ready for the flesh to double

& double. I end the alphabet at U. I point, I click, I catch
the second when your head was turned, or when a dog leapt from
a puddle at a bird. I shutter the world in two; your two hands
separate from you.

Between this world and the next hour I will gaze at you &
you & you. I am behind the eye that froze you feeling a dasheen.
I am behind the gloss, behind the print, behind the page.
Behind the blunt lens that cut you out and kept you.

PETE KALU

Old Radicals

Hot with indignation
apartheid, Special Patrol and the NF
we nailed placards together, wrote speeches
flung each other over barricades
our hands on rocks and riot shields

We cried, hugged, slept, dreamed
made the 5 a.m. calls from cells
brothers for the Cause

Years intervened
the Anti Deportation Campaign calls came
your support phoned through
signature on the fifth page of the petition,
an approving onlooker to the march
at length your name appeared only on campaign chain emails
occasionally and then never

Me? I found myself worrying about fresh nappies
as we marched
grew content to listen to others' speeches
traded in the car that constantly broke down
found jackets and trousers easy to wear

That afternoon we met on Liverpool Street, fumbled
with the old handshakes
and as you pulled away again I glanced
back at a friendship cooled

SIDDHARTHA BOSE

Sex and the City

She brings me striped shirts cos her father wore them, my love
in the afternoon. Blue and white stripe Calcutta – enter her parlour
shocked with revolving wooden chandelier darting spots of light,
dust in light.

She maps me in her web, spinning limbs.

– Give give, I'll do, she groans in that salt tone, as she grips
me in skin that bubbles in sores. Some like galaxies sweat pus, not
stars. Room is wet with rain that never comes. The floor heaves
under us, instinctive as nitrate.

A Tom Waits razor growl chops me up.

I lie on her single bed the clay of hash in my hair. Black and
wet like Kali, she plays the piston.

I am stung on a rack, flayed.

We go to a play by a temple, and as the blackyellow cab turns
to Ballygunge by the kebab shop with men wrapped in loincloth,
passing the day watching smoke gather on tram tracks, we see two
stray dogs doing what is natural with a insistence that frightens,
as we hike up our reserve in a giddy laughter.

Not in London – dogs fucking, fleas on backs, stone as my
pocket alley in the east end, which is home more or less than
home. Sometimes, on a late Saturday when the gods crawl outta
their holes, I see a man taking the piss by a bin, and the smell,
not the trickle – a branch of veins – reminds me of where I'm
from, and I glow like a lantern, holy.

SIDDHARTHA BOSE

Swansong, Mile End

Pigeons on a tiled roof.
Foreground – bus stop shines in the rain.

Swans – patches of cloud –
float along Regent's Canal, its

skin, moving fish scales.

Shirt of sky opens.
Hair of stars sprout.

Plastic bags crackle like
pellets of rain in a tin can, like fire

bled in wood.

A southbound train lunges over a
bridge.

The night is radioactive.

The two swans screech their song of love,
shake their manes,

proud as horses.

LIZZY DIJEH

Stratford City

I lie still sometimes and feel a sense of readiness blowing East:
trail along the ruts and juts of the soft tarmac, skirt the freshly
        laid railway
track like a blind man with his Braille,

glimpse its past secrets glossed over with a fresh coat,
judder with the anticipation weaving through the stands,
the stench of cut grass, its waft of splayed blades
flying up with rubber feet through the arena –
that polite pinch of newness teasing an old game.

I spot a world through a rising platform, and
once the cranes and scaffolds fall away,
in comes the human highway, flooding
venue after venue in thick greedy bands, pumping
excitement past the street stalls
that presents its sea of flags,
its stacks of London maps,
its bowls of whistles, flyers, cuddly toys
and hats dangling like fine jewellery,
the rich colours sparkle
in rows and rows of souvenir stands,
both tempting and extortionate.
Ticket touts eat the air in relays,
flag down passing cars like bull-fighters,
begging to buy our future
by selling their stories.

Westfield stands tall above the new city,
a giant glass spectre full of prim, pressed
suits, sparkling shoes turned red
with the love of new money
riding the air in waves.
The roar of the crowds deepen
as the athletes leave the village
in a procession of robes and banners like a grinning army.
There are men across the river in stiff white shirts and headsets
seated in the mouth of the BBC,
a high-rise building block of commentaries
in several hundred languages
over-looking the mayhem below
with careful applause.

I wake up,
plunged back into silence, the stillness of a new dawn
except for the slow hum of the moving diggers.

I move towards it, see the spider's web of scaffolds
still creeping up the walls,
the floating white hard hats running around the soft tarmac like mice:
my window on a world of greatness –
The picture promises much,
five continents brought together, a medal in every colour,
to each other we are an event, we are all winners here,
even Mr *McDonald's* with his tent already pitched squarely in the mud,
his great big billboard swelling red and yellows,
looking down on the starving city, smiling.

SHAMSHAD KHAN

Isosceles

you were obvious targets

shaven heads
with big fat black beards

bang
a flash of orange
a bloody shoulder

you heard your mother
break london's 4 a.m. silence
through the sounds of your own shouts
and theirs to

shut the fuck up
shut the fuck up
confusion

at the press conference
you said your head bounced down the stairs
when they dragged you by the foot

heavy handed incompetence
asymmetric warfare
this wobbly triangle

bush and blair and the rest of us
teetering

(Police raid in Forest Gate, London of a Muslim family home. 15 police officers
entered their home unannounced, the remaining 235 stayed in the street. One
of the two brothers arrested, Mohammed Abdulkahar was shot without warning.
Both brothers were released without charge. The investigation [June 2006]
did not charge the policeman, the shooting was classed as a mistake.)

NICK MAKOHA

Promise to my unborn son

It used to be enough, to be my father's son,
until he was gone. Neither of my two languages
could reach down the phone and ask him to stay.

Even when we lived in the same city. His voice only
ever spoke to me about the news. So when your mother
told me, our second child will be a boy, I panicked.

There were no memories to show me
how to love you and I knew a day would come when
I would stare back at you – without words

like faces on the billboards of the Barking Road.
This road will always lead you home.
It is important to be from somewhere.

I am Ugandan, living in the East End of London.
At your birth, look for me. My voice will be a river
flowing from my mouth, waiting to tell you – everything.

FRED D'AGUIAR

I Buried My Father A Complete Stranger

One close day in E5 or E6, the mute hearse
rounded the corner and filled his street.

At the parlour I looked and looked
at the boy asleep. I could have kissed him
on his brow with every hair in place or wept.

We stood by empty seats shifting our weight,
drove deliberately to a hole made for him,
buried the child and took the man away.

E.A. MARKHAM

At the Redland Hotel, Stamford Hill

1

The basement room lets in the light
and breeze through the grille of the open window.
As the TV doesn't work I lie in bed
reading Lowell's *Life Studies*
killing an hour or so in contrition
before the necessary telephone call of the morning.

This might be punishment enough: to wake
in a low time, loo and shower shared
along the corridor, family pride honoured
only in the clean sheets (the Australian patron
true to her word that nothing would crawl
and scuttle here during the night).
And somehow Lowell's absurd and beguiling
family seem OK in this light.

Yesterday, not knowing the future
I was thinking how to write up
that old scene at the Paddington Baths
in – was it – '57? with Sunday morning orators
and their congregation of the unwashed,
staged for my education.

Those amateur Ciceros, less of *The Murder Trials*,
more of the *Letters to Friends* brought
Grenadian and Tobagian accents
to the poor Roman theatre of bath-time
urging Khrushchev & Co. to do the black man
a favour, and go to war.

Despite everything I think of myself without irony
as a man of property, lucky in my world.
So I wake in a basement on the Seven Sisters Road.
(Who were those sisters? Lowell's
would be dream institutions housing
our brightest lesbian daughters;
though if we're talking families, then a grandmother,
a mother from Montserrat would not lack
the colour of these New Englanders.)

And I, too, remember taking a body home
to be buried, though I doubt, whether like Lowell's
mother, she travelled First Class in her DC10.
These thoughts, stirring my weakness
to be blown off-track, will swirl into something
like resentment, unless I call home now.

2

Heading for the phone I try not to think
of the other man's nine month's daughter
signalling him, with a dab of water on her cheek
to shave. *I will be at fault. I am at fault.*
I mean it. The phone-box broken, I think
of options in life, like owning America,
and wonder if that, too, will drive you mad.
Like Commander Lowell, my new twin,

I have a mock title and am growing irrelevant;
and must tread that line (I'm sober, mother, lover)
between dignity and ridicule
Lowell's nostalgic last afternoon with Uncle
Devereux Winslow was when he was five.
I am sixty-three: how far is that now, from five?

JOHN AGARD

Toussaint L'Ouverture Acknowledges Wordsworth's Sonnet 'To Toussaint L'Ouverture'

I have never walked on Westminster Bridge
or had a close-up view of daffodils.
My childhood's roots are the Haitian hills
where runaway slaves made a freedom pledge
and scarlet poincianas flaunt their scent.
I have never walked on Westminster Bridge
or speak, like you, with Cumbrian accent.
My tongue bridges Europe to Dahomey.
Yet how sweet is the smell of liberty
when human beings share a common garment.
So, thanks brother, for your sonnet's tribute.
May it resound when the Thames' text stays mute.
And what better ground than a city's bridge
for my unchained ghost to trumpet love's decree.

> *...Thou has left behind*
> *Powers that will work for thee; air, earth, and skies;*
> *There's not a breathing of the common wind*
> *That will forget thee; thou has great allies;*
> *Thy friends are exultations, agonies,*
> *And love, and man's unconquerable mind.*

– from Wordsworth's sonnet to Toussaint L'Ouverture,
a former slave, who led a revolution that would lay the
foundation for Haiti to become the first Black republic (1804).

PATIENCE AGBABI

The London Eye

Through my gold-tinted Gucci sunglasses,
the sightseers. Big Ben's quarter chime
strikes the convoy of number 12 buses
that bleeds into the city's monochrome.

Through somebody's zoom lens, me shouting
to you, *Hello!...on...bridge...'minster!*
The aerial view postcard, the man writing
squat words like black cabs in rush hour.

The South Bank buzzes with a rising treble.
You kiss my cheek, formal as a blind date.
We enter Cupid's capsule, a thought bubble
where I think, 'Space age!', you think, 'She was late.'

Big Ben strikes six. My SKIN .Beat™ blinks, replies
18·02. We're moving anticlockwise.

MALIKA BOOKER

Hungerford Bridge

Since you jumped
I have wondered
what death was like

On sweltering nights, hay fever attacks,
I awake starved of wind, oxygen scarce
listless, clogged up by a sticky cork, gasping,
gaping mouth working like a fish,
my tongue coated with white spots
where my mouth attempted to keep me alive

and I fight crying, trumpeting my nostrils
with mighty heaves.

Then I think of you.

For three years you have been
submerged
missed your step off the tall red barrier
your stride into air
blinked and you were air walking
feet scissoring with nothing
then
landing like a life raft on the Thames
pinstriped suit ballooned
brief case dislodged
for a moment   time stopped

now every time I walk across Hungerford Bridge
I see you step, land, and balloon

I took a bath the other day
and thought of you
landing.

MAHMOOD JAMAL

Apples and Mangoes

The exotic fruit
was placed upon the table
and invited comment:
'I prefer to eat apples at home,'
said the professor from SOAS
'But when out I like a slice or two
of mango;
that is what it is no doubt?'

'Easy to get hold of these days,'
said the liberal host
who wrote guilt ridden plays about blacks.
'A transplant, I can see
by its shape and colour,
from India on African soil,'
remarked the social worker from Battersea.
'A good thing surely
in the cause of internationalism,'
muttered the pale bespectacled revolutionary.
'I like its pink blush, subtle
not too obvious in natural light
tastes nice if eaten late at night,'
said the artist, adding,
'almost nipple like its eye
where all the juice can be sucked through.'
'No! No! It's not one you can suck!'
screamed the professor, hands shaking
with age and anticipation as he picked
the knife. 'Surely this is one for slicing.'
'Some of these mangoes,' said the poet,
'look ok but taste like apples
and are the same colour inside.'
'Hmm,' said the professor as everyone smiled,
'A cross between an apple and a mango!
Science has indeed made great strides.'
'Hmm,' added everyone as they had a slice.

JOHN AGARD

Listen Mr Oxford don

Me not no Oxford don
me a simple immigrant
from Clapham Common
I didn't graduate
I immigrate

But listen Mr Oxford don
I'm a man on de run
and a man on de run
is a dangerous one

I ent have no gun
I ent have no knife
but mugging de Queen's English
is the story of my life

I dont need no axe
to split/ up yu syntax
I dont need no hammer
to mash/ up yu grammar

I warning you Mr Oxford don
I'm a wanted man
and a wanted man
is a dangerous one

Dem accuse me of assault
on de Oxford dictionary/
imagine a concise peaceful man like me/
dem want me serve time
for inciting rhyme to riot
but I tekking it quiet
down here in Clapham Common

I'm not a violent man Mr Oxford don
I only armed wit mih human breath
but human breath
is a dangerous weapon

So mek dem send one big word after me
I ent serving no jail sentence
I slashing suffix in self-defence
I bashing future wit present tense
and if necessary

I making de Queen's English accessory/to my offence

ROGER ROBINSON

The Wedding Picture

I do not know any of these women,
these bridesmaids at my mother's wedding.

My mother knows just what beehive hairdo
ground her kneecaps away praying for her son

who everybody said was gay, even though he
swore to her that he was not, and she would

make the sign of the cross and drop
to her knees every time she thought about him.

My mother also knows which smile broke
down from too much alcohol and bad men,

who shaved off her hair and walked naked
and barefoot down Clapham High Street.

And mother knows which fuchsia satin dress
had been living with her man for fourteen years

and had two children and a house with him
till he went away on holiday to Miami,

only to hear from a friend three weeks later
that he got married and he wasn't coming back

and that same woman took him back
when everyone abandoned him

because his body was so riddled with cancer
that he smelled like compost.

MARSHA PRESCOD

Community Policing!

Dey say dey ha to keep de peace
And when dey lik Erral,
So hard,
He pedal *clean up Brixton Hill*
Widout chain on he bicycle,
He feel like it wus a piece of he
Dey did keep in truth.

Dey carry Eunice mudder,
Outa Woolworth in han'cuff,
Swearing blind dat she steal de paira panty
She buy in Tesco,
She start to bawl in de van,
De hurt of twenty-five years of sweat
'Employers' tief off she, widout pay
Bursting her chest.

Winston change he name, to Afetbutu,
One night,
Dey hold he up for ganga,
And when dey fine out he name,
Dey figger he illegal
An decide to 'repatriate' he
(Doe he born in Tottenham)
He reach *quite in Zaire*
Before it sort out.

So when time come dat,
Errol, decide to pick up brick,
Eunice mudder, reach for she husban' machete,
An Winston put he paraffin
In sumptin udder dan he heater,
An when de day done,
Shopping centre looking....
...*radically diff'rent*

Evrybody get vex!
Evrybody excited!
Voices rise,
In riotous indignation

'Dese people are criminals!
Dese people do not understand
How we do things, in dis country,
An,
How we have a tradition of
Justice, (trust us)
Fair play (fear prey)
An,
COMMUNITY POLICING!'

DESMOND JOHNSON

Mass Jobe

And so
we all gone old in inglan
mi an sister lizza
brada ferd
an sister matty
an inglish man
an inglish woman
with a yard
with a yard
with a yard identity
our memories of the past
are so plenty
how we first come here
in winter time
got a bustraining
to earn little dime
did train shunting
and office cleaning
did road sweeping
and can-packaging

did bread baking
and house building
did hospital work
on various wings
were aux-
iliary
nurse
and kitchen porter
guardman
teawoman
and cleaner
am speaking
from a standpoint of age
'perience
my sones and daughters
experience!
we were railman
railwoman
train drivers
signal man
and controller
collectors of tickets
and night workers
our best years spent
on british rail
our years went by
like a fairy tale
am speaking
from a standpoint of age
'perience
my sons and daughters
experience!
we sen back money
to o' people a yard
say life is good
it was tough and hard
and we have children
plus those back a yard
we have children
o lord! lord! lord!
and to make enns meet

we work seven days a week
on sundays as well
till we body get weak
at nights as well
till we run right down
with physical ailments
and nerves breakdown
am speaking
from a standpoint of age
'perience
my sons and daughters experience!
the beauty that we had
the strength that we had
was reduce and reduce
dear lord my God!
like wasted life
and wasted time
we have nothing to show
not a penny
not a dime
only fruits of our body
our blood children
who are thrown like dogs
in a lion's den
I am looking
from a standpoint of age
'perience
at my sons and daughters
experience
in
Bristol
Brixton
Moss Side
and Merseyside
bawling to myself
there is little difference
still a wasted like
wasted time
without a job
without a dime
fuming

and raging
against this crime
it's from a standpoint of age
and experience
that I know they shall win
and overcome
but for us it's late
to say 'if we know'
much too late to make a show
jus thank massa God
that mi live so long
to have a walk with the wife
still feeling strong
holding the wife
by a bus stop stand
going to friends
in the heart of Brixton
Railton Road
our new Kingston.

DESMOND JOHNSON

Ole Charlie Boy

Ole charlie boy
you still deh a inglan
charlie boy
you still deh a london
yes
   mi sey
      mi sey
         mi sey
            mi sey
yes
   mi sey
      mi sey
         mi sey
            mi sey

razing mi voice a likkle
e did fass
fe ask mi dat question
cause we both is in
de same position
for we both come
here in de fifties
a kinda runaway
from yard perplexities
an we all come find
de same sin-ting
low paid jobs
bad housing
so yes
   mi sey
      mi sey
         mi sey
            mi sey
yes
   mi sey
      mi sey
         mi sey
            mi sey
mi still on de dole
still in de hole
still is as bruck
and can't find no wok
what about your children
charlie boy
what about you plan dem
charlie boy
well
   mi sey
      mi sey
         mi sey
            mi sey
well
   mi sey
      mi sey
         mi sey
            mi sey

mi only boy is as worser than mi
dem sen him to prison
on dem new sus law
dem sen him to prison
cause dem catch him with a draw
and de gals dem a breeding agen
dem total children come to ten
de mada an mi is not so sweet
she sey all mi do is to walk de street
ole johnny boy
   time is rough
      ole johnny boy
         time is tough
mi save up so money
mi waa fe go home
telephone de airport people dem
ole johnny boy
   time is rough
      ole johnny boy
         time is tough
de cost fe de flight
is more dan wha mi have
coulda sell de house
if belong to mi
ole johnny boy
   time is rough
      ole johnny boy
         time is tough
mi ago die in inglan
johnny boy
we ago die in inglan
johnny boy
cause mi bruck in inglan
johnny boy
cause we bruck in inglan
johnny boy
ole johnny boy
   time is rough
      ole johnny boy
         time is tough!

LINTON KWESI JOHNSON

Five Nights of Bleeding
(for Leroy Harris)

1

madness...madness...
madness tight on the heads of the rebels
the bitterness erupts like a hot-blast
                            broke glass
rituals of blood on the burning
served by a cruel in-fighting
five nights of horror an of bleeding
                           · broke glass
cold blades as sharp as the eyes of hate
an the stabbings
it's war amongst the rebels
madness...madness...war.

2

night number one was in BRIXTON
SOPRANO B sound system
was a beating out a rhythm with a fire
coming doun his reggae-reggae wire
it was a soun shaking doun your spinal column
a bad music tearing up your flesh
an the rebels them start a fighting
the yout them jus turn wild
it's war amongst the rebels
madness...madness...war.

3

night number two doun at SHEPHERD'S
right up RAILTON ROAD
it was a night named Friday
when everyone was high on brew
or drew a pound or two worth a kally
soun coming doun NEVILLE KING'S music iron

the rhythm jus bubbling an back-firing
raging an rising, then suddenly the music cut
steel blade drinking blood in darkness
it's war amongst the rebels
madness...madness...war.

4

night number three
over the river
right outside the RAINBOW
inside JAMES BROWN was screaming soul
outside the rebels were freezing cold
babylonian tyrants descended
pounced on the brothers who were bold
so with a flick
of the wrist
a jab an a stab
the song of blades was sounded
the bile of oppression was vomited
an two policemen wounded
righteous righteous war.

5

night number four at a blues dance
                      a blues dance
two rooms packed an the pressure pushing up
hot. hot heads. ritual of blood in a blues dance
                                    broke glass
splintering fire, axes, blades, brain – blast
rebellion rushing doun the wrong road
storm blowing doun the wrong tree
an LEROY bleeds near death on the fourth night
                            in a blues dance
on a black rebellious night
it's war amongst the rebels
madness...madness...war.

6

night number five at the TELEGRAPH
vengeance walked through the doors
so slow
so smooth
so tight an ripe an smash!
                              broke glass
a bottle finds a head
an the shell of the fire-hurt cracks
the victim feels fear
              finds hands
              holds knife
              finds throat
o the stabbings an the bleeding an the blood
it's war amongst the rebels
madness...madness...war.

LINTON KWESI JOHNSON

Di Great Insohrekshan

it woz in april nineteen eighty wan
doun inna di ghetto af Brixtan
dat di babylan dem cauz such a frickshan
dat it bring about a great insohreckshan
an it spread all ovah di naeshan
it woz truly an histarical occayshan

it woz event af di year
an I wish I ad been dere
wen wi run riat all ovah Brixtan
wen wi mash-up plenty police van
wen wi mash-up di wicked wan plan
wen wi mash-up di Swamp Eighty Wan
fi wha?
fi mek di rulah dem andahstan
dat wi naw tek noh more a dem oppreshan

an wen mi check out di ghetto grape vine
fi fine out all I coulda fine
evry rebel jussa revel in dem story
dem a taak bout di powah an di glory
dem a taak bout di burnin an di lootin
dem a taak bout di smashin an di grabin
dem a tell mi bout di vanquish an di victri

dem seh di babylan dem went too far
soh wi ad woz fi bun two cyar
an wan an two innocent get mar
but wha
noh soh it goh sometime inna war ein star
noh soh it goh sometime inna war?

dem seh wi bun dung di George
wi coulda bun di lanlaad
wi bun dung di George
wi nevvah bun di lanlaad
wen wi run riat all ovah Brixtan
wen wi mash-up plenty police van
wen wi mash-up di wicked wan plan
wen wi mash-up di swamp eighty wan

dem seh wi comandeer cyar
an wi ghaddah ammunishan
wi bill wi baricade
an di wicked ketch afraid
wi sen out wi scout
fi goh fine dem whereabout
den wi faam-up wi passi
an wi mek wi raid

well now dem run gaan goh plan countah-ackshan
but di plastic bullit an di waatah cannan
will bring a blam-blam
will bring a blam-blam
nevvah mine Scarman
will bring a blam-blam

JEAN 'BINTA' BREEZE

The Wife of Bath speaks in Brixton Market

My life is my own bible
wen it come to all de woes
in married life
fah since I reach twelve,
Tanks to Eternal Gawd,
is five husban I have
            (if dat is passible)
but all of dem was wort someting
in dem own way
doah dem say
dat troo Jesas only go to one weddin
in Canaan
we no suppose fi married
more dan once
but den again
dem say Im tell de Samaritan woman
by de well
dat doah she did have five husban
de laas one never count
        is wat Im mean by dat
        why jus de fif one lef out
        ow much she can have den
            four?
Im don't give no precise number
Well,
        people can argue it forever
        but me sure of one serious ting
        Im order we to sex an multiply
Im also say dat
        de man mus lef im madda an im fadda
        an cling to me
        but Im never say
        how many
        mi no hear no mention of bigamy
        or polygamy

so why me or anyone
should tink it is a crime
An wat about de wise king Soloman
look how much wife im tek, Lawd,
ah wish ah did have as much in bed as him!
God mus did give him some 'great' gif
No one alive did ever have such fun
But still
I will tank de Lawd
fah doah I have only five
I shall welcome de sixt one
wenever im choose to arrive
because I nat lacking up my foot at all
if one husban dead
anadda christian man will surely come
fah even de apostle say dat den mi free
to tek anadda man dat can please me
                betta to married dan to bun

Abraham, Joseph,
nuff adda holy man
did have nuff wife
Whey God forbid dat?
Yuh see no clear word?
Where Im ever order virginity?
            Dere is no such commandment!
is de apostle Paul come talk bout maidenhead
an him never qualify fi talk bout dat.
Im say a man may counsel a woman
but counselling is nat command
wat I do wid my body is my personal business
an if God did command virginity
nobady wouldn married
fah married woulda dead
an no more pickney wouldn born
so no new maidenhead.

How Paul him want to tek command
wen Jesas wouldn dweet
we all know pum pum is someting sweet

an nuff sword will falla it.
Whoever, jus like de apostle,
want to do widdouten sex
is free to choose dat,
but wid we, no badda vex
fah if my husban wear out an im dead
you free to marry me
dat is nat bigamy
an to enjoy good sex
is nat a frailty
nat unless yuh did decide, like Paul,
fi tek up chastity
because a man don't want pure gold pot
in im house
im want some mek wid good wood
as a spouse
an God did give we all a different gif
we choose wat we is suited for
everyone don't have to give up everyting fah Christ
Im neva aks we dat
dat is fah who want perfect peace
an you all know already
dat is nat me
I gwine mek de bes of all my years
fah dat is de joy an fruit of marriage
an why we have dese private parts so sweet
dem cyan jus mek so an don't put to use
except to piss
or tell man apart from woman
das wat you tink?
fram wat me feel already
dat could nat be so
a man mus give im wife er tings
Piss yes, an tell we apart
but wat pleasure dese instrument brings!

JACOB SAM-LA ROSE

After Lazerdrome: McDonalds, Peckham Rye...

> *What's clear, now, is / that there was music, that it's lasted, that it /*
> *doesn't matter whether a player played it, / or whether it just played itself,*
> *that it still is / playing, / that at least two gods exist...*
> ABDULAH SIDRAN, 'A Dispute About God'

where I say goodbye to south-east London for the next 3 years
a gaggle of us   still damp   spilling in from the night before

early flock for a Sunday   six or seven A.M.   sleepless
drowning in light and all this quiet   after all that sweat
and darkness   all that flighty noise

this is the year one of the guys says music is the one thing
that won't ever let him down   that music is his religion

the year we're stopped and searched because we
fit the description   the year jungle music passes
out of fashion   stripped down

to naked beat and bass   and we club together   to dance
alone   in the dark   let the music play us   meat and bone

let music fill the empty spaces   rhythm in wads and scads
scattershot   crashing   wall to wall   to be baptised
by filtered drums   pressed snares and swollen b-lines

be baptised by city songs   urban hymns   seamless
sound   a brimming sea of sound   poured out

from towering speaker stacks   this is the year we stand
close enough   to feel the music   rise   its wing-beats
on our faces   drawing salt from our skin   released

then morning   small fries and a strawberry milkshake
counting coins for the cab back   sitting around a table

slouching in moulded seats   drowning in silence
light-headed   leavened   waiting
for the right moment to move

awake for too long   ears
still ringing   drum-drunk

eyes still adjusting to the light
a weight coming down

INUA ELLAMS

GuerillaGardenWritingPoem

The mouth of the city is tongued with tar
its glands gutter saliva, teeth chatter in rail
clatter, throat echoes car horns and tyre's
screech, forging new language: a brick city
smoke-speak of stainless steel consonants
and suffocated vowels. These are trees and
shrubbery, the clustered flora battling all
hours, staccato staggered through streets.

Meet Rich and Eleanor on Brabourn Grove
as he wrestles her wheelbarrow over cobble-
stones to the traffic island by Kitto Road
where this night, coloured a turquoise-grit,
cathedral-quiet and saintly, makes prayer
of their whispers and ritual of their work:
bend over, clear rubble, cut weed and plant.

But more than seeds are sown here. You
can tell by his tender pat on tended patch;
the soft cuff to a boy's head – first day to
school, by how they rest with parent-pride
against stone walls, huff into winter's cold,

press faces together as though tulips might
stem from two lips, gather spades, forks,
weeds and go. Rich wheelbarrows back to
Eleanor's as vowels flower or flowers vowel
through smoke-speak, soil softens, the city
drenched with new language thrills and
the drains are drunk with dreams.

The sky sways on the safe side of tipsy
and it's altogether an alien time of half-
life and hope, an after-fight of gentle fog
and city smog, where the debris of dew drips

to this narrative of progress, this city tale;
this story is my story, this vista my song.
I cluster in the quiet, stack against steel
seek islands, hope, and a pen to sow with.

AMRYL JOHNSON

Circle of Thorns

(in memory of the New Cross victims – 18 January 1981)

There is a ring which shines brightly
It is the answer to our prayers
I am not afraid

There is a ring of rusty iron
which grates along concrete
until your blood crawls
And
I have seen
I have seen
I have seen the young willow
sink beneath the waves
    beneath the waves
    beneath the hand which does not
replenish

316

So
when they ask
For whom the bell tolls?
Tell them
     Male black aged nineteen
     Female black aged seventeen
Two faces
in
a storm

KIMBERLY TRUSTY

Fireworks, New Cross Road, 1981

There were fireworks
pink and white star shower
green and gold clouds
the night I met you
New Year's Eve 1980
we watched the night sky spark up
from behind the glass
of a shop front window

A bashment in a Brixton record shop
I was trendy and tragic
in skinny, paint-splattered jeans
and battered Nike high tops
my hair wet and curly
like Coco from *Fame*

You? you were all
roots   rock   rebel
baby dreads sticking out
from your head like a satellite
army fatigues and a red
'black market Clash' t-shirt
you held out a record sleeve
asked if I liked Black Uhuru

I sipped my beer and wondered
if you could tell from the crinkle
between my eyebrows that
the last record I bought
was 'We got the beat' by the Go-Go's
thank God for fireworks
those pyrotechnic fireflies

A year later
we celebrate your 21st birthday
at a friend's house in
New Cross Road where
two girls, Angela and Yvonne,
are also celebrating birthdays
we are antisocial socialisers
standing in a corner in the front room
alone together in a room full of people

I know who Black Uhuru are now
and sometimes I catch you singing
the *Fame* theme song under your breath
when you think I'm busy with something else
random velocities of our molecules
have made us one

The glow from red paper Chinese lanterns
takes the sharpness out of your cheekbones
we hold each other tight and rock
to 'Guava Jelly' unaware that the Lion is ailing
my fingers twisted in
your shoulder-length locks
the heat from your body a spark
that sets off fireworks in the pit of my stomach

And then...

I see red.
Not from paper lanterns.
I see orange.
Not from 21 candles on your cake.
I feel heat.
Not from your body.

And it is red and orange and heat and people running and young women screaming and it's then that I lose you, get carried out in a wave of colour and noise. Still hot from your body and the party and the... I don't notice New Year cold. I move from person to person, grabbing at jumpers, t-shirts and coats, screaming above the screaming and the fire and the sirens, 'Where is he? Have you seen him?' but no one answers. I see fireworks behind my eyes, trip over someone prone in the street and sit down heavily on the pavement. I scream so loudly and so long that a lifetime passes. A lifetime passes before I notice your arms around me and although you're whispering my name I can hear it above the screaming and the fire and the sirens and my own sobs because we share molecules; are one.

My Coco curls are smoke and ash
your dreads are singed, your 21st year a house on fire
but energy is kinetic; our molecules' random velocity
and we are one

And the following day?
the following day we are one
one with the 13 dead
one with the 20 injured
one with the 15,000 people
who take to the streets
and put a too silent police force
on notice

Our fear
our anger
our sorrow
our determination
our new awareness
diffuses across the nation
and we are one

JOHN AGARD

The Embodiment

since spider feel at home
with thread and rope

I thought I'd try Eu-rope
(the name sounded promising)

so I headed for England
land of hope and unfinished glory
like Schubert's symphony

leaving Amsterdam to Surinam spinners
and Paris to Martinique weavers

arrived at Heathrow not quite light
eight nothing-to-declare suitcases
balanced on eight metropolis-dreaming legs

soon got used to juggling eight cups of tea
like I was spider embodiment of Earl Grey

and nobody made any comment
till I metamorphosed into proper
tophat ascot gent

and bought a piece
of property in Kent

then the pauses
became pregnant

and I heard myself say

No I'm not on holiday
Spider is here to stay

MAGGIE HARRIS

Timeline Whitstable

1976
…a timeline, a roll and a lime
bell-bottomed and **patchouli-oiled**
bottle-green beat-up **VW Beetle**
coughing down the High Street
and its **sea of stones**

unfold the **baby buggy** with its **flailing fists**
in a wind of **raw rains** and **fish-gut stains**
on **concrete cracks** pass the **fishing shacks**
where the **oysters** fall on their **broken backs**

        and the stones listened and the sea sung
        and the tide crept in with fingers of foam
        and slices of polystyrene
        and the blue buoys and the fishlines spun
        old tales of shanty songs and ice-cream

1992, the kids at school, and it's time to be cool
a mature stude up the hill at the universe/city
into **Whitstabubble** for the night for the vibe
where the **Africans** played in the **Oyster Stores** and
that's where **Miriam danced**
busting **djembe rhythms** through **English arteries**
that's where **Miriam danced**
and we danced like crazy **crazy** crazy
maybe we knew she'd be dead by '93
and the **cute guy** with the **lead guitar**
couldn't take his eyes off me in my **blue 'alter top**
or maybe was the **busty bitch** at the back
waving her arms like she was on **crack**

        and the stones listened and the sea sung
        and the tide crept in with fingers of foam
        and slices of polystyrene
        and the blue buoys and the fishlines spun
        old tales of shanty songs and ice-cream

1992 European poets and me
are eating **posh fish** at tables with the powers that be
talking of the trip the **P&O ships** will   hoist us across the **sea**
and **fish** will be the **taste** that lines our **tongue**
from **Nord pas de Calais** to **Bruges**
the **Irish poet** who **didn't like fish**
nipped out each course for a **fag** and a **craick**
        there had to be a **catch** to this **poetry lark**

                                    and the stones listened...

2010 and we tumble off the train   walk
the long walk pass the **antique shops**
100 quid! for the *washboard* your gran chucked out in 1959
and the caf's brought back *the old wood floors*
they'd *linoed* back in '78
£6.95! for a bowl of carrot soup **12 quid**
a *bag of lavender* wrapped in violet check
but what the heck it's called living

                                    and the stones listened...

a voice across the way
'Ah don't give a monkey's fart about Art
Ave cummere for the charity shops!'

                                    and the sea sung...
                        and the tide creeps in with fingers of foam...
                    old tales of shanty songs   and ice-cream.

DALJIT NAGRA

Look We Have Coming To Dover!

> *So various, so beautiful, so new...*
>   MATTHEW ARNOLD, 'Dover Beach'

Stowed in the sea to invade
the alfresco lash of a diesel-breeze
ratcheting speed into the tide, brunt with
gobfuls of surf phlegmed by cushy come-and-go
tourists prow'd on the cruisers, lording the ministered waves.

Seagull and shoal life
vexing their blarnies upon our huddled
camouflage past the vast crumble of scummed
cliffs, scramming on mulch as thunder unbladders
yobbish rain and wind on our escape hutched in a Bedford van.

Seasons or years we reap
inland, unclocked by the national eye
or stabs in the back, teemed for breathing
sweeps of grass through the whistling asthma of parks,
burdened, ennobled – poling sparks across pylon and pylon.

Swarms of us, grafting in
the black within shot of the moon's
spotlight, banking on the miracle of sun –
span its rainbow, passport us to life. Only then
can it be human to hoick ourselves, bare-faced for the clear.

Imagine my love and I
our sundry others, Blair'd in the cash
of our beeswax'd cars, our crash clothes, free,
we raise our charged glasses over unparasol'd tables
East, babbling our lingoes, flecked by the chalk of Britannia!

GRACE NICHOLS

Seven Sisters

Seven sisters standing
shoulder to chalky shoulder –
Seven sisters huddling to Sussex mist
open-armed to sun's expansive kiss
yet straight and firm as Victorian maidens
all kin to Dover – the green-shawled
                    grandmother of all cliffs.

GRACE NICHOLS

Hurricane Hits England

It took a hurricane, to bring her closer
To the landscape
Half the night she lay awake,
The howling ship of the wind,
Its gathering rage,
Like some dark ancestral spectre,
Fearful and reassuring:

Talk to me Huracan
Talk to me Oya
Talk to me Shango
And Hattie
My sweeping, back-home cousin.

Tell me why you visit
An English coast?
What is the meaning
Of old tongues
Reaping havoc
In new places?

The blinding illumination,
Even as you short-
Circuit us
Into further darkness?

What is the meaning of trees
Falling heavy as whales
Their crusted roots
Their cratered graves?

O why is my heart unchained?

Tropical Oya of the Weather,
I am aligning myself to you,
I am following the movement of your winds,
I am riding the mystery of your storm.

Ah, sweet mystery,
Come to break the frozen lake in me,
Shaking the foundations of the very trees
within me,
Come to let me know
That the earth is the earth is the earth.

GRACE NICHOLS

Long Man

(For Barbara Cole who first introduced us to the Long Man;
for Jan and Tim who came along, and to
The Druid Way *by Philip Carr-Gomm)*

On open downland we're as open as he
Me and Jan, Tim and John,
Kalera and Ayesha,
and the cracked-sun
has once again withdrawn
leaving us to windy shawls
and pewtery greys
to newly mowed down
fecund-earth, which the rains
have furrowed into clay.

Plod-Plod
through the caking-blood
of England's sod,
our good shoes growing
sulkier by the minute,
as is my five-year-old,
whose hand, a sixth-sense
tells me to hold,
despite her intermittent tugging –.
on this our Hill-God pilgrimage.

And even when she manages
to break free, I'm after her
a wiser Demeter –
swift-footed and heavy
with apprehension –
sensing the weald-spirits.
A primitive pull
of the pagan dimension.

'We're off to see the Long Man.
the wonderful Long Man of Wilmington,'
I chant, humouring her
over the timeless witchery
of the landscape.

Meanwhile as always, he's there
looming out of the green coombe
of Windover's womb.

In our heart-searching
and soul-yearning
we stand before him.
But soon our luminous eyes
are nailing him with
a crucifixion of questions
Who and Why and How
he came to be. Male, female,
or ancient presage of androgyny?

With the sun back out
surely he is benevolent Corn-God
and Shepherd of the good harvest?

Sun-in and he's
the Phantom-symbol
of all foreboding;
the Gate-Keeper-Reaper
who would reap us in;
the faceless frozen traveler;
Moon-gazer;

Green-man-mirror
tricking our eyeballs on –
the cunning chameleon.

But going back over
the wet green swelling,
the presumptuous goddess in me
looks back and catches him
off guard –
poor wounded man
the staves in his arms
no barrier for –
She-who-would-break-them
and take him in her arms.

LOUISA ADJOA PARKER

Forest-child

That night we made you
in the forest,
lying in the orange two-man tent
in the middle of tall trees
dark like patterned cloth.

I woke next morning
listening to woodpigeons
rolling the sounds of summer
like toffees in their throats.
(The first time I ever really heard
the rhythm of their coos.)

      I dreamed you into being –
a child-shaped star falling
through the forest sky, lighting it with hope
like a Catherine wheel;
finding me, finding your home in me.

LOUISA ADJOA PARKER

Velvet Dresses

I want to climb under Dorset's skin
curl up in her folds, wrap her around me
like a patchwork quilt, stained
yet stitched with years of love,
taste the colours of green and gold,
run my fingers over rough textures
of ancient earth.

I want to crawl under her pavements,
her roads; lift great slabs of tarmac,
climb every craggy, awkward hill,
every cliff like a tooth capped with gold;
trek for miles through woods
and green fields like velvet dresses
with skirts fanned out wide;

I want to sink my fingers into the earth
let the tiny stones and grit and bones
run through my hands;
search for the past along with
fossils spiralling to dust
in clay-rich soil.

I want to let Dorset's past soak
like cocoa butter into my skin,
let its history merge with mine:
talk of Africa and her slaves.
I want to know it will be fine
for anyone with *not from here* etched
like tribal markings into their skin,
to sink into Dorset like a warm rock-pool,
with fingers stretched out towards the sun;
to walk her beaches, green-velvet fields
with pride, say

I live here, belong here, she's mine.

KIM O'LOUGHLIN

Play

You climbed the shingle mountain
and threw yourself down

your descent a dark scar
on the sun-dried stones

the wind stole
your laughter

your mouth
filled with sand.

I followed your scratch-line
as it looped around rocks,

as it spiralled dangerously
close to the tide.

We fought
with driftwood swords.

We argued
about when to leave.

So you wandered away
too far for me to call you back.

I yelled your name
until my throat was sore.

Then discarded child's play
like a too-small coat

and marched you home.

KIM O'LOUGHLIN

Burton Beach

The day is a murmur, the sun has blinded it, scorched
out its tongue. I walk towards a headland eaten by heat.
Where tide pulls back over shingle it leaves a ribbon of mauve
that slithers into a distance alive with gulls

that wheel and dive and seem to wait like vultures.
At my feet green seaweed, bright as stained glass, glistens.
Three women strip to seduce the sun, stretch out their silvered bodies,
their sand-haired children squeal in the surf.

I think of him too often. He steps into my head
like an actor on cue with lines that take me by surprise.
The day should scream and wail,
but the sun has made it dumb.

I write his name on stones and bury them.
I write his name on stones and hurl them into the sea.

KIM O'LOUGHLIN

The Dream

Beneath the quilt's plump skin her body fights
as sleep rolls clammy palms around her limbs,
below the house a cow screams in the night;
mellow hoops of sound shot through with pins.

Hordes of Friesian children flood her dreams
like whitebait surf-thrown onto shingle.
They writhe and drown in piebald silver gleams
slubs of light where child and cattle mingle.

As birdsong wrestles for its field of air
she emerges, fog-headed from the deep;
the morning whistles secrets through her hair
of all she knew, that now skips out of reach.

Sunshine swaddles flesh in golden robes,
gilds fishscales, dries out eyes to paper globes.

SUDEEP SEN

Line Breaks
a fragment from a longer work

PROOF-READING ON THE PHONE, POEMS IN PROSE,
ON MILK-WHITE PAGES, AS MARY AND I WALKED,
TALKING IN THE RAIN

1 *Devon*

Far from Edinburgh
here at Arvon's

hot drying room,
where a shrivelled

pair of jeans
hung on a hanger,

amidst copper pipes,
glass-encased books

of poems, and an
open bathroom door,

the telephone rang,
and rang repeatedly.

2 *Moor*

Mary asked me
if I would go out

for a walk with her
in the rain, to feel

the white backs
of sheep on the hill.

'Only after
the telephone call,'

I said, that is if she
could wait that long.

3 *Line Breaks*

I remember
talking

about the
peculiarities of

page-proofs,
type-faces,

paper-weights,
trying to

proof-read every
line-break,

long-distance
on the line.

LOUISA ADJOA PARKER

Beach Huts on Paignton Beach

Next to bone-white beach huts
in the half-dark, where red and green lights

hang like beaded necklaces, strung
against the sky, I want to tell the woman

with the little boy who trails behind her,
while she calls out *Charlie*

every now and then as though the word
will reach him, wrap itself around him

like rope; pull him close, I want to say
I lived here once, I lived here, me.

KAREN McCARTHY WOOLF

The Beach at Clovelly

Although Melissa dropped
her birthday cake in a strop
it didn't matter
because we'd had such fun
walking up cliffs
with the wind on our faces.
Wavey-Davey brewed tea
on his camping stove
and everyone gathered round him
as if he were a bonfire.
We drank like Vikings
squeezing red wine
out of a silver bladder,
courtesy of Larry
who retrieved a dead pheasant

from a tunnel in the rocks.
Manda wanted to look like
Marianne Faithfull in *Girl on a Motorcycle*
– and she did.
Gary filmed everything on his Super 8
while Jean strode about in a hat.
People took photos
of people taking photos.
Bim was quiet.
The tide was coming in.

KAREN McCARTHY WOOLF

Looe

Oh yes, we're friendly to strangers who flock
to the seaside, we like to make new pals.
You're a seedling I plan to harden off.

You bob about in me like a beach ball.
A mother wades out with her teenage daughter
whose waist contracts with every icy swell.

I wonder if I'll be enough of a layer.
You'll be fine she nods as I close my eyes
and plunge my head under the water.

LEMN SISSAY

A Black Man on the Isle of Wight

Faces cold as the stone stuck
to the sea's belly
with seaweed for hair
sculpted into expressions of fear.

LIZZY DIJEH

United Kingdom

A small island of three countries from across the ocean,

A Crown hand-delivered to the Pied Piper – *her* Ring-O-Roses –
Her cartwheel of blind mice – once

as impenetrable as set cement,
as flawless as an untouched wedding-cake,

twisted round and round like mixed mortar, talking in rhymes,
meaning different things to different people.

Once I sought to break in, suggested a re-union,
offered up stately hymns and selected a line of clear vows

we could all sing to. But all three insisted on veils
and I grew tired of standing at the altar.

I remember how I shied when Solitaire beamed
her undisguised brilliance,

how I cried when the teeth of Eternity flashed
her hard diamonds,

The Good, The Bad –
two-thirds of the same band

seated like proud parents on either side of the solid hoop,
a heavy blanket of spun metal wrapped around her carat-finger,

and I, now the sole witness who threw them at her.

CONTRIBUTORS

Leila Aboulela was born in Cairo and grew up in Khartoum. Her novels, *The Translator* and *Minaret*, were longlisted for the Orange Prize. She lives between Doha and Aberdeen.

Shanta Acharya was born in India, educated at Oxford and Harvard and lives in London. An internationally published poet, the latest of her five collections is *Dreams That Spell The Light* (Arc Publications, 2010). Penelope Shuttle describes her as a poet with 'a wondrous gift for evoking place'. www.shantaacharya.com

John Agard. Once described as a 'Guyanese-born word magician', Agard has been a pivotal figure of the black British poetry scene for the past 30 years. His work gives 'an outsider-insider view of British life in poems which both challenge and cherish our peculiar culture and hallowed institutions'.

Patience Agbabi was born in London in 1965, and educated at Oxford and Sussex Universities. She is a renowned performance poet whose work has also appeared on the London Underground. She has taught Creative Writing in Kent and Cardiff.

Rizwan Akhtar was born in Lahore, Pakistan. He is currently reading for his PhD at the University of Essex. His poems have appeared in *Poetry Salzburg Review*, *Poetry NZ*, *Wasafiri*, *Postcolonial Text*, *decanto*, *Poesia*, *Exiled Ink*, *Pakistaniat: A Journal of Pakistani Studies*, *Solidarity International*, *Orbis*, *Other Poetry*, *South Asian Review*, *Gutter*, *ScottishPen*, *tinfoildresses*, and in anthologies.

Moniza Alvi was born in Pakistan and grew up in Hertfordshire. After living in London for many years, she now lives in Norfolk. Her most recent collections of poetry are *Split World: Poems 1990-2005*, *Europa*, and *Homesick for the Earth*, her versions of the French poet Jules Supervielle.

Panya Banjoko is a graduate of Nottingham Trent and Nottingham universities. Her first published work was 'Brain Drain' published in *IC3: An Anthology of New Black Writing in Britain* (2000). Her work includes *Bibi's Museum Adventure* (2008) and *Hari at the Castle* (2010). She writes a blog called hair encounters: http://hairencounters.blogspot.com

Louise Bennett was born in Kingston, Jamaica in 1919, and lived and worked in London during the 1940s. Her often humorous poems, written and performed in Jamaican creole, earned her regular slots on the BBC during WWII. Notable works include *Jamaica Labrish* (1966), *Anancy and Miss Lou* (1979) and *Aunty Roachy Seh* (1993).

Jay Bernard is from London. She is the 2011/2012 writer-in-residence at the NUS University Scholars Programme and The Arts House, Singapore. Her first chapbook *Your Sign is Cuckoo, Girl* (Tall Lighthouse) was PBS pamphlet choice for summer 2008.

James Berry remains one of the most influential poets and anthologisers of black British poetry. Born in Jamaica, he came to England in 1948 and took a job working for British Telecom. His two seminal anthologies are *Bluefoot Traveller* (1976) and *News for Babylon* (1984). His most recent book is *A Story I Am In: Selected Poems* (2011).

Rajat Kumar Biswas was born in India and graduated from Presidency College, University of Calcutta. He worked in London's public libraries and was interested in travel, cricket and photography. A bilingual poet, his publications include: *A Flat for Sale and Other Poems, Mukhosh O Anyanya Kabita* and *The Lascar's Song*.

Malika Booker is a writer, spoken word and multidisciplinary artist. She has performed internationally and was Hampton Court Palace Writer in Residence in 2004. She jointly runs Malika's Kitchen, a writers' collective based in London and Chicago.

Siddhartha Bose is a writer, performer, and a Leverhulme Fellow in Drama at the University of London. He grew up in India, lived in the US and now resides in Hackney. His first book, *Kalagora*, appeared in 2010, and his one-man play recently completed an acclaimed run at Edinburgh Fringe. www.kalagora.com

Kamau Brathwaite was born in Barbados in 1930 and lived in Britain during the 1950s and 1960s, becoming a leading figure the London-based Caribbean Artists Movement (CAM). One of the leading poets of his generation, Brathwaite is also an internationally respected historian of the West Indies and is currently Professor of Comparative Literature at New York University.

Jean 'Binta' Breeze is a poet, storyteller and choreographer internationally recognised for her artistry and writing on the 'Dub' art form. She is the author of five poetry collections including *Riddym Ravings, Spring Cleaning* and her latest, *Third World Girl: Selected Poems*. Cited as a 'one-woman festival' she was the recipient of a NESTA Award and in 2011, became an Honorary Fellow at University of Leicester.

Sue Brown was born in Birmingham in 1961, and her parents came from Jamaica. She says 'I've seen many changes along my journey; people, places, rules, the spoken and the unspoken all have had an impact on my life and creativity. My writing explores and reflects these moments.'

Jeff Caffrey's love of film was fuelled by Ridley Scott. This led to studying graphic design, graduating into a recession, lengthy unemployment and enrolment on a film MA course, which introduced him to scriptwriting. After an eclectic 20 years he has discovered an AfroCelt voice gilt-edged by Mancunian sensibilities.

Christian Campbell was a Rhodes Scholar at Oxford University and currently lives in Toronto. His first collection of poems, *Running the Dusk* (2010), was described as 'remapping Caribbean, British and African American geographies'. It won the 2010 Aldeburgh First Collection Prize and was shortlisted for the 2010 Forward Prize for the Best First Collection in the UK.

Vahni Capildeo was born in Trinidad and currently lives in the UK. Now a Contributing Editor for the *Caribbean Review of Books*, after a Research Fellowship at Girton College, Cambridge she worked as an academic, an Oxfam volunteer, and on the Oxford English Dictionary. Her third book is *Dark & Unaccustomed Words* (2011).

Eric Ngalle Charles was born in Buea, Cameroon. After crossing many oceans and time zones he ended up in the UK where Cardiff became his 'city of choice'. He has run poetry workshops across South Wales and his work was translated into Welsh at the St David's Eisteddfod (2002).

Leon Charles was born in Wales' Cosmopolitan Capital, Cardiff. He qualified in Mechanical Engineering, Media Studies, and toured with Welsh National Opera as a theatre technician. A member of Academi's excellent Writers On Tour scheme, Leon has taken his educational, motivational workshops, 'Beyond The Barrage', to schools, libraries and youth clubs throughout Wales.

Debjani Chatterjee has been called 'Britain's best-known Asian poet' (Elisabetta Marino). Her many books include *Namaskar: New & Selected Poems* and *Words Spit and Splinter*. She is a patron of Survivors' Poetry. Sheffield Hallam University awarded her an honorary doctorate and in 2008 she received an MBE. www.debjanichatterjee. moonfruit.com

Kayo Chingonyi was born in Zambia in 1987 and came to the UK in 1993. He has since lived in Newcastle, London, Sheffield and Essex. Chingony studied English at Sheffield University where he co-founded a poetry night called 'Word Life'. His debut pamphlet, *Some Bright Elegance*, appeared in 2012.

Maya Chowdhry is a poet and inTer-aCtive artist born in Edinburgh, part of the Asian diaspora, currently residing in Lancashire. Published in *The Seamstress and the Global Garment*, many anthologies and magazines such as *Ambit*. Accolades include the Cardiff International Poetry Competition. Currently exploring haiku sewn in cress. www.mayachowdhry.net

Merle Collins was born in 1950 in Aruba to Grenadian parents. Her first collection of poetry was *Because the Dawn Breaks* (1985), followed by *Rotten Pomerack* in 1992. Collins also writes fiction and her second novel, *The Colour of Forgetting*, was published in 1995. She taught in London from 1984 to 1995 and is currently Professor of Comparative Literature and English at the University of Maryland.

Fred D'Aguiar was born in London in 1960 to Guyanese parents and currently teaches in Virginia where he is Professor of English and African Studies. His highly influential collections include *Mama Dot* (1985), *British Subjects* (1993), *Bill of Rights* (1998) and *Continental Shelf* (2009). He has also been Northern Arts Literature Fellow at Newcastle University.

David Dabydeen was born in 1955 in Guyana, moving to England in 1969. Director of the Centre for Caribbean Studies at the University of Warwick, he is also Guyana's Ambassador-at-Large and a member of UNESCO's Executive Board. His poetry collections include *Slave Song* (1984) and *Turner* (2002). Since the 1990s he has focused increasingly on fiction, most recently *Molly and the Muslim Stick* (2008).

Kwame Dawes is the author of over thirty books. Born in Ghana in 1962, he is currently Professor of English at Nebraska, and a regular visitor to England. Evocative place-based collections like *Midland* (2001) follow what Eavan Boland describes as 'the painful and vivid theme of homelessness in and out of the mysteries of loss and belonging'. His latest collection is *Wheels* (2011).

Imtiaz Dharker is an artist and documentary film-maker, and has published four books with Bloodaxe, *Postcards from god* [including *Purdah*] (1997), *I speak for the devil* (2001), *The terrorist at my table* (2006) and *Leaving Fingerprints* (2009); all include her own drawings. Born in Pakistan, she grew up in Scotland, and now lives between India, London and Wales.

Lizzy Dijeh is a playwright and poet born and raised in East London.

Her play, *High Life*, debuted at the Hampstead Theatre in 2009 and was also shortlisted for the Alfred Fagon Award in 2007. Her poetry has been performed at venues including London's Southbank Centre.

Tishani Doshi is an award-winning poet and dancer of Welsh-Gujarati descent. She was born in India, in the city formerly known as Madras, in 1975. She has lived in the United States, Britain and Italy, but finds herself calling Madras home. *Everything Begins Elsewhere* (Bloodaxe, 2012), is her latest book.

Roshan Doug was born in India in 1963 but since then has lived in Britain. He has travelled extensively both at home and abroad and is currently based in the Midlands. He is a former Poet Laureate of Birmingham (2000-01) and an academic at the university. His poetry deals with belonging and cultural identity.

Richard Grant writes and performs under the name **Dreadlockalien**. An Anglo Indo Caribbean slam poet and a strict advocate for live literature, rarely appearing in print. Birmingham Poet Laureate in 2005-06, his appearances include radio, television and youtube as well as British council trips to India, Japan Poland and South Africa.

Creswell Durrant's recent movements are not known by the editors of this anthology, but his work first appeared in James Berry's influential collection, *News for Babylon* (1984). He was born in St Vincent in 1937 and came to London in 1961 where he became a library worker.

Inua Ellams is a poet, playwright and performer. Descending from the nomadic Hausa people of North Africa, he has lived in Plateau State in Nigeria, Dublin, and London, where he currently resides. He has five books published including his second pamphlet *Candy Coated Unicorns and Converse All Stars* (flipped eye, 2011).

Bernardine Evaristo was born in London to an English mother and Nigerian father. She is the author of two critically acclaimed novels-in-verse, *Lara* (1997/2009) and *The Emperor's Babe* (2001), her novel-with-verse, *Soul Tourists* (2005), and her latest novel, *Blonde Roots* (2008). She was awarded an MBE in 2009.

Marsden Falcon is out of bounds.

John Figueroa was born in Jamaica. He published three collections, and *The Chase* (1991), which collects his poetry into an organisation which reflects his lifelong preoccupations: a synthesising of the spirit and the flesh, the Caribbean and Europe in one vision. He died in 1999.

Bashabi Fraser was born in West Bengal and has since played on the banks of the Thames, travelled along the romantic Tay and settled in the city watered by the Forth and the Water of Leith. A lecturer at Napier University and an Honorary Fellow at Edinburgh University, she lives in Edinburgh with her husband and has one daughter who considers Edinburgh 'home'.

Martin Glynn was born in Nottingham of a Jamaican father and Welsh mother in 1957. His early poems appear in *De Ratchet a Talk* (1985). Now a criminologist, he has also gained an international reputation for his commissioned work in theatre, radio drama, live literature, short fiction for children, and poetry.

Lorna Goodison was born and grew up in Jamaica, where she still has a home. She has taught in Canada and in the United States. She has been a major participant in literature festivals in New York, London and Erlangen, and her poetry and prose are widely anthologised.

Romesh Gunesekera grew up in Sri Lanka and moved to England in 1972, first living in Merseyside, then in London. He is the author of the novel, *Reef*, which was shortlisted for the Booker Prize in 1994. His other books include *Monkfish Moon*, *The Sandglass*, and most recently, *The Prisoner of Paradise* (2012). He is a Fellow of the Royal Society of Literature. www.romeshgunesekera.co.uk

Tajinder Singh Hayer is from Bradford and teaches Creative Writing at Bradford University. Aside from poetry, he has worked in theatre and radio. His writing has been broadcast on BBC Radio 3 and Radio 4; he has had work produced by the West Yorkshire Playhouse and Menagerie Theatre Company.

Maggie Harris was born in Guyana and has lived in Kent since 1972, and Wales since 2006. She has written five collections of poetry, a memoir, *Kiskadee Girl*, a short story collection, *Canterbury Tales on a Cockcrow Morning* and edited *Sixty Poems for Haiti*. She has performed her work internationally and her awards include the Guyana Prize for Literature and Arts Council England New Writing.

Ralph Hoyte is a Bristol-based poet, writer, GPS-triggered locative soundscape writer, director and producer. Residencies/work include Tintagel/English Heritage and Japan/Arts Council Bursary. 'Chew Stoke' was composed as part of his residency with the 'Seven Ages' Project of Bristol European Capital of Culture 2008. The material was derived from talking with Chew Stoke Women's Institute.

Michelle 'The Mother' Hubbard is a founder member of 'Blackdrop', a monthly spoken word event in Nottingham. Freelance workshop facilitator, poet, storyteller, and African drummer. She defines herself as 'Irish-Jamaican' and is the winner of several Slam competitions. Her work is included in several anthologies.

Sadi Husain is currently out of bounds. We'd be delighted to hear from anybody who knows his whereabouts.

Khadijah Ibrahiim is of Jamaican parentage, born in Leeds. She is the Artistic Director of Leeds Young Authors and executive producer of 'Voices of a New Generation' Lit & Slam Festival. Her poetry chapbook, *Rootz Runnin'*, was published in 2008, and her first full-length collection is due in 2012.

Mahmood Jamal is an award-winning filmmaker and poet, he is the editor/translator of *The Penguin Book of Modern Urdu Poetry* (1986) and *Islamic Mystical Poetry* (2009). Jamal has several poetry collections to his name and has been widely anthologised. His *Sugar-coated Pill: Selected Poems* (2006) received critical acclaim. Jamal has produced several documentaries, notably a series called *Islamic Conversation*.

Nabila Jameel is a proud Prestonian, poet and short story writer. Her work has been published by Crocus Books, *Stand*, *Poetry & Audience* and various anthologies. She was runner-up in the Manchester Cathedral International Religious Poetry Competition in 2010.

Amryl Johnson was born in Trinidad and came to England when she was 11. Much of her poetry is concerned with exploring the space she felt she occupied between British and Caribbean culture. Her most famous works include *The Long Road to Nowhere* (1985), *Sequins for a Ragged Hem* (1988) and *Let it be told* (1988). She died in 2001.

Desmond Johnson is the author of *Deadly Ending Season* (Akira Press, 1984). His biography in this collection notes that he 'was born in Kingston, Jamaica in 1962 and came to London in 1980, where he now lives and works'.

Linton Kwesi Johnson was born in Jamaica in 1952. In 1963 he joined his mother in London, and went to Tulse Hill Comprehensive, Brixton. His many acclaimed volumes include *Dread Beat An' Blood* (1975), *Inglan Is A Bitch* (1980), *Tings An' Times* (1991), and *Mi Revalueshanary Fren: Selected Poems*, published in Penguin Modern Classics in 2002. Johnson has performed all over the world, and has been the recipient of many awards. He is an Honorary Fellow of his alma mater, Goldsmiths College.

Anthony Joseph was born in Trinidad and has lived in England since 1989. He writes prose, fiction and poetry and is the author of three poetry collections, *Desafinado* (1994), *Teragaton* (1997) and *Bird Head Son* (2009), and a spoken word CD, *Liquid Textology: Readings From The African Origins of UFOs*.

Pete Kalu is a poet, playwright and novelist. Of Nigerian-Danish heritage, he was born and lives in Manchester. He attended the 'Moss Side Write' black writers workshop in the 1980s, with Lemn Sissay, SuAndi and others. Much of his writing has been focused on the themes of Home and Belonging.

Jackie Kay was born in Edinburgh to a Scottish mother and Nigerian father before being adopted as a baby by a white couple. Kay's awareness of her different heritages inspired her first book of poetry, *The Adoption Papers*, which won the Scottish Arts Council Book of the Year. Subsequent poetry collections, short stories and novels have gone on to win numerous awards. In 2006 Jackie was awarded an MBE. She currently lives in Manchester.

Anthony Kellman is a Barbados-born writer and musician. He edited the celebrated anthology of English-speaking Caribbean poetry, *Crossing Water*, and is the originator of the Caribbean poetic form, Tuk Verse, a poetry form in three 'movements' derived from melodic and rhythmical patterns of Barbados' indigenous folk music.

Shamshad Khan was born in Leeds and now lives and works in Manchester. As well being involved in Commonword (a writing collective) and co-editing poetry, she has published her own volume, *Megalomaniac* (2007) to critical acclaim.

Aimé Kongolo grew up in the Congo and is studying at Swansea University. His poetry has appeared in anthologies, and he has recently published his first solo volume, *Reciprocities / Réciprocités* (Hafan Books, 2009). This collection is in both English and French, and explores contemporary African politics. Aimé writes bilingual free verse, often about contemporary African politics and war, and finding a refuge in love in Wales.

Roi Kwabena was born in Trinidad in 1956. His first collection was *Lament of the Soul*, and marked the beginning of a prolific body of work over the following three decades, including other poetry collections, journals, essays, and children's stories. He was Birmingham's Poet Laureate in 2001-02. He died in 2008.

Judith Lal attended The Norwich School of Art and Design and completed a BA in Cultural Studies before doing an MA in Creative Writing at UEA. She received an Eric Gregory Award in 2001. Her *Flageolets at the Bazaar* was a winner in the 2006 Poetry Business Book and Pamphlet Competition.

George Lamming was born in Barbados in 1927 and came to England in the spring of 1950. Before establishing himself as one of the leading novelists and essayists of his generation, Lamming's poetry was published in the Caribbean Little Magazine, *Bim* and broadcast on the BBC's *Caribbean Voices* programme. He returned to the Caribbean in the 1960s, and has since lived and worked in various parts of the world.

Tariq Latif was born near Lahore before coming to England. After graduating from Sheffield University he working in Manchester for fifteen years in the family printing business. He has recently moved to the outbacks of Argyll and Bute where he spends his free time roaming the Scottish Highlands. His most recent collection is *The Punjabi Weddings* (2007)

Segun Lee-French is a 'Nigerian Mancunian' and a singer, poet, composer, playwright and film-maker. He believes that, given the desire and the opportunity, anybody can do anything. Segun's work is inspired by jazz, reggae, hiphop and the Beat poets. Segun has lived and worked in France and Spain, and is fluent in French and Spanish.

Carol Leeming was born and partly raised in Leicester and Jamaica. She describes herself as a Mother, Grandmother, Polymath, Cultural Visionary and Activist. She writes poetry and plays for the stage and for broadcast and describes herself as 'Madame of the Poetry Brothel UK, an urban griot chronicling from the heart of the Middle Lands of England'.

Hannah Lowe was born in Ilford to an English mother and Jamaican-Chinese father. She studied American Literature at the University of Sussex and has a Masters degree in Refugee Studies. Currently she lives in Brixton and teaches literature and creative writing. She has published a pamphlet, *The Hitcher* (2011), and her first book-length collection, *Chick*, is out from Bloodaxe in 2013.

John Lyons was born in Trinidad, and studied at Goldsmiths College and the Newcastle University. His many part-time jobs range from factory cleaner to creative writing lecturer at Bolton Institute of Higher Education. He has six published collections, most recently

Cool-up In a Trini Kitchen (2009). His work was also collected in *Sun Rises in the North* (1991) a pioneering volume in bringing a regional British perspective to black and Asian poetry.

Roy McFarlane was born in Birmingham of Jamaican parentage and writes poetry, plays and short stories. His poems have appeared in magazines and anthologies including *Celebrate Wha* (2011) which he co-edited. He is a former Starbucks poet in residence, Birmingham Poet Laureate and is presently working on his first collection of poetry.

Claude McKay was a poet, novelist and short story writer, and a foundational figure in the Harlem Renaissance. His early dialect verse appears in *Songs of Jamaica* (1912) and *Constab Ballads* (1912). He lived in London between 1919 and 1921.

Sheree Mack was born in Bradford to a Trinidadian father and a Geordie mother of Bajan and Ghanaian heritage. She has recently completed a PhD in Creative Writing at Newcastle University. Her first full collection of poetry is called *Family Album* (2011).

Nick Makoha fled Uganda, because of the civil war during the Idi Amin dictatorship. He has lived in Kenya, Saudi Arabia and currently resides in London. As a Spoke-Lab resident he developed a one-man show, 'My Father & Other Superheroes', which reveals how pop culture raised him in the absence of his father.

Hazel Malcolm was born and grew up in the Black Country, West Midlands. She comes from a large Caribbean family which has been a source and inspiration for much of her writing. She enjoys experimenting with various forms of writing, but mainly produces poetry and short stories.

Jack Mapanje was born in Malawi and imprisoned without trial by the Malawian government between 1987 and 1991 on the basis of his first collection *Of Chameleons and Gods* (1981). This was followed by *The Chattering Wagtails of Mikuyu Prison* (1993) which he composed in jail. Mapanje has taught at the Universities of Leeds and Newcastle and currently lives in York. His latest publications are two poetry books, *The Last of the Sweet Bananas* (2004) and *Beasts of Nalunga* (2007), and his prison memoir *And Crocodiles Are Hungry at Night* (2012).

E.A. Markham was born in Montserrat in 1939 and based mainly in Britain and elsewhere in Europe after 1956. As well as living in London he made his home in Hull, Lampeter, Manchester, Newcastle, and in Sheffield, where he was Professor of Creative Writing. As a poet and short story writer he was prolific (he wrote over 30 volumes), if relatively neglected during his lifetime. He was also an influential editor of poetry. He died in 2008.

D.S. Marriott was born in Nottingham in 1963 of Jamaican parentage and was educated at the University of Sussex. He has lived and worked in Brighton and London and currently teaches at the University of California. He is the author of *Incognegro* (2006), *Hoodoo Voodoo* (2008) and *The Bloods* (2011).

Una Marson was born in Jamaica in 1905. In 1928 she launched her own magazine, *The Cosmopolitan*, followed in 1930 by her self-published collection of poems, *Tropic Reveries*. Between 1932 and 1945, Marson lived mostly in England and London, and her poetry was marked by her confrontation with racism there. Her work with the BBC led to the creation of the hugely influential *Caribbean Voices* programme.

Cheryl Martin was born in Washington, DC, and educated at Cambridge. Her poetry appears in the anthologies *The Fire People* (Payback Press) and *The Sun Rises in the North* (Smith/Doorstop Press). She wrote the poetry documentary *Lush Life* (dir. John Akomfrah) which was screened by Granada and Manchester's Cornerhouse Cinema, and the Granada television drama *Blue Irises*.

Tariq Mehmood's first two novels *Hand on the Sun* (1983) and *While There is Light* (2003) are set against a youth fight back against racism in Yorkshire, where he lived, campaigned, was imprisoned and acquitted. He is the co-director of *Injustice*, a film that deals with deaths in police custody. He teaches at the American University of Beirut, Lebanon.

Irfan Merchant was born in Liverpool in 1973, and brought up in Ayr. He has lived in Edinburgh and London, and has recently returned to live in Ayr. His poetry has been published in diverse places, including *Wish I Was Here: A Scottish Multicultural Anthology* and *The Redbeck Anthology of British South Asian Poetry*. The poems here are previously unpublished.

Kei Miller was born in Jamaica and currently teaches Creative Writing at the University of Glasgow. He has published collections of poetry (*Kingdom of the Empty Bellies, There Is an Anger That Moves, A Light Song of Light*) and short fiction (*The Fear of Stones*) to critical acclaim. He is editor of *New Caribbean Poetry: An Anthology* (2007).

Sudesh Mishra was born in Suva and educated in Fiji and Australia. He taught at Stirling University in the late 1990s and early 2000s. He is author of four books of poems, including *Tandava* and *Diaspora* and the *Difficult Art of Dying*, two critical monographs, and two plays

(*Ferringhi* and *The International Dateline*). He is currently a Professor at the University of the South Pacific.

Raman Mundair writes poetry, short stories and plays. She was born in India and came to live in the UK at the age of five. She is the author of two volumes of poetry, *A Choreographer's Cartography* and *Lovers, Liars, Conjurers and Thieves*, both published by Peepal Tree Press.

George Murevesi was born and raised in Zimbabwe but in 2007 he relocated to Scotland where he currently lives. In Scotland he started writing and performing poetry with the Seeds of Thought Poetry Group. His other activities and interests include radio broadcasting, organising community events and reading.

Tinashe Mushakavanhu was born in Harare, Zimbabwe. He graduated with a first class honours degree in English from Midlands State University and became the first African to receive an MA Creative Writing from Trinity College, Carmarthen in Wales. He co-edited *State of the Nation: Contemporary Zimbabwean Poetry* (2009).

Daljit Nagra was born and raised in West London, then Sheffield, and currently lives in Willesden. His first collection, *Look We Have Coming to Dover!* won the 2007 Forward Prize for Best First Collection and was shortlisted for the Costa Poetry Award. In 2008 he won the South Bank Show / Arts Council Decibel Award. His latest collection is *Tippoo Sultan's Incredible White-Man-Eating Tiger Toy-Machine!!!*

Grace Nichols came to Britain from Guyana at the age of 27 is the celebrated author of *I is a long memoried woman* (1983) and *The Fat Black Woman's Poems* (1984). Her recent collection, *Picasso, I Want My Face Back* (2009) weaves together art, landscape and memory. Of Nichols it has been said 'she has carried the warmth of the Caribbean sensibility through many a cold English winter'.

Kim O'Loughlin was born in Birmingham in 1958. At seventeen she escaped to the dramatic hills of County Durham. With her first taste of the English countryside she began writing about landscape and her place within it. Kim now lives on the West Dorset coast and works on the land.

Louisa Adjoa Parker has lived in the West Country (Devon then Dorset) since she was 13. Her poetry collection, *Salt-sweat and Tears* was published in 2007. Louisa is of Ghanaian heritage, and started writing to talk about the racism she experienced in rural areas. Her poetry is inspired by, and reflects, the landscape in which she lives.

Nii Ayikwei Parkes is an author and performance poet who has performed on major stages across the world. Nii is the Senior Editor at flipped eye publishing. His first full-length poetry collection is *The Makings of You* (Peepal Tree Press), and his latest novel is *Tail of the Blue Bird* (Jonathan Cape).

Sandeep Parmar was born in Nottingham and raised in California. She has written on the modernist poets Mina Loy and Hope Mirrlees. Her debut poetry collection was *The Marble Orchard* (2012). She is the Reviews Editor for *The Wolf* poetry magazine and a Visiting Fellow at Clare Hall, Cambridge.

R. Parthasarathy is an Indian poet, translator, critic, and editor. His books include *Rough Passage* (1977), a long poem; *Ten Twentieth-Century Indian Poets* (1976), an anthology; and *The Tale of an Anklet: An Epic of South India* (1993), a translation of a Tamil epic. He is a Professor Emeritus of English and Asian Studies, Skidmore College, Saratoga Springs, New York.

Gabriela Pearse was born in Columbia of a Trinidadian mother and English father and raised in South America, the Caribbean and England. One of Britain's pioneering black women poets of the 1980s, her work was collected in the landmark volume, *A Dangerous Knowing* (1984).

Marsha Prescod was born in Trinidad and came to England in the 1950s. Her first collection of poetry was *Land of Rope and Tory*. Her work often combines humour and politics and, as the blurb on her first collection puts it 'the flavour of her language is undoubtedly Nation Language'.

James Procter teaches at Newcastle University. His publications on black British and British Asian writing include *Writing Black Britain* (MUP, 2000) and *Dwelling Places* (MUP, 2003).

Shampa Ray is a regular contributor to the *Edinburgh Review*. Her work has been collected in *Wish I Was Here: A Scottish Multicultural Anthology* (2000).

Gemma Robinson teaches at the University of Stirling. She is the editor of Martin Carter's *University of Hunger: Collected Poems and Selected Prose* (Bloodaxe Books, 2006).

Roger Robinson is a Trinidadian writer and performer who has lived in London for 20 years. He has received numerous commissions and was chosen by the Arts Council England and Decibel as one of the most influential writers on Black-British writing canon over the past

50 years. He is a co-founder of Malika's Kitchen and was programme co-coordinator of Apples & Snakes. Roger has published a two poetry collections, *Suitcase* (2004) and *Suckle* (2009), which won The People's Book Prize.

Kokumo Rocks was born in Dundee, but was raised in the Fife mining village of Cowdenbeath. Hers was the only black family in the area, and she left school with no qualifications and an inability to spell. Since then, she has published two books and spoken to countless individuals about the appreciation of poetry. She has performed in the UK, USA, Canada, India and Africa.

Joy Russell is a Belize born writer, poet and assistant producer. She lived in London for many years. Her writing has appeared most recently in *The Fire People: A Collection of Contemporary Black British Poets* (1998), *IC3: The Penguin Book of New Black Writing in Britain* (2000), and *Bluesprint: Black British Columbian Literature and Orature* (2001).

Suhayl Saadi, the Glasgow-based novelist, playwright and radio writer has been described as 'one of the most prolific and innovative British Asian writers of the past decade...'. His novel *Psychoraag* was described by *The List* magazine/Scottish Book Trust as one of the hundred most important Scottish books of all time. His latest novel, *Joseph's Box* was nominated for the IMPAC Prize 2011. www.suhaylsaadi.com

Andrew Salkey was born in Panama in 1928 and died in Massachusetts in 1995. He was a leading artist of the first wave of West Indian migrants to Britain after World War II. As well as poems, short stories and novels, Salkey was an influential editor of Caribbean poetry and prose.

Jacob Sam-La Rose is a London-based poet, freelance artistic director and editor. His poetry has been described as 'fresh, vivid and masterly in its evocation of contemporary Britain' (Poetry Book Society) and he's known for his work in support of emerging poets through educational settings and arts institutions around the world. His first book-length collection, *Breaking Silence*, came out in 2011.

Ashna Sarkar was born in 1992 in London to two imminently divorcing social workers. A young writer with more eyeliner than sense, Ashna's poetry takes you on a guided tour from Camden Lock to the Surrey Downs, charting the perils of adolescence. She was dubbed 'Britain's hippest young Asian poet' by Roddy Lumsden.

Michelle Scally-Clarke is a performance poet based in Leeds. Her turbulent early life was recounted in *I Am*, a memoir written when she was 30. Her first full collection *She Is* was published in 2003. Both books are published by Route and contain CDs of Michelle in performance.

Moqapi Selassie has been a performance poet in the West Midlands for many years. Selections of his work can be found in *Black Men and Black Women in Love* (1997), *Five Birmingham Poets* (2006) and *Celebrate Wha? Ten Black British Poets from the Midlands* (2011).

Sudeep Sen's books include *Postmarked India: New & Selected Poems* (HarperCollins), *Distracted Geographies, Rain, Aria|Anika* (A.K. Raman-ujan Translation Award), *Ladakh, Blue Nude: Poems & Translations 1977-2012* (Jorge Zalamea International Poetry Prize) and *The Harper-Collins Book of English Poetry* (editor). He is editorial director of AARK ARTS and editor of *Atlas.* www.sudeepsen.net

Seni Seneviratne is a poet, creative artist and qualified psychotherapist. Her debut poetry collection, *Wild Cinnamon and Winter Skin,* was published in 2007, and her second collection, *The Heart of It,* from Peepal Tree in 2012.

John Siddique is the author of *Full Blood, Recital – An Almanac, Poems From A Northern Soul,* and *The Prize.* He is the co-author of the story/memoir *Four Fathers.* He has contributed poems, stories, essays and articles to many publications, including *Granta, The Guardian, Poetry Review* and *The Rialto.* www.johnsiddique.co.uk

Anita Sivakumaran was born in Madras, India, and lived in Lan-caster through her mid-20s before marrying a Londoner and moving to Leicester. She recently won the Grassroutes commission to write about Leicester. She has been long-listed for the Montreal International Poetry Prize, and her first collection of poetry, *Sips That Make A Poison Woman,* is published by Ravenglass.

Siffre, Labi: Born: 1945. Since 1949: Homosexual. Since 1951: Atheist. Since 1959: Thinker. Since 1960: Black. Since 1961: Muscian. Since 1963: Songwriter. Since 1964: In (now 'civil') partnership. Since 1984: Poet (collections: *Nigger/Blood on the Page/Monument*). Embraces critical thinking. Opposes nationalism/conservatism. Made own place/ location (see 'La Grande Illusion' in *BOTP*).

Gerry Singh was born in Glasgow in 1957 of an Indian father and Scottish mother, and brought up by foster parents. His great love of the Scottish Highlands is reflected in his poetry

Lemn Sissay is the author of five collections of poetry. Published by Canongate Books, his sculpture poem *Gilt of Cain* was unveiled by

Bishop Desmond Tutu. He has also written plays for stage and BBC radio. He is the first poet to write for the Olympics 2012 and received an MBE from the Queen for Services to Literature.

Tawona Sithole was raised in Zimbabwe with oral traditions that celebrate the values of his ancestral family, Moyo Chirandu. Co-founder of Seeds of Thought, an arts collective in Glasgow, he expresses his heritage through mbira music, poetry and as a playwright and educator.

Dorothea Smartt is a poet and live artist of Bajan descent. She is the author of two collections of poetry, *Connecting Medium* and *Ship Shape*, both published by Peepal Tree Press. Her work is widely anthologised, most recently in *Caribbean Erotic*, and in *Red: Contemporary Black British Poetry*.

Rommi Smith is a poet and playwright. In 2007 she was appointed Parliamentary Writer in Residence, the first such appointment in British history. In 2010-11 Rommi was Poet in Residence at Keats House, London. Her *Selected Poems* is a Poetry Book Society Pamphlet Choice. Rommi has been awarded a Hedgebrook Fellowship in the US, to complete her next collection. www.rommi-smith.co.uk

Mahendra Solanki was born in Nairobi in 1956 of Indian parents. He is the author of *What You Leave Behind*, *Exercises in Trust* and *Shadows of My Making*. His poems have appeared in *The Observer*, *Poetry Review* and *The Rialto* and broadcast on Radio 4. He teaches at Nottingham Trent University.

Saradha Soobrayen was born in London in 1974. She is the Poetry Editor of *Chroma*. Her poems have been published in *Poetry Review*, *Wasafiri*, *Red: Contemporary Black British Poetry*, *The Forward Anthology 2008* and *Oxford Poets Anthology 2007*. She received an Eric Gregory Award in 2004. *The Guardian* named Saradha as one of the 'Twelve to watch', up and coming new generation of poets.

Wole Soyinka is a Nigerian playwright and poet who lived in Leeds and London in the 1950s. He was awarded the Nobel Prize in Literature in 1986.

SuAndi was born, raised and cultivated in Manchester. She is a Nigerian daughter of a Liverpool mother and has lived and worked internationally yet she always returns home. In 1999 she was awarded an OBE in the Queen's Honours list for her contributions to the Black Arts Sector.

Maud Sulter was born in Glasgow in 1960 of Scots and Ghanaian descent. She was a gifted visual artist, writer, playwright and cultural historian. *As a Blackwoman* is the title of her first volume of poems (1985), and remained the perspective for her explorations across genres. She died in 2008.

Levi Tafari was born in Liverpool. He is the author of four poetry collections: *Duboetry* (1987), *Liverpool Experience* (1989), *Rhyme Don't Pay* (1998) and *From the Page to the Stage* (2006). His plays have been performed at the Unity Theatre and the Playhouse in Liverpool, as well as at the Blackheath Theatre in Stafford. He made a well received film about Rastafarianism for BBC television's Everyman programme entitled *The Road to Zion*.

Kimberly Trusty is a Canadian writer and a secondary school teacher based in Birmingham, the author of a solo collection of poetry, *Darker than Blue*. Her poems have been anthologised in Canada, the United States and the United Kingdom.

Derek Walcott was born in St Lucia, in the West Indies, in 1930. The author of many plays and books of poetry, he was awarded the Queen's Medal for Poetry in 1988, and the Nobel Prize in Literature in 1992. His latest collection, *White Egrets*, won the T.S. Eliot Prize.

Gopi Warrier is a poet, playwright, philanthropist and businessman. He is the author of a number of poetry collections including *Lament of JC: Poems by Gopi Warrier* (1999) and *Vahara: The Secret of Evolution: New and Selected Poems* (2009).

Marie Guise Williams is described in *ICA3: The Penguin Book of New Black Writing* (2000) in Britain as 'a Mancunian who recently moved to London'. Her work has also appeared in *The Fire People* (1998).

Karen McCarthy Woolf is a poet, playwright, editor and short story writer. Her poetry collection *The Worshipful Company of Pomegranate Slicers* (2006) was selected as a *New Statesman* book of the year. A selection of her poems also appeared in *Ten New Poets* (Spread the Word/Bloodaxe). She is the editor of *Bittersweet: Black Women's Poetry*.

Benjamin Zephaniah has said that he lives in two places, Britain and the world. He is also one of Birmingham's most famous poetic exports. As well as poetry collections including *City Psalms* (1992), *Propa Propaganda* (1996), *Too Black, Too Strong* (2001) and *To Do Wid Me* (2012), he has published several novels and children's books.

Zhana was born in New York and moved to London in 1982. She co-founded numerous Black Women's Writing workshops and edited the historically important anthology of poetry and prose, *Sojourn* (1988).

ACKNOWLEDGEMENTS

The poems in this anthology are reprinted from the following books, all by permission of the publishers listed unless stated otherwise. Thanks are due to all the copyright holders cited below for their kind permission:

Leila Aboulela: 'When I First Came to Scotland...' from *Wish I Was Here* (Pocketbooks, 2000). **Shanta Acharya**: 'Aspects of Westonbirt Arboretum' from *Dreams that Spell the Light* (Arc Publications, 2010); 'The Vulnerable Plot of Green' from *Not This, Not That* (Rupa & Co, 1994), by permission of the author. **John Agard**: 'Toussaint L'Ouverture Acknowledges Wordsworth's Sonnet to Toussaint L'Ouverture', 'Listen Mr Oxford don', 'The Embodiment', 'Caribbean Eye Over Yorkshire' and from *Alternative Anthem: Selected Poems* (Bloodaxe Books, 2009). **Patience Agbabi**: 'North(West)ern', 'The London Eye' and 'Postmod:' from *Bloodshot Monochrome* (Canongate, 2008); 'Weights and Measures and Finding a Rhyme for Orange' from *Transformatrix* (Canongate, 2000). **Rizwan Akhtar**: 'Aberdonian Winter', first published in 'New Writing' Scottish PEN (25 May 2011) http://www.scottishpen. org/new-writing/aberdonian-winter **Moniza Alvi**: 'Spring on the Hillside', 'Rural Scene', 'Go Back to England', 'The Double City', 'Arrival 1946' and 'Luckbir' from *Split World: Poems 1990-2005* (Bloodaxe Books, 2008).

Panya Banjoko: 'Arriving', previously unpublished, by permission of the author. **Louise Bennett**: 'De Victory Parade' from *Jamaica Labrish* (Sangsters, 1966). Jay Bernard: 'F12' from *City State: New London Poetry* (Penned in the Margins, 2009), by permission of the author. **James Berry**: 'Roomseeker in London' from *Fractured Circles* (New Beacon Books, 1979) and 'Wanting to Hear Big Ben' from *Windrush Songs* (Bloodaxe Books, 2007), by permission of PFD. 'Beginning in a City, 1948' and 'Migrant in London' from *A Story I Am In: Selected Poems* (Bloodaxe Books, 2011). **Rajat Kumar Biswas**: 'Cambridge' from *The Redbeck Anthology of British South Asian Poetry* (Redbeck Press, 2000), by permission of Mrs Sobha Biswas. **Malika Booker**: 'Hungerford Bridge' from *A Storm Between Fingers* (flipped eye, 2006). **Siddhartha Bose**: 'Sex and the City' and 'Swansong, Mile End' from *Kalagora* (Penned in the Margins, 2010). **Kamau Brathwaite**: 'The Emigrants' from *Rights of Passage* (Oxford University Press, 1967). Jean 'Binta' Breeze: 'The Wife of Bath speaks in Brixton Market' and 'Mi Duck' from *Third World Girl: Selected Poems* (Bloodaxe Books, 2011). **Sue Brown**: 'Birmingham', previously unpublished, by permission of the author.

Jeff Caffrey: 'A Brief History of Manny', previously unpublished, by permission of the author. **Christian Campbell**: 'Ballad of Oxfraud' from *Running the Dusk* (Peepal Tree, 2010). **Vahni Capildeo**: 'Winter: II. Harewood Estate' from *Undraining Sea* (Egg Box Publishing, 2009); 'Monolithicity', first published in *Stand Magazine*; 'Night in the Gardens', first published in the *Caribbean Review of Books*; 'La Poetessa', previously unpublished; 'Shell', first published in *Oxford Magazine*; all by permission of the author. **Eric Ngalle Charles**: 'A Mountain and a Sea' from *Between a Mountain and a*

Sea (Hafan Books, 2003), by permission of the author. **Leon Charles:** 'Tiger Bay (Heart of Wales)', previously unpublished, by permission of the author. **Debjani Chatterjee:** 'Reason for Coming' from *Jade Horse Torso: Poems and Translations* (Sixties Press, 2003); 'Visiting E.M. Forster' from *I Was That Woman* (Hippopotamus Press, 1989); both by permission of the author. **Kayo Chingonyi:** 'Baltic Mill', from *Bedford Square 5* (Ward Wood Publishing, 2011) and subsequently published in *Some Bright Elegance* (Salt Publishing, 2012); 'Denouement', originally appeared in *Verbalized* (British Council South Africa, 2010); 'Andrew's Corner', from *Wasafiri* and subsequently published in *The Best British Poetry 2011* (Salt Publishing, 2011) and *Some Bright Elegance* (Salt Publishing, 2012); 'Berwick Street', commissioned by Inua Ellams for The Mini Midnight Run 2009; all by permission of the author. **Maya Chowdhry:** 'Hurry Curry' and 'Four Corners', from *The Seamstress and the Global Garment* (Crocus Books, 2010); 'My Eyes', from *The Redbeck Anthology of British South Asian Poetry* (Redbeck Press, 2000). **Merle Collins:** 'For the Lumb Bank Group, December 1991', 'Soon Come', 'The Lumb Bank Children', and 'Visiting Yorkshire – Again', from *Rotten Pomerack* (Virago, 1992).

David Dabydeen: 'Coolie Odyssey', from *Coolie Odyssey* (Hansib/Dangaroo, 1998), reprinted with corrections by permission of the author. **Fred D'Aguiar:** 'At the Grave of the Unknown African', 'Home', 'Domestic Flight', and 'I Buried My Father a Complete Stranger', and 'Sonnets from Whitley Bay', from *British Subjects* (Bloodaxe Books, 1993), by permission of the author. **Kwame Dawes:** 'Bristol', 'Umpire at the Portrait Gallery', and 'Birthright', from *New and Selected Poems* (Peepal Tree, 2003). **Imtiaz Dharker:** 'Campsie Fells', 'Lascar Johnnie 1930: Lascar', and 'How to Cut a Pomegranate' and 'Mersey Crossing', from *The terrorist at my table* (Bloodaxe Books, 2006); 'Being good in Glasgow', from *I speak for the devil* (Bloodaxe Books, 2001); all by permission of the publisher; 'Speech balloon', uncollected poem, by permission of the author. **Lizzy Dijeh:** 'Stratford City' and 'United Kingdom', previously unpublished, by permission of the author. **Tishani Doshi:** 'Memory of Wales' from *Everything Begins Elsewhere* (Bloodaxe Books, 2012), by permission of the author. **Roshan Doug:** 'Flash of Independence', 'Sound Bites' and 'Slow Motion', from *The English-knowing Men* (Castle View, 1999), by permission of the author. **Dreadlockalien:** 'Fires burn in Bradford, Rockstone fling innah Oldham', published at http://www.birminghampoets.contactbox.co.uk/dreadlock1.htm; by permission of the author. **Creswell Durrant:** 'Colours', from *Bluefoot Traveller*, ed. James Berry (Thomas Nelson and Sons Ltd, 1981).

Inua Ellams: 'GuerillaGardenWritingPoem', from *Untitled* (Oberon Books, 2010). **Bernardine Evaristo:** extract from *Soul Tourists* (Hamish Hamilton, 2005), by permission of the author; '1949: Taiwo', from *Lara* (Bloodaxe Books, second edition, 2009), by permission of the publisher.

Marsden Falcon: 'It's a big ask...', previously unpublished, by permission of the author. **John Figueroa:** 'Hartlands/Heartlands' from *The Chase* (Peepal Tree, 1992). **Bashabi Fraser:** 'Do' care' and 'Tartan and Turban' from *Tartan and Turban* (Luath, 2004).

Martin Glynn: 'Highfields Style' from *De Ratchet a Talk* (Akira Press, 1985), reprinted with corrections by permission of the author. **Lorna Goodison:** 'To Mr William Wordsworth, Distributor of Stamps for Westmoreland', from *Turn Thanks*, copyright © 1999 by Lorna Goodison, used by permission of the poet and the University of Illinois Press; 'Bam Chi Chi La La: London, 1969' and 'At the Keswick Museum' from *Controlling the Silver* (University of Illinois Press, 2005) and *Goldengrove: New and Selected Poems* (Carcanet Press, 2006). **Romesh Gunesekera:** 'Turning Point', first published in the *London Review of Books* (1989), and 'Frontliners', first published in *Poetry Matters* (1988), both reprinted in *The Redbeck Anthology of British South Asian Poetry* (Redbeck Press, 2000).

Maggie Harris: 'Cwmpengraig, place of stones' and 'Montbretia, Wales' from *After a Visit to a Botanical Garden* (Cane Arrow Press, 2010); 'Timeline Whitstable' and 'Llamas, Cwmpengraig', both previously unpublished, by permission of the author. **Tajinder Singh Hayer:** 'Holy Man' and 'A Seasonal Picture', first published in *Bradford Square* http://www.bradfordsquare.net/sqtexts.asp, and envelope of texts edited by Steve Dearden for Bradford's Stir Festival in 2007. **Ralph Hoyte:** 'Chew Stoke', previously unpublished, by permission of the author. **Michelle Hubbard:** 'Take the girl out of Notts, but you can't take Notts out of the girl!', previously unpublished, by permission of the author. **Sadi Husain:** 'Not in India', from *The Poetry of Protest* (BBC/Longman, 1991), permission outstanding.

Khadijah Ibrahiim: '56 Cowper Street', 'Homespun', 'Home Schooled', 'Grandad's Home Brew', '*Roots* on TV', from 'A Snapshot of Leeds', from *Rootz Runnin'* (Peepal Tree, 2008).

Mahmood Jamal: 'Two Women (I)' and 'Apples and Mangoes' from *Sugar-Coated Pill: Selected Poems* (Word Power Books, 2006). **Nabila Jameel:** 'The Island in Preston', previously unpublished, by permission of the author; 'A Book Closer to Home', first published in *Paraxis*, October 2011, by permission of the author. **Amryl Johnson:** 'Circle of Thorns', previously unpublished, by permission of the author's estate. **Desmond Johnson:** 'Mass Jobe' and 'Ole Charlie Boy' from *Deadly Ending Season* (Akira Press, 1984). **Linton Kwesi Johnson:** 'Di Great Insohrekshan', 'Five Nights of Bleeding', 'It Dread inna Inglan', from *Mi Revalueshanary Fren: Selected Poems* (Penguin Modern Classics, 2002), by permission of the author. **Anthony Joseph:** 'Who passed on Haymarket, winter night?' and 'Blues for Brother Curtis' from *Bird Head Son* (Salt Publishing, 2009).

Pete Kalu: 'Manchester', first published by the Urbis Museum, Manchester; 'The Poet's Song', from *KISS* (Crocus Books, 1994); 'Old Radicals' from *Red: Contemporary Black British Poetry* (Peepal Tree, 2010); all by permission of the author. **Jackie Kay:** 'George Square' and 'In my country' from *Darling: New & Selected Poems* (Bloodaxe Books, 2007); 'Granite', '85th Birthday Poem for Dad' and 'Windows, Lakes' from *Fiere* (Picador, 2011). **Anthony Kellman:** 'Roofs of Yorkshire' from *Wings of a Stranger* (Peepal Tree, 2000). **Shamshad Khan:** 'pot' and 'Isosceles' from *Megalomanic* (Salt Publishing, 2007). **Aimé Kongolo:** 'Non-toxic trust' from *Reciprocities/Réciprocités* (Hafan, 2009), by permission of the author. **Roi Kwabena:** 'From Location:Re' from *In the Moment* (Raka, 2006).

Judith Lal: 'Kestrel' and 'Swallowtail Day' from *Flageolets at the Bazaar* (Smith/Doorstop Books, 2007). **George Lamming:** 'Swans', published in 'Three Poems' in *Bim*, 4.15 (1951). **Tariq Latif:** 'Western Ferry', 'After Lights over Girvan', 'MoonMen' and 'Trefor' from *Punjabi Weddings* (Arc Publications, 2007). **Segun Lee-French:** 'So Many Undone' and 'Rain' from *Praise Songs for Aliens* (Crocus Books, 2009), by permission of the author. **Carol Leeming:** 'Highfields Fantasia' and 'Valley Dreamers', previously unpublished, by permission of the author. **Hannah Lowe:** 'Sausages', forthcoming in *Chick* (Bloodaxe Books, 2013), by permission of the author. **John Lyons:** 'Home is Weyever Yuh Is' from *Lure of the Cascadura* (Bogle-L'Ouverture Publications Ltd, 1989); 'Weather Vane', previously unpublished; 'Drinking up the Drizzle' from *The Sun Rises in the North* (Smith/Doorstop Books, 1991); all by permission of the author.

Roy McFarlane: 'I found my father's love letters', previously unpublished, by permission of the author. **Claude McKay:** 'London' and 'La Paloma in London', from *Complete Poems* (University of Illinois Press, 2004).

Sheree Mack: 'Bonny Baby Contest', previously unpublished, by permission of the author. **Nick Makoha:** 'To My Unborn Son', previously unpublished, by permission of the author. **Hazel Malcolm:** 'Blues in the Black Country', from *Red: Contemporary Black British Poetry* (Peepal Tree, 2010), by permission of the author. **Jack Mapanje:** 'The Seashells of Bridlington North Beach', 'After Celebrating Our Asylum Stories at West Yorkshire Playhouse, Leeds' and 'The First Train to Liverpool (Enfield: Liverpool 1, Stoke 0, 1972)', from *The Last of the Sweet Bananas: New & Selected Poems* (Bloodaxe Books, 2004). **E.A. Markham:** 'Epilogue', 'Ladbroke Grove, 58', 'At the Redland Hotel, Stamford Hill', 'To My Mother, the Art Critic' and 'A Politically-Correct Marriage' from *Looking Out, Looking In, New and Selected Poems* (Anvil Press Poetry, 2009). **D.S. Marriott:** 'The Day Ena Died' from *Hoodoo Voodoo* (Shearsman Books, 2008); 'The Ghost of Averages' from *Incognegro* (Salt Publishing, 2006). **Una Marson:** from 'Spring in England' from *The Moth and the Star* (Una Marson, 1937). **Cheryl Martin:** 'Driving Back from Durham' and 'The Coffee Bearer' from *The Sun Rises in the North* (Smith/Doorstop Books, 1991). **Tariq Mehmood:** 'Mined Memories', first published in English and Pothowari (also called Pahari), in *Bradford Square* http://www.bradfordsquare.net/sqtexts.asp, and envelope of texts edited by Steve Dearden for Bradford's Stir Festival in 2007, English version printed by permission of the author. **Irfan Merchant:** 'The Indian Upon Scotland', 'The World Is More Real Than It Is' and 'Address Tae Chicken Tikka Masala', previously unpublished, by permission of the author. **Kei Miller:** 'The only thing far away' from *There Is an Anger that Moves* (Carcanet Press, 2007). **Sudesh Mishra:** 'Suva; Skye' from *Diaspora and the Difficult Art of Dying* (University of Otago Press, 2002), by permission of the author. **Raman Mundair:** 'Name Journeys' and 'Welsh Postcard' from *Lovers, Liars, Conjurors and Thieves* (Peepal Tree, 2003); 'Shetland Muse', 'Stories fae da Shoormal' and 'Sheep

Hill, Fair Isle' from *A Choreographer's Cartography* (Peepal Tree, 2007). **George Murevesi**: 'Pleas', previously unpublished, by permission of the author. **Tinashe Mushakavanhu**: 'The Green Man Festival', previously unpublished, by permission of the author.

Daljit Nagra: 'Look We Have Coming to Dover!', 'Parade's End', 'Darling & Me', 'Our Town with the Whole of India' and 'University', from *Look We Have Coming to Dover!* (Faber and Faber, 2007); 'Raju t'Wonder Dog!', from *Tippoo Sultan's Incredible White-Man-Eating Tiger Toy-Machine!!!* (Faber and Faber, 2011). **Grace Nichols**: 'Opening Your Book', 'Angel of the North', 'Seven Sisters' and 'Outward from Hull', from *Picasso, I Want My Face Back* (Bloodaxe Books, 2009); 'Hurricane Hits England' and 'Long Man' from *I Have Crossed an Ocean: Selected Poems* (Bloodaxe Books, 2010); 'The Queen of Sheba replies to Kathleen Jamie' from *Sunris* (Virago, 1996); all by permission of Curtis Brown.

Kim O'Loughlin: 'Play' and 'Burton Beach', previously unpublished; 'The Dream', first published in *Poetry Review* (1992); all by permission of the author.

Louisa Adjoa Parker: 'Forest-child' and 'Velvet Dresses' from *Salt, Sweat and Tears* (Cinnamon Press, 2007); 'Beach Huts on Paignton Beach', revised version of 'Beach Huts' from *Wasafiri* 64 (2010), by permission of the author. **Nii Ayikwei Parkes**: 'A Familiar Voice at the V&A Museum' from *The Makings of You* (Peepal Tree, 2010), by permission of the publisher; 'Common/wealth', previously unpublished, by permission of the author. **Sandeep Parmar**: 'Archive for a Daughter' from *The Marble Orchard* (Shearsman Books, 2012), by permission of the author. **R. Parthasarathy**: 'A Northern City' from *London Magazine* (Dec-ember 1969), © 2012 by R. Parthasarathy; by permission of the author. **Gabriela Pearse**: 'Grenada...Heathrow...London' from *A Dangerous Knowing* (Sheba Feminist Publishers, 1984). **Marsha Prescod**: 'Community Policing' from *Land of Rope and Tory* (Akira Press, 1985).

Shampa Ray: 'My India' from *Edinburgh Review: Calcutta Connects*, 119. **Roger Robinson**: 'Parallel' from *Suckle* (Waterways, 2009); 'The Wedding Picture', 'Sleep' and 'Conversion', from *Suitcase* (Waterways, 2004); all by permission of the author. **Kukomo Rocks**: 'Shopping Trip Tesco in Fife' from *Badass Raindrop* (Luath Press, 2002). **Joy Russell**: 'On the Tube' from *The Fire People* (Payback Press, 1998).

Suhayl Saadi: 'Glasgow: Mantle of Green Hollow' from *Paradise Gardens Carpet*, previously unpublished, by permission of the author. **Andrew Salkey**: 'Notting Hill Carnival, 1975' from *Away* (Allison and Busby, 1980), by permission of Mrs Patricia Salkey. **Jacob Sam-La Rose**: 'After Lazerdrome: McDonalds, Peckham Rye...' from *Breaking Silence* (Bloodaxe Books, 2011). **Ashna Sarkar**: '99 Flakes and The End of Something' from *City State: New London Poetry* (Penned in the Margins, 2009), by permission of the author. **Michelle Scally-Clarke**: 'Granny Betty Scally Bates' from *I AM* (Route, 2001). **Moqapi Selassie**: 'Tellin de stori', from http://www.rastafari westmidlands.co.uk/tellin_de_stori.html by permission of author. **Sudeep Sen**: 'Over May Day' and extract from 'Line Breaks', by permission of the author, from *Postmarked India: New and Selected Poems* (HarperCollins) where the full version of 'Line Breaks' is available. **Seni Seneviratne:** 'Frame Yourself', 'Yorkshire Childhood' and 'A Wider View' from *Wild Cinnamon and Winter Skin* (Peepal Tree, 2010). **John Siddique:** 'A Map of Rochdale' and 'Industrial Landscape' from *Poems from a Northern Soul* (Crocus, 2007); 'Jali', first published as part of Lancaster University's 'Moving Manchester' commission; 'One New Years Eve' from *Recital* (Salt Publishing, 2007); all by permission of the author. **Labi Siffre:** 'Foreigner', 'Incoming Calls' and 'Across the Great Divide' from *Monument* (Xavier Books, 1997). **Gerry Singh:** 'India Gate', from *Wish I Was Here* (Pocketbooks, 2000); 'Ladhar Bheinn', from *The Redbeck Anthology of British South Asian Poetry* (Redbeck Press, 2000). **Lemn Sissay:** 'A Black Man on the Isle of Wight' and 'Mill Town and Africa' from *Rebel Without Applause* (Canongate, second edition, 2000); 'This Train' and 'Flags' from *Listener* (Canongate, 2008). **Tawona Sithole:** 'Climbing Hills', previously unpublished, by permission of the author. **Anita Sivakumaran:** 'Ice and Ice Age', previously unpublished, by permission of the author. **Dorothea Smartt:** 'Bringing It All Back Home', 'A Few Words for Samboo' and 'Today on Sunderland Point', from *Ship Shape* (Peepal Tree, 2008). **Rommi Smith:** 'Night River' from *Writ in Water* (London Metropolitan Archives, 2010), by permission of the author. **Mahendra Solanki:** 'In a Jar' from *The Redbeck Anthology of British South Asian Poetry* (Redbeck Press, 2000), by permission of the author. **Saradha Soobrayen:** 'On the water meadows' from *New Poetries IV* (Carcanet Press, 2007), by permission of the author. **Wole Soyinka:** 'Telephone Conversation' from *Reflections* (African Universities Press, 1962), by permission of the author. **SuAndi:** 'Sambo's Grave' and 'Bolton Safari', previously unpublished, by permission of the author. **Maud Sulter:** 'Scots Triptych' from *As a Black Woman* (Akira Press, 1985); 'Flight' from *Zabat: Poetics of a Family Tree* (Urban Fox, 1985); both by permission of the estate of Miss Maud Sulter.

Levi Tafari: 'Toxteth Where I Reside' from *Rhyme Don't Pay* (Headland, 1993). **Kimberly Trusty:** 'Alcester Road, Moseley, 50 Bus' and 'New Vic Theatre, Stoke-on-Trent, ring bell for service', previously unpublished, by permission of the author; 'Fireworks, New Cross Road, 1981', from *Red: Contemporary Black British Poetry* (Peepal Tree, 2010).

Derek Walcott: Extracts 'XXIII', 'XXXIX', 'XXXV', 'XXXVI' and 'L' from *Midsummer* (Faber and Faber, 1984) and extract from *Tiepelo's Hound* (Faber and Faber, 2001), by permission of the publisher. **Gopi Warrier:** 'Cricket at Lords' from *Not Just a Game* (Five Leaves Publications, 2006). **Marie Guise Williams:** 'My Mother's Porch #1: First Love at 15' from *The Fire People* (Payback, 1998). **Karen McCarthy Woolf:** 'The Beach at Clovelly' from *I Am Twenty People!* (Enitharmon Press, 2007); 'Looe', previously unpublished; both by permission of the author.

Benjamin Zephaniah: 'Master Master' and 'I Have a Scheme', from *Propa Propaganda* (Bloodaxe Books, 1996), and 'The Big Bang' and 'Knowing Me', from *Too Black Too Strong* (Bloodaxe Books 2001), by permission of the publisher; 'Call It What You Like!', from *News for Babylon* (Chatto, 1984), by permission of the author. **Zhana**: 'Apartheid Britain 1985 (Or Kenwood Ladies Pond)' from *Sojourn* (Methuen, 1988); by permission of the author.

Every effort has been made to trace copyright holders of all work included in this book. The editors and publishers apologise if any material has been published without permission or without the appropriate acknowledgement, and would be glad to be told of anyone who has not been consulted. Anyone wishing to reprint any poems from this anthology in other books should contact the rights holders listed above and not Bloodaxe Books Ltd (except in the case of poems whose publication rights are controlled by Bloodaxe).

The editors would like to acknowledge the support of the UK's Arts and Humanities Research Council. A major research grant under the project title, 'Devolving Diasporas', funded the editors' research and permissions costs. The Carnegie Trust for the Universities of Scotland awarded a Carnegie Publication Grant to the editors and The Humanities, Arts, and Social Sciences Faculty, Newcastle University and School of Arts and Humanities, University of Stirling provided further support.

We also extend our sincere thanks to the following people and organisations for their invaluable assistance and advice: Melanie Abrahams at Renaissance One, Africa in Motion Film Festival, Apples and Snakes, Viccy Adams, Linda Anderson, Neil Astley and Suzanne Fairless-Aitken at Bloodaxe Books, Nii Ayikwei Parkes, Martin Banham, Hannah Bannister and Peepal Tree Press, Stewart Brown, Lorna Burns, Claire Chambers, Leon Charles, Nigel Corbett, Jonathan Davidson and Writing West Midlands, Eric Doumerc, Femi Folorunso, Corinne Fowler, Lucy Gallagher, James Gibbs, Chloe Garner at Ledbury Poetry Festival, Cathy Grindrod, Elizabeth Guest, Exiled Writers Ink, Hafan Books, Pete Kalu and Commonword, Don Kinch, Kay McArdle, Frances Mather, Gavin MacDougall and Luath Press, Karen McCarthy Woolf, Henderson Mullin and Writing East Midlands, Susheila Nasta and *Wasafiri*, Bohdan Piasecki, David Richards, Salt Publishing, the Scottish Poetry Library, John Siddique, Angela Smith, Emma Smith, SuAndi, Lleucu Siencyn and Yr Academi Gymreig/The Welsh Academy, Rory Watson, Kirsty Wilson and Canongate.

INDEX OF WRITERS

Italicised numerals are references to the writer or writer's work.

INDEX OF TITLES

INDEX OF FIRST LINES